also a little wine

Soak the beans overnight; in the morning dra[in]
off and put them into fresh wat[er]
Set them over the fire to boil slowly for [an hour]
Put in a separate kettle the meat, carrots and
Strain the soup, when done, through a fine s[ieve]
rubbing through all the beans that will [go.]
Pour into a Tureen adding in slices the [le]
and hard boiled eggs; — Put in the wine
If it is too thick after straining, put it ba[ck]
in the kettle and add hot water; if too
thin, let it boil until thick enough.

Take eight large mealy potatoes, peel
and cut in small slices, slice one
large onion, boil in three pints of w[ater]
until tender, then pulp through a
cullender, add a small piece of butter,
little cayenne pepper and salt,
Just before serving add two table spoons
full of cream. Do not let it boil
after the cream is added.
This is sufficient for three or four pe[ople]

Purchased on our New England trip Oct 5-16, 2005 in Boothbay Harbor, Maine on Monday Oct. 10 in a bookstore in downtown area shops. We stayed with Sandy Terry at her PEO B&B. (See page 39 for recipe that is similar to a delicious appetizer we had in Wolfboro, NH at Ramona & Bob Lockhart's PEO B&B).

THE
EAST HAMPTON

L.V.I.S.

CENTENNIAL COOKBOOK

Wonderful recipe for a tomato bisque from Sandy:
  1 qt. chicken broth
  1 jar spaghetti sauce
Heat together and add seasonings as desired for additional ingredients to create a unique soup (i.e., basil leaves, parsley, whole tomatoes, shrimp, etc.)

CELEBRATING THE 100TH ANNIVERSARY OF THE LADIES' VILLAGE IMPROVEMENT SOCIETY OF EAST HAMPTON, L.I.

Main Street about 1910. The building at left is now
White's Pharmacy. It was Hooper's Furniture Store.

The Ladies' Village Improvement Society

CENTENNIAL COOKBOOK COMMITTEE

CHAIRPERSON	DIANE DUNST
ART DIRECTOR. DESIGNER	DOLORES FREY
HISTORIAN	EUNICE JUCKETT MEEKER
RECIPE COMMITTEE	DEBBIE CLEMENCE. EDITOR
	MARY BRETT. CO-EDITOR
	DEBBIE WALTER. ASSISTANT EDITOR
	BARBARA DUBITSKY
	PATTI FERRIN
	ELIZABETH J. MAGILL
	ANNE TREGELLAS
PROOF READERS	ANN K. WILLARD
	HARRY L. WILLARD
FINANCE COMMITTEE	BONNIE KRUPINSKI
	RUTH M. LIZARS
	CAROLINE PREISCHE
MAP COORDINATION	PATTI FERRIN
	RUTH M. LIZARS
MARKETING	JENNIFER D'AURIA
	LISBETH DIRINGER
	ELIZABETH J. MAGILL
	MARY T. MACDONALD
	MARTHA MURRAY
	ETHEL ROSNER
PUBLIC RELATIONS	JANE PALEY
WORD PROCESSING	KATE KOPLOWITZ

$\mathcal{T}$ABLE OF $\mathcal{C}$ONTENTS

L.V.I.S. Fair on the Village Green. circa 1916.

THE $\mathcal{L}$ADIES

Main Street directly opposite South End Cemetery. Notice the well-worn bicycle path and horse grazing on the Village Green.

Determination and dedication have, for a full century, enabled the members of East Hampton's women's oldest organization, The Ladies' Village Improvement Society, to truly live up to its name.

Begun in 1895 and strengthened from generation to generation, the Ladies' original goals were designed to make and "KEEP EAST HAMPTON BEAUTIFUL."

Their vision was largely responsible for the Village's growth from a simple farming and fishing community to one recognized as one of the most beautiful villages in America.

A hundred years ago, when 21 housewives banded together to help eliminate many of the problems of a growing East Hampton, they had no idea their efforts would have such far-reaching results, not only in East Hampton but all over the country. Who could imagine that a century later, their little group would

have grown to over 400 strong and that their year-round programs would include environmental, conservation, preservation issues, and local scholarship grants.

What were the problems back in 1895?

Steam locomotive at East Hampton Railroad Station.

Well, in those days, Main Street, which was then unpaved, was unbearably dusty during the long hot summers. And, also, the eagerly awaited, and newly constructed Long Island Railroad Station left the surrounding area a shambles. The Ladies set out to see what they could do.

In order to pay for the manpower needed to regularly water down the dusty streets, and also to clean up the railroad station, The Ladies' Village Improvement Society set out to raise funds. A New England Supper on New Year's Eve, 1895, successfully launched the first L.V.I.S. fund-raising endeavors. Soon to follow, the first cookbook was introduced in July 1896 at the first annual L.V.I.S. Fair.

It was a wonderful collection of favorite local recipes entitled, The Way We Cook in East Hampton. It provided an insight into the abundant natural resources of the region by using local seafood, crops such as potatoes and tomatoes, wild cranberries, beach plums, and grapes. And thus, a tradition was born.

To provide

Typical East Hampton picket fence. In 1891, all Main Street houses stood behind such fences.

more funds for additional environmental and social projects, The L.V.I.S embarked on the ambitious undertaking of making the summer fair an annual event. And, this too, has become a most successful tradition.

East Hampton was growing. It provided a haven for artists and writers of the day. New York families also began to discover East Hampton's cool ocean breezes, beautiful wide beaches, and spectacular scenic landscapes.

Local first families, such as the Hands, Mulfords, Osbornes, Daytons, Parsons and Hedges began to share their family homes on Main Street, and rented rooms to city dwellers. People like Juan Trippe (the founder of Pan Am Airlines) and his family came, found summer accommodations along Main Street, and returned joyfully, summer after summer.

Soon, lovely changes took place, as summer visitors became residents. A new architecture was born as native Villagers developed Three Mile Harbor, and built "cottages" along the shore. Dune homes began to dot the ocean landscape and summer "cottages" appeared along Ocean Avenue. Indeed, a house at the seashore was a *cottage*.

An early East Hampton beach scene.

As The Ladies' Village Improvement Society became better known, women emerged from their traditional role in the home and became actively and vigorously involved in the greater community problems.

The East Hampton elected officials and The L.V.I.S. members soon combined forces. When the Ladies said there should be bicycle paths, there soon were. Billboards must come down. They disappeared. Parking should be parallel, not headed in. The blatant red and black weekend For Sale signs in shop windows had to go. They did.

Dancing on the Village Green, L.V.I.S. Fair Ca. 1915

Ladies preparing booths for early L.V.I.S. Summer Fair.

Photo Concession at 1945 L.V.I.S. Fair. Persons unknown.

Woman, two children and artist on float at 1945 L.V.I.S. 50th Anniversary Parade.

Jacqueline Bouvier
Kennedy Onassis
modeling at L.V.I.S.
fashion show.

The cookbook booth at the 1965 L.V.I.S. Fair. Left to right: Mrs. Frank Conklin, Mrs. Arnold Rattray and Mrs. Frank Dayton.

1981 L.V.I.S. Summer Fair barbecue. Person unknown.

Main Street in front of The L.V.I.S. Headquarters.

Joining the by now well-entrenched year-round L.V.I.S. group, the city Ladies found there was more to the group's sway-power than showed on the surface. The L.V.I.S. had already become a true force in the community. Year after year, The Ladies found ways to improve the already attractive Village: grass plots on Main Street, manicured greens along Town Pond and Main Street, at Hook Mill, and the Sheep Pound, even flowers on Main Street.

Mother Nature threw a curve at East Hampton in 1938, sending the first major hurricane in over 100 years. Far too many of the huge elms that had marched in stately fashion along Main Street were toppled like match sticks.

The aftermath of the storm was chaos - but only briefly. The Ladies of The L.V.I.S. knew the village trees were vital. The trees that needed to be righted were. Those that couldn't be were replaced. To fund the expensive program, the industrious Ladies initiated a memorial fund. Today's street trees now include not only East Hampton's famous elms, but also zelkova, and four disease-resistant elms, the Delaware, Pioneer, Homestead, the Liberty Elm, among others.

Incidentally, the 1994 circumference of one of the old-timers, strategically located in front of The L.V.I.S. headquarters, measures over twenty feet. Tender, loving care has paid off!

Today's fantastic tree display has brought East Hampton to the attention of community planners all across the country.

Through the years, The L.V.I.S. Tree

Historic Elm

This tree is hereby designated a historic landmark to be honored and preserved for future generations.

ELM RESEARCH INSTITUTE
HARRISVILLE N.H. 03450

The Ladies' Village Improveme...

Committee has become more zealous and committed to see that healthy, well-shaped trees continue to grace the main streets of the village with an arboreal canopy. A significant percent of the funds raised annually by L.V.I.S. goes to maintaining the trees of East Hampton Village.

A large L.V.I.S. committee keeps active tabs on each individual tree, seeing that new street trees are purchased, and professionally planted, watered, sprayed, fed, and pruned. Some bear memorial plaques, indicating they've been given in memory of a deceased L.V.I.S. member or a community figure.

The Ladies care for another specially important project begun by The L.V.I.S. many years ago and carried on faithfully year after year. On holidays, seventy-five American flags fly along Main Street and its intersecting Newtown Lane. The impressive East Hampton flag display is frequently noted in metropolitan papers.

The June 9 flag showing may come as a surprise to visitors. This is the date of John Howard Payne's birthday. He is an early East Hampton VIP - the lonely Long Islander who wrote the poignant words about the cottage that still looks out over the Village Green. The weathered saltbox birthplace is now, with the persuasion of The L.V.I.S., the Village-owned museum, "Home, Sweet Home."

In 1987, The L.V.I.S. purchased the spacious Gardiner Brown House near the Village Center. The beautifully treed home was badly run-down but included a sunken garden. Through revenues generated from the fundraising efforts of the Ladies, the mortgage has been totally paid off. The 1740 house, restored to its former beauty, is the proud headquarters of The L.V.I.S.

The headquarters houses the well-known Bargain Books and Bargain Box. The two shops, staffed by volunteers and selling contributed merchandise, enable The L.V.I.S. to generate greater income and thus expand its commitments. The annual L.V.I.S. Fair (100 years old in July 1996) is now held on the grounds of the house. A late Saturday in July finds the grounds dotted with colorful booths and tents as the Ladies display

Flag Pole on East Hampton Village Green.

a great variety of items to tantalize the eager fairgoers. Highly attended, the community looks forward to it with pride.

Working enthusiastically together, the multi-faceted membership of The L.V.I.S. has grown in recent years to include women with full-time careers. Lawyer or housewife, teacher or publishing executive, local or part-time resident, the membership of The Ladies' Village Improvement Society has expanded its goals.

Today, in addition to its environmental, conservation, and preservation endeavors, The L.V.I.S.' most important project is the many scholarships it offers to outstanding local high school graduates. Additionally, L.V.I.S. has a broad-reaching book program to encourage those in the lower grades to read.

The twelfth regional cookbook of The L.V.I.S. is, by far, the most ambitious it has published in its century-long tradition. Like its predecessors, produced in 1896, 1897, 1908, 1911, 1916, 1924, 1939, 1948, 1955, 1965, and 1975, the new cookbook is an update on the culinary history of East Hampton.

Earlier cookbooks, thinner volumes supported by advertisements, carried old family recipes and were

interspersed with hints on such things as how to thwart cramps and to return black silk to its original lustre. The later books included old-time favorite recipes from (to name just a few) celebrity chefs: a beef stew from President Eisenhower, a clam chowder from New York Governor Averill Harriman, and a molasses cookie recipe from the White House, courtesy of East Hampton's own Jackie Bouvier Kennedy. And, of course, Craig Claiborne, Clementine Paddleford, Henri Soule, and Pierre Franey could always be called upon to supply L.V.I.S. with many of their famous dishes.

The following cookbook hint comes from a 12th generation resident. "Young brides should purchase their Centennial cookbook as soon as it appears. L.V.I.S. cookbooks sell out early, and almost never turn up at Bargain Books. We think of them as being worth their weight in gold. Everyone knows if you weren't born into one of the old families, you try your darndest to marry into one - just for their cookbook collection."

"So I give you this advice: buy each new one as soon as it comes out, so you'll have one to leave to your daughter. Better make that two, so your son will have one to give to his bride." Your purchases will help "KEEP EAST HAMPTON BEAUTIFUL".

- Eunice Juckett Meeker

L.V.I.S. Annual Summer
Fair Committee 1990

Officers of L.V.I.S. and Mayor of East Hampton in The L.V.I.S. 50th Anniversary Parade. Left to right: Hester Cheney, Mrs. Bouvier Scott, Judd Bannister, June Kelly, Maude Taylor, Helen Gay, unidentified person.

The Ladies' Village Improvement Society

Presidents Past & Present

1895 – Mrs. Henry D. Hedges	1942 – Mrs. Edwin Ewen Anderson
1897 – Mrs. William A. Hedges	1944 – Mrs. Bouvier Scott
1898 – Mrs. E.H. Dayton	1946 – Mrs. J. Edward Gay, Jr.
1899 – Mrs. William A. Hedges	1946 – Mrs. Russell Hopkinson
1900 – Mrs. E.H. Dayton	1949 – Mrs. Juan T. Trippe
1902 – Mrs. William A. Hedges	1951 – Mrs. Donald Carse
1903 – Mrs. B.H. Van Scoy	1954 – Mrs. Victor Harris
1904 – Mrs. N.H. Dayton	1955 – Mrs. E.H. Siter
1909 – Mrs. Henry D. Hedges	1957 – Mrs. Ellery S. James
1911 – Mrs. N.H. Dayton	1960 – Mrs. Condie Lamb
1913 – Mrs. E.T. Dayton	1962 – Mrs. Alfred L. Loomis
1916 – Mrs. N.W. Barns	1965 – Miss Eleanor Tingley
1918 – Mrs. John W. Hand	1966 – Mrs. M. Anderson Kennard
1920 – Mrs. N.H. Dayton	1969 – Mrs. Philip M. Brett
1922 – Mrs. E.T. Dayton	1971 – Mrs. Thomas A. Kelly
1923 – Mrs. Frederick Russell	1974 – Mrs. Ann Jones Light
1924 – Mrs. Frederick Russell	1977 – Mrs. William C. Parr
1925 – Mrs. George Ethridge	1979 – Mrs. Bambi King
1932 – Mrs. George Ethridge	1981 – Mrs. John Kennedy
1933 – Mrs. Frank P. Shepard	1984 – Mrs. Harry Willard
1934 – Mrs. William R. Maloney	1987 – Mrs. Walter Preische
1938 – Mrs. Nelson C. Osborne	1990 – Mrs. James Briggs
1940 – Mrs. Howard Morris	1993 – Mrs. Leonard L. Cooper

L.V.I.S. Summer Fair
1982.

Appetizers

Caviar Cake

GAIL PARKER

en particularly like this appetizer. Perhaps they're not as calorie conscious as women.

INSTRUCTIONS: Prepare this dish 24 hours in advance. In a 6-inch springform pan, layer the ingredients in the following order: 8 ounces cream cheese, onions, 8 ounces cream cheese, eggs, 8 ounces cream cheese, caviar. Cover with plastic wrap. Refrigerate overnight. To remove cake, run knife around the inside of the pan. Loosen. Lift off. Transfer to a round plate lined with lemon leaves. Serve with Bremner wafers.

INGREDIENTS FOR 6 SERVINGS:
3 (8 ounce) containers softened cream cheese
2 medium red onions, finely chopped
3 hard cooked eggs, chopped
1 (2 ounce) jar black lumpfish caviar, very well drained

Crab Dip

MRS. BETH FIELD

his is a terrific dip for entertaining a crowd. It can be easily doubled.

INSTRUCTIONS: Crumble sealegs into coarse pieces. Combine remaining ingredients. Fold in sea legs.

Spray baking pan with oil. An 8x8-inch glass or ceramic pan or a 9-inch quiche dish is suitable. Bake at 400° for 20 to 25 minutes until slightly brown and bubbly. Serve hot with cocktail rye or pumpernickel bread.

INGREDIENTS FOR 6 SERVINGS:
1½ pounds sealegs
16 ounces cream cheese, softened
¾ cup mayonnaise
¼ cup lemon juice
¼ cup chopped onions
2 teaspoons minced garlic
⅛ teaspoon white or black pepper
cocktail rye or pumpernickel bread

Mom's Clam Dip

BARBARA STRONG BORSACK

This is a recipe my mother always makes when she has company. It has become the traditional hors d'oeuvre in our family!

INSTRUCTIONS: Drain clams, reserving 1 tablespoon of clam juice. Combine all ingredients. Chill well. Serve with chips.

INGREDIENTS:
1 (6½ ounce) can of minced clams
1 tablespoon reserved clam juice
8 ounces cream cheese, softened
1 teaspoon grated onion
1 tablespoon Worcestershire sauce
squeeze of lemon juice

Shrimp Cheese Dip

MARION EDWARDS

This dip is suitable for stuffing celery or for serving with crackers.

INSTRUCTIONS: Drain and mash shrimp with a fork. Combine all ingredients together and mix well.

INGREDIENTS:
1 (4½ ounce) can shrimp
8 ounces cottage cheese
¼ cup mayonnaise
3 tablespoons catsup
1 teaspoon lemon juice
dash garlic salt
freshly ground pepper, to taste

Bar Cheese

MRS. B.W. KINSELLA

INSTRUCTIONS: Melt cheese in the top of a double boiler. Stir in remaining ingredients. Refrigerate in sterilized jars.

INGREDIENTS:
1 pound Velveeta cheese
6 ounces horseradish
½ cup plus 1 tablespoon mayonnaise
2 drops Tabasco sauce

Hot Creamy Beef Dip

HELEN SHEEHY

INSTRUCTIONS: Beat cream cheese with sour cream until light and fluffy. Stir in beef, onion, and seasonings.
Place mixture in a shallow baking dish. Top with nuts. Bake at 350° for 20 minutes. Serve with cocktail bread.

INGREDIENTS:
8 ounces cream cheese, softened
1 cup sour cream
3 ounces dried beef, finely chopped
1 tablespoon minced onion
¼ teaspoon garlic salt
¼ teaspoon pepper
½ cup pecans or walnuts, chopped

Hummus

LANCE ROLL, CHEF, THE RED HORSE MARKET

INSTRUCTIONS: Soak the beans for at least 2 hours, preferably overnight. Discard water. Place beans in a large pot with carrot, celery, onion, garlic, and water to cover. Cook approximately 2 hours, until beans are very soft. Drain and reserve the cooking liquid*. Discard carrot and celery. Let beans, onion, and garlic cool.

Place ¼ of the beans, ½ of the lemon juice, 4 ounces of the tahini, and the dry spices into a food processor. Pulse the processor, adding enough reserved liquid to smooth out the hummus. Repeat this process until all of the ingredients, except the parsley and scallions, have been added. Be careful not to add too much of the reserved liquid. Use just enough to keep the mixture smooth. Salt to taste.

Fold in parsley and scallions.

Serve with crostini, crackers, or crudités.

*Note: The reserved liquid from the cooked beans makes an excellent stock for vegetarian soups. Feel free to add more vegetables, a bay leaf, and other fresh herb stems such as thyme or parsley. This liquid truly enhances the flavor of the hummus. Don't be surprised when you serve this to guests if they ask, "Who made the hummus?"

INGREDIENTS:

1 pound garbanzo beans
1 carrot
1 stalk celery
1 onion, peeled
6 cloves of garlic, peeled
juice of 3 lemons
12 ounces tahini
1 tablespoon cumin
1 teaspoon cayenne, or less to taste
2 tablespoons soy sauce
¼ cup extra virgin olive oil
salt to taste
2 ounces chopped parsley
1 bunch scallions, chopped

Marvelous Onion Appetizers

JANE KIRK KIMBRELL

*I*NSTRUCTIONS: Soak the onions, covered, for 2 days in water, sugar, and vinegar. Drain well. Stir in mayonnaise and seasonings. Serve with cocktail rye or pumpernickel bread.

INGREDIENTS:

2 large sweet onions, thinly sliced
2 cups water
1 cup sugar
½ cup vinegar
1 to 2 tablespoons mayonnaise
celery salt, to taste
salt and freshly ground pepper, to taste

Poor Man's Caviar

NATASHA LARY

*T*his makes a delightful summer appetizer. It gets its name from the fact that it looks like caviar.

INSTRUCTIONS: Bake eggplant at 375° for 40 minutes. Let cool sufficiently to handle. Remove skin. Chop finely.

Sauté onion in 1 tablespoon oil until translucent. Add eggplant and tomato purée. Simmer, uncovered, on low heat for 15 minutes. Stir occasionally.

Continue to cook, gradually adding the remaining 3 tablespoons of oil. Cook until quite thick. Stir in lemon juice, salt, and pepper. Chill well before serving. Thin slices of black bread make a nice accompaniment.

INGREDIENTS:

1 large eggplant
4 tablespoons olive oil
2 small onions, minced
4 tablespoons tomato purée
2 teaspoons lemon juice
salt and freshly ground pepper, to taste

TAPENADE

BARBARA DUBITSKY

INSTRUCTIONS: Process all ingredients in a food processor to create a coarse spread. Chill. Serve with toasted pita wedges.

INGREDIENTS:
3 ounces Olivetta
1 (6½ ounce) can tuna fish in oil
2 cans anchovies
¼ cup capers
1 garlic clove
¼ cup olive oil
1 tablespoon fresh lemon juice
pita bread

WATERCRESS SPREAD

KATE CAMERON

For some reason, almost no one will guess all of the ingredients in this spread. This does not keep well overnight, and should be prepared 1 to 2 hours before serving.

INSTRUCTIONS: Chop watercress leaves by hand. Discard stems. Do not use a food processor. Combine watercress leaves with sour cream. Add white horseradish to desired tartness. Spread on pumpernickel squares to serve.

INGREDIENTS:
2 bunches watercress
1 (16 ounce) container sour cream
white horseradish, to taste
dark brown pumpernickel bread squares

Zesty Artichoke Chili Dip

MRS. RICHARD B. GORDON

Add a little South-of-the-Border touch to your next cocktail party!

INSTRUCTIONS: Drain artichokes and chilies. Chop coarsely. Place in medium bowl.

Add mayonnaise, cheese, and lemon juice.

Mix thoroughly.

Bake in a small oven-proof ramekin at 375° until hot and bubbly, about 15 minutes.

Place ramekin on a serving platter. Surround with tortilla chips.

This dip can be made ahead, and refrigerated until baking time.

INGREDIENTS FOR 8 SERVINGS:

1 (16 ounce) can imported artichokes

1 (4 ounce) can peeled mild green chilies

¼ cup mayonnaise

½ cup grated Parmesan cheese

1 tablespoon lemon juice

1 (12 ounce) package tortilla chips

Creamy Paté

RUTH MCCREA LIZARS

INSTRUCTIONS: Sauté onion in butter until soft. Add livers, sauté. Add apple, and continue to cook a few minutes longer.

Do not let the apples get too soft.

Purée mixture with the cream, sherry, and seasonings*.

Pour into a mold and chill. Serve with bland crackers.

*Note: If the liver taste is too strong, add more cream, sherry, and spices. If you would like the paté to be thick enough to slice, increase the butter.

INGREDIENTS:

4 tablespoons butter

1 onion, finely chopped

1 pound chicken livers

1 green apple, peeled, cored, and chopped

2 tablespoons heavy cream

1 tablespoon sherry, Madeira, or Marsala

½ teaspoon thyme

½ teaspoon rosemary

salt and freshly ground pepper, to taste

Avocado Paté

CRISTA G. MARTIN

This is a great recipe to serve with drinks in the evening. The recipe was given to me by a fellow Stanford classmate in 1965. I have adapted its preparation to a food processor, which makes it very simple and fast.

INSTRUCTIONS: Soak gelatin in cold water for 3 minutes. Place over hot water and stir until dissolved. Set aside.

With motor running, drop scallions, shallots, and garlic in food processor. Add remaining ingredients. Process until smooth. Blend in gelatin.

Place in 5-cup mold (a ring mold works well). Refrigerate at least 6 hours, or overnight. Unmold on platter. Garnish with salsa or pistachio nuts and parsley. Serve with crackers or tortilla chips.

*Chef's Secret: If avocados aren't fully ripe, store covered in flour for a couple of days.

INGREDIENTS:

1 envelope unflavored gelatin
¼ cup water
2 scallions
2 small shallots
2 medium cloves of garlic
4 ripe avocados*
16 ounces softened cream cheese
1 to 2 tablespoons fresh lemon juice
1 teaspoon chili powder
½ teaspoon salt
Tabasco sauce, to taste

GARNISH:

red salsa or ¼ cup chopped pistachio nuts and ¼ cup chopped parsley

Paté Maison

MRS. LAWRENCE CLARKE

Instructions: Process all ingredients in a food processor or blender. Put mixture in a 2-quart paté mold or soufflé dish. Bake at 350° in a water bath for 1½ hours, or until the juices are clear.

Remove from oven. Weigh the top down with a heavy plate. Let cool for 6 to 8 hours before serving. Slice with a sharp knife, placing the knife in water in between each slicing. Serve with lemon wedges and crackers.

INGREDIENTS FOR 12 SERVINGS:
1 pound veal, finely ground
1 pound chicken cutlets, finely ground
1 pound chicken livers, finely ground
2 cups heavy cream
8 egg whites
½ cup Madeira, sherry, or cognac
1 teaspoon garlic salt
1 teaspoon nutmeg
1 teaspoon thyme
1 teaspoon paprika
1 teaspoon liquid Maggi
1 drop Tabasco sauce

Brie Cheese Pastry Rounds

RUTH MUELLER

Instructions: Combine flour and brie cheese. Add egg and seasonings. Knead mixture. Allow to set for one hour in a cool place.

Roll dough out to ¼-inch thick. Cut rounds with a 3-inch cookie cutter. Place the rounds on a buttered baking dish. Brush them with a beaten egg, to which a pinch of salt is added.

Bake at 300° for 6 to 8 minutes.

INGREDIENTS:
2 cups flour
8 ounces very ripe Brie cheese, crust removed
1 egg
pinch of salt
pinch of nutmeg
pinch of cayenne

GLAZE:
1 egg, beaten
pinch of salt

Fantastic Cheese Squares *

OLIVIA BROOKS

his recipe was given to me by my friend, Marylu Payne Stephenson, over 20 years ago. It is still, by far, my most favorite hors d'oeuvre and everyone adores it! Try it - you'll love the results.

INSTRUCTIONS: Trim crusts off bread, then quarter the bread slices.

Blend the cheese, butter, spices, and Worcestershire sauce.

Spread some mixture on top of one quarter piece of bread. Top with another quarter piece of bread, and spread mixture on top. Top with another quarter piece of bread. There should be 3 bread layers with cheese mixture in between.

Next, coat the four sides and then top with cheese mixture. Do not coat the bottom.

Place squares on cookie sheets and freeze for 30 minutes. Bake now or store squares in plastic bags in freezer until ready to use. Bake at 350° for 15 to 18 minutes until golden brown.

INGREDIENTS FOR 80 APPETIZERS:
2 large loaves of Wonder bread
4 (5 ounce) jars of Kraft Old English Cheese
1 pound butter or margarine, softened
2 teaspoons Beau Monde
2 teaspoons dill weed
1 ½ teaspoons Worcestershire sauce

* Ramona Lockhart in Wolfboro, NH made a similar appetizer using whole loaf bread cut into large cubes and frosted on all sides (except for side facing pan) with a mixture of Kraft Old English/Cheddar cheese and 1 stick butter softened. Can be frozen ahead + baked when ready to serve.

Roquefort Roll Waldorf

LYNN KROLL

his recipe originated from the collection of Claude Philippe of the Waldorf-Astoria Hotel. It is excellent as an hors d'oeuvre or served sliced with a green salad.

INSTRUCTIONS: Bring cheeses and butter to room temperature. Blend well. Blend in remaining ingredients. Form mixture into a ball. Chill 4 hours.

When chilled, roll in finely ground nuts to coat. Serve with crackers or thin slices of tart apple.

INGREDIENTS FOR 1 BALL:
¼ pound Roquefort cheese
6 ounces cream cheese
1½ tablespoons sweet butter
1 celery stalk, chopped fine
½ green pepper, chopped fine
3 sprigs parsley, chopped fine
1 teaspoon chopped walnuts
1 teaspoon dry sherry
3 drops Tabasco sauce

COATING:
finely ground nuts

Bruschetta

MRS. ADRIENNE VITTADINI

INSTRUCTIONS: Use the best tomatoes you can find. Cut the tomatoes into ¼-inch dice. Chop basil. Drizzle with olive oil. Season to taste with salt and pepper. Do not allow the tomatoes to stand too long, as the liquid will drain from them.

Slice and toast the bread. While still warm, rub one side of the bread slices with a whole, peeled clove of garlic. Top bread slices with the tomato mixture and serve.

INGREDIENTS:
tomatoes
fresh basil
extra virgin olive oil
salt
pepper
Tuscan bread
garlic clove

East End Tomato Tart

LYS A. MARIGOLD

 hin, crisp, and delicious. Beautiful and colorful, too.

INSTRUCTIONS: Line a 12-inch tart pan with pastry dough. Chill 15 minutes.

Brush bottom of tart shell with Dijon mustard. Line with mozzarella or chèvre. Starting at outer edge, overlap tomato slices to form concentric circles.

Sprinkle tomatoes with garlic, oregano, salt, and pepper. Drizzle with olive oil. Bake at 375° for 40 minutes.

INGREDIENTS FOR 8 SERVINGS:
pastry for 12-inch tart pan

1 tablespoon Dijon mustard
4 ounces fresh mozzarella, shredded (or chèvre, crumbled)
8 ripe tomatoes, sliced very thin
1 clove garlic, minced
¼ teaspoon oregano
salt and freshly ground pepper, to taste
olive oil

Lobster Canapés

FRANK 'SPRIG' GARDNER, 1965 L.V.I.S. COOKBOOK

lace the liver, fat, and coral from a large lobster in a bowl. Add mayonnaise, an egg, and a pinch of baking powder. Stir into a smooth paste. Spread mixture on quarters of bread (not toast); sprinkle with grated Parmesan cheese and paprika. Place under broiler until tops are brown.

Marinated Shrimp

BEBE ANTELL

've used this recipe for the past 25 years as an hors d'oeuvre for cocktail parties, or as a first course for dinner.

INSTRUCTIONS: Place shrimp and onion rings in alternate layers in a large bowl. Combine remaining ingredients and pour over shrimp. Marinate 2 to 3 days. To serve, drain marinade and place shrimp and onions on a platter. Garnish with parsley.

INGREDIENTS:
2 pounds medium shrimp, cooked
2 small red onions, cut in rings
1½ cups olive oil
¾ cup red wine vinegar
1 clove garlic, crushed
1 teaspoon Worcestershire sauce
2 tablespoons sugar
1 teaspoon freshly ground black pepper
1 teaspoon salt
several dashes of Tabasco sauce

GARNISH:
¼ cup chopped fresh parsley

Mussels Vinaigrette

ELLEN PHILIPS SCHWARZMAN

INSTRUCTIONS: Scrub and debeard mussels well, scraping away any dirt and barnacles.

In a large pot, bring water, wine, lemon juice, and butter to a boil. Add mussels. Cover and steam at medium high for about 10 minutes, or just until mussels are opened.

Meanwhile, prepare vinaigrette. Whisk together oil, vinegar, and mustard. Season to taste.

Drain mussels. Transfer them to a large serving dish. Drizzle warm mussels with vinaigrette. Sprinkle with onion and parsley. Toss gently to coat mussels evenly. Serve now or refrigerate until serving. This dish is best served on the same day it is prepared.

INGREDIENTS FOR 8 SERVINGS:
8 pounds mussels
2 cups water
1 ½ cups white wine
4 tablespoons butter
juice of ½ lemon
2 red onions, finely chopped
½ cup chopped parsley

VINAIGRETTE:
1 ½ cups olive oil
¼ cup red wine vinegar
1 tablespoon Dijon mustard
salt and freshly ground pepper, to taste

Stuffed Baked Clams

SANDRA CONKLIN

his recipe was Isabelle Hawxhurst's, my mother. Unfortunately, all she had written down for this recipe were the ingredients, not the amounts. My husband and I have experimented over the years, trying to get these clams as close to hers as possible. I hope you enjoy them!

INSTRUCTIONS: Open the clams, reserving the juice. Grind or finely chop clam meat. Wash clam shells thoroughly.

Fry bacon; when partially cooked, add onions and green pepper. Cook until tender, add garlic. Cook until garlic is clear.

Combine this mixture with the clam meat, bread crumbs, mayonnaise, parsley, thyme, oregano, mustard, salt, and pepper. This mixture should be a thick paste. If too dry, add some reserved clam juice.

Fill clean shells with clam mixture. Sprinkle heavily with Parmesan cheese. Sprinkle with paprika.

Bake at 400° for 20 minutes until brown and bubbly. These clams freeze very nicely. Freeze them on cookie sheets; then place them in Ziploc freezer bags.

INGREDIENTS:

5 or 6 dozen large cherrystone clams
    (3 pints clam meat)
5 bacon strips, cut in small pieces
2 large onions, chopped
1 large green pepper, chopped
1 clove garlic, crushed
1 cup soft bread crumbs
1 cup Italian bread crumbs
2 tablespoons mayonnaise
2 tablespoons fresh parsley, minced
¼ teaspoon thyme
¼ teaspoon oregano
dash of powdered mustard
salt and freshly ground black pepper, to taste
1 cup Parmesan cheese
paprika

Glazed Chicken Wings

LENORE PICARD

These wings are good finger food for cocktail parties. They work equally well as part of a casual buffet dinner.

INSTRUCTIONS: Combine all ingredients for marinade. Marinate wings for several hours, or overnight. Bake wings and marinade, uncovered, at 350° for 1 hour. Baste occasionally. The result should be wings that are beautifully glazed — brown and shiny.

INGREDIENTS:
3 to 4 dozen chicken wings, tips removed

MARINADE INGREDIENTS:
4 tablespoons melted butter
½ cup soy sauce
½ cup red wine
¼ cup lemon juice
1 cup brown sugar
2 teaspoons dry mustard
½ teaspoon salt
¼ teaspoon pepper

Stuffed Mushrooms

DEBBIE CLEMENCE

INSTRUCTIONS: Remove stems from mushrooms. Reserve for another use. Wipe mushroom caps clean with a damp cloth.

In small skillet, sauté onions in oil and butter until translucent. Add garlic and pine nuts. Sauté several minutes longer. Add arugula; cook 5 minutes longer. Remove from heat. Cool slightly.

Stir in cheeses, parsley, salt, and pepper.

Arrange mushroom caps in a shallow baking dish. Divide the filling evenly among the mushroom caps.

Bake at 400° for 8 to 10 minutes until lightly browned.

INGREDIENTS:

12 large mushrooms
1 tablespoon olive oil
1 tablespoon sweet butter
½ cup finely chopped yellow onion
1 clove of garlic, minced
2 tablespoons pine nuts, coarsely chopped
1 cup fresh arugula, torn into small pieces
3 ounces feta cheese, crumbled
1 ounce Gruyère cheese, crumbled
2 tablespoons parsley, chopped
salt and freshly ground black pepper, to taste

Stuffed Grape Leaves

RUTH C. DIEFENDORF

While traveling throughout the southern Mediterranean and the Middle East, these quick snack items could be bought at side street stalls. They were delicious and fun to eat. Upon returning home, I have tried to put my own "twist" on the recipe over the years. They still delight my husband, Pete. Each time I serve them they bring back numerous memories of good times.

INSTRUCTIONS: For filling, combine all ingredients except grape leaves and olive oil.

Unroll the grape leaves. Be sure the underside of each leaf is facing upward. Place 1 tablespoon of the filling in the center of each leaf. Roll the sides of the leaf towards the middle; then roll the whole leaf into a tight roll.

Place stuffed leaves seam side down in a pan. Pour olive oil over the top. Cover and refrigerate overnight. To serve, garnish with lemon slices.

Note: This recipe can be made up to 2 days ahead.

INGREDIENTS FOR 3 DOZEN HORS D'OEUVRES:

1 pound feta cheese crumbled

or

1 pound ground beef, cooked and crumbled

2 cups cooked rice, cooled

2 tablespoons cumin

1 tablespoon curry powder

1 teaspoon garlic paste

1 tablespoon tomato paste

3 tablespoons lemon juice

salt and freshly ground pepper, to taste

1 (16 ounce) jar of Krinos Grape Leaves in brine

¼ cup olive oil

GARNISH:

1 lemon, thinly sliced in rounds

Zucchini Appetizers

HELEN J. ADAMS

INSTRUCTIONS: Mix all ingredients together in a large bowl. Spread mixture into a greased 9x13-inch baking pan. Bake at 350° until golden brown, 25 to 30 minutes. To serve, cut into 2x1-inch rectangles. Cut each rectangle diagonally. Serve hot or cold.

INGREDIENTS FOR 96 HOR D'OEUVRES:

3 cups (about 4 small) zucchini, unpared and thinly sliced
½ cup finely chopped onion
1 clove of garlic, minced
2 tablespoons fresh parsley, chopped
½ cup vegetable oil
4 eggs, lightly beaten
½ cup Parmesan cheese
1 cup Bisquick
½ teaspoon marjoram or oregano
½ teaspoon salt
½ teaspoon seasoned salt
dash of pepper

Susan's Peanut Butter Sticks

ELIZABETH J. MAGILL

his recipe came from the late Whiting Hollister, a lifelong summer resident of East Hampton. He was a great cook!

INSTRUCTIONS: Trim crusts from bread. Place crusts on cookie sheet.

Cut trimmed bread slices into ½-inch fingers. Place fingers on another cookie sheet.

Place crusts and fingers in a 300° oven for 30 minutes until crisp. Watch them! Do not let them get brown.

Heat oil and peanut butter in the top of a double boiler. Mix thoroughly. Remove from heat.

Crumble crisp crusts until fine crumbs form. Place crumbs on waxed paper.

When fingers are cool, dip them into the peanut butter mixture. Then roll in crumbs. Dry them on a wire rack. Have a happy, messy time!

INGREDIENTS:
1 loaf white bread
¼ cup salad oil
1 (12 ounce) jar creamy peanut butter

Soups

Black Bean Soup

1 qt black beans
4 qts fresh water
A small piece of lean pork, or a bone of beef
A couple of carrots
An onion stuck with cloves and allspice
Salt and pepper to taste
Sliced lemon and hard boiled eggs
Also a little wine

Soak the beans overnight; in the morning draw off and put them into fresh water
Set them over the fire to boil slowly for four hours
Put in a separate kettle the meat, carrots and onion
Strain the soup, when done, through a fine sieve, rubbing through all the beans that will go.
Pour into a Tureen adding in slices the lemons and hard boiled eggs; — Put in the wine last
If it is too <u>thick</u> after straining, put it back in the kettle and add hot water; if too thin, let it boil until thick enough.

Potato Soup

Take eight large mealy potatoes, peel and cut in small slices, slice one large onion, boil in three pints of water until tender, then pulp through a cullender, add a small piece of butter, a little cayenne pepper and salt,
Just before serving add two table spoons full of cream. Do not let it boil after the cream is added.
This is sufficient for three or four persons.

Page from Mrs. J. Alexander Tyler's recipe book. November 28, 1910.

Soups

Borshock Soup

DINA MERRILL HARTLEY

This is a simple but delicious soup that came from Mrs. Bartley Crum, who had something called "Menus by Mail" in the '50s. They were excellent recipes for people who don't know much about cooking.

INSTRUCTIONS: Mix broths, beet juice, and dill seed. Bring to a boil. Reduce heat. Simmer 15 minutes. Strain dill seed. Salt and pepper to taste. Lastly, add Madeira. To serve, garnish with a twist of lemon and a sprig of fresh dill. Cheese straws make a nice accompaniment.

INGREDIENTS FOR 6 SERVINGS:
1½ (13¾ ounce) cans College Inn chicken broth
1 (10½ ounce) can Campbell's beef bouillon
1¼ cups beet juice
1 teaspoon dill seed
salt and pepper, to taste
¼ cup Madeira wine

GARNISH:
lemon twists
fresh dill sprigs

Cold Carrot and Dill Soup

ANNE SAGER

This soup tastes best if made one day ahead of serving.

INSTRUCTIONS: Steam or microwave carrots and leeks separately, until soft.
Purée carrots, leeks, broth, cumin, thyme, salt, and pepper in a food processor until smooth.
Place mixture in bowl. Blend in dill and buttermilk. Correct seasonings, if necessary. Chill well before serving.

INGREDIENTS FOR 8 SERVINGS:
1 pound young carrots, thinly sliced
2 to 3 leeks, white part only, well washed and chopped
1 (13¾ ounce) can chicken broth, with the fat removed
1¼ teaspoons ground cumin
pinch of thyme
salt and freshly ground pepper, to taste
1½ tablespoons fresh dill, snipped
1 to 1½ quarts buttermilk

BUTTERNUT SQUASH SOUP WITH GINGER AND LIME

JODY AND LARRY CARLSON

The farms of the Hamptons are rich with squash. Our family is always on the lookout for ways to use this nature's bounty. Friends and family love this recipe so much that we always double it and make a meal of it. You only need to provide good bread!

INSTRUCTIONS: In large saucepan, sauté onion and ginger root in butter until the onion is soft.

Add squash, broth, water, and garlic. Bring to a boil. Reduce heat. Cover and simmer 15 to 20 minutes.

Using a food processor or a blender, purée the mixture in batches. Return to pan. Stir in lime juice, salt, and pepper. Heat on low until hot. Recipe may be prepared 1 to 2 days in advance up to this point.

FOR GARNISH: Heat oil in a small skillet until it is hot, but not smoking. Fry ginger root strips until golden, about 1 minute. Drain well on paper towels.

To serve, float a lime slice in each bowl. Top soup with fried ginger root.

INGREDIENTS FOR 4 SERVINGS:

½ cup chopped onion

1 ½ tablespoons peeled, fresh ginger root, minced

3 tablespoons butter

4 cups butternut squash, peeled, seeded, and thinly sliced

2 cups canned chicken broth

2 cups water

3 cloves garlic, minced

2 tablespoons fresh lime juice

salt and freshly ground pepper, to taste

GARNISH:

⅓ cup vegetable oil

3 tablespoons julienne strips of ginger root

4 thinly cut lime slices

Cabbage Roquefort Soup

DOLORES FREY

I had a Cabbage Roquefort soup at La Colombe D'Or in New York City, and tried to duplicate it. This is the result. It's wonderful for lunch on a cold winter day.

INSTRUCTIONS: Gently sauté carrots, potatoes, and leeks in butter. Stir constantly until vegetables are soft. Do not let them brown.

Add broth and water. Simmer on low heat for about 1 hour, or until vegetables are tender.

Add cabbage and garlic. Simmer an additional 30 minutes. To serve, top each bowl with a thin slice of Roquefort cheese. Warm, buttered French bread is a nice accompaniment.

INGREDIENTS FOR 8 SERVINGS:

3 medium carrots, pared and grated

3 medium potatoes, pared and grated

1 or 2 leeks, trimmed, washed, and sliced into rounds

1 tablespoon butter

3 cans chicken broth

5 cups water

1 small head cabbage, thinly sliced

1 to 2 cloves garlic, chopped

Roquefort cheese, cut in thin slices

Cauliflower and Roasted Garlic Soup

LANCE ROLL, CHEF, THE RED HORSE MARKET

Instructions: Place all garlic cloves in saucepan with olive oil. Bring to a boil. Reduce heat and simmer until garlic is a golden brown. Reserve.

In a large stockpot, sauté onions with butter and all of the garlic and oil. When onions are translucent, add cauliflower and potatoes. Sauté vegetables until they begin to sweat. Be careful not to let them brown.

Stir in flour. Slowly add stock, continually stirring with a wooden spoon or wire whisk. Bring to a boil. Reduce to a simmer. Cook, stirring from time to time, until vegetables are tender.

Add cream. Return soup to a boil for one or two minutes. Season with salt and pepper.

At this point, the soup is done cooking. However, it needs to be puréed. This process can be done most easily with a hand blender. A food processor will also work, although it is not recommended. For a heartier soup, only purée partially. The soup should be off-white in color and smooth.

INGREDIENTS FOR 12 SERVINGS:

12 cloves garlic
1 cup olive oil
2 large Spanish onions, diced
4 ounces butter
3 heads cauliflower, cut in small pieces
4 large russet potatoes, peeled and diced
1½ cups all-purpose flour
1 gallon chicken stock
2 cups cream, half and half, or milk
1 tablespoon white pepper
salt, to taste

Curried Carrot Soup

MRS. IRENE KUZYK

NSTRUCTIONS: Sauté onions in butter until translucent. Stir in curry powder until well blended.

Add remaining ingredients, except the sherry. Simmer, covered, until carrots are tender. Cool.

Purée soup in batches using a food processor or blender. If desired, add sherry.

Serve soup hot or cold. Garnish with a dollop of sour cream and a sprig of fresh dill.

INGREDIENTS FOR 4 TO 6 SERVINGS:

1 onion, coarsely chopped
2 tablespoons butter
2 teaspoons curry powder
8 medium carrots, diced
6 cups chicken stock
½ teaspoon lemon peel, finely chopped
1 teaspoon sugar
salt and pepper, to taste
3 tablespoons sherry (optional)

GARNISH:
sour cream
fresh dill sprigs

Tomato Carrot Soup with Basil

ANNA PUMP, OF LOAVES AND FISHES

This soup is an all time favorite at Loaves and Fishes. It is excellent as a first course, when chicken or fish is the entrée.

INSTRUCTIONS: Heat olive oil in a large soup pot. Add onions, garlic, and carrots. Sauté over medium heat for about 10 minutes. Do not brown the vegetables. Add tomatoes, chicken stock, and salt. Bring to a boil; simmer for 20 minutes.

Remove from heat. Add orange rind, juice, and the basil leaves.

Purée in batches in a food processor or blender. Serve hot or cold. Garnish with fresh basil leaves.

INGREDIENTS FOR 8 SERVINGS:

2 tablespoons olive oil
3 cups peeled and chopped onion
1 clove garlic, peeled and minced
3 large carrots, peeled and chopped
3 cups peeled, chopped fresh tomatoes or 3 cups canned crushed tomatoes
5 cups homemade chicken stock
1 teaspoon salt
grated rind of 1 orange
1 cup fresh orange juice
10 basil leaves

Tomato Soup

ANN KIRK WILLARD

Instructions: Sauté carrot, onion, and celery in butter until soft. Add tomatoes, sugar, basil, salt, and pepper. Bring to a boil. Reduce heat. Cover and simmer for 15 to 20 minutes. Purée in a food processor or blender. Return to saucepan. Add chicken broth. Heat through and serve.

INGREDIENTS FOR 4 SERVINGS:
- 1 carrot, shredded
- 1 large onion, sliced
- ½ cup chopped celery
- 3 tablespoons butter
- 1 (28 ounce) can tomatoes
- ½ teaspoon sugar
- 1 tablespoon basil
- ½ teaspoon salt
- ⅛ teaspoon white pepper
- 1 (14 ounce) can chicken broth

Gazpacho

ANNE TREGELLAS

Instructions: Finely chop or process tomatoes, cucumber, and green pepper until a mush is achieved. Process in remaining ingredients. Season to taste. Chill.
To serve, place an ice cube in the center of each mug or bowl. Ladle soup over ice cube. You can also hollow out firm, ripe tomatoes to create tomato cups!

INGREDIENTS FOR 4 SERVINGS:
- 2 large, ripe tomatoes, peeled
- ¼ cucumber, peeled
- ¼ green pepper
- 1 teaspoon grated onion
- 1 clove garlic, pressed
- 1 cup tomato juice
- 2 tablespoons vegetable oil
- 1 tablespoon wine vinegar
- 1 teaspoon Worcestershire sauce
- salt and freshly ground pepper, to taste

Cold Zucchini Soup

MR*S*. FREDERICK *S*. WILLIAMS*

*T*errific on a hot day!

INSTRUCTIONS: Cook zucchini and onions in stock over medium heat until tender. Stir occasionally.

Purée in batches in food processor or blender (I like it chunky). Add curry powder, half and half, and milk. Blend. Season to taste with salt and freshly ground pepper. Chill before serving.

INGREDIENTS FOR 6 SERVINGS:

6 medium zucchini, cut into chunks
2 onions, coarsely chopped
4 cups chicken stock or broth
½ teaspoon curry powder
1 cup half and half
½ cup milk
salt and freshly ground pepper, to taste

Flo's Apple Soup

MARGOT C. DOWLING

*I*NSTRUCTIONS: Sauté onions and celery in butter in oven-proof skillet until soft. Add apples. Place skillet in oven. Cover and cook for 20 minutes at 350°.

Remove skillet from oven and stir in broths, spices, and lemon juice. Mix well. Strain, yielding a smooth soup. Return skillet to stove top. Bring to a boil. Remove from heat. Slowly whisk in cream or yogurt.

INGREDIENTS FOR 4 SERVINGS:

1 large onion, chopped
4 stalks celery, chopped
2 tablespoons butter
3 large green apples, peeled, cored, and sliced
1 cup chicken broth
1 cup beef broth
1 teaspoon curry powder
1 teaspoon paprika
juice of 1 lemon
½ cup heavy cream or low fat yogurt

PHILIP TILEARCIO

INSTRUCTIONS: Sauté onions and garlic in oil until golden. Stir in flour and spices. Cook 2 to 3 minutes longer.

Add stock, corn, salsa, and pimento. Bring to a boil. Remove from heat.

Gradually stir in cream cheese. Blend well.

Add milk and return to heat. Heat gently. To serve, garnish with fresh cilantro or parsley.

INGREDIENTS FOR 6 SERVINGS:

1 ½ cups chopped onions

3 large cloves garlic, minced

2 ½ tablespoons olive oil

1 ½ tablespoons flour

1 ½ to 2 tablespoons chili powder

1 to 1 ½ tablespoons ground cumin

2 cups chicken stock

16 ounces corn kernels, fresh or frozen

2 cups mild salsa

4 ounces red pimento, chopped

8 ounces cream cheese, softened

1 cup milk

GARNISH:

fresh cilantro or parsley, chopped

Roasted Eggplant Soup with Citrus and Ginger

MIRKO'S RESTAURANT, WATER MILL

Instructions: Brush eggplant quarters with oil. Season with salt and pepper. Roast at 350° for 45 minutes. Cool, and discard skins.

In a medium saucepan, sweat onions in butter until translucent. Add eggplant.

In another saucepan, add wine, citrus juices, scallions, and ginger root. Heat to reduce by ⅓. Strain and pour liquid over eggplant and onions. Purée.

Return puréed mixture to pot. Thin with chicken stock. Heat through. Season to taste with salt and pepper.

Ingredients for 12 servings:

2 large eggplants, quartered

olive oil

salt and pepper, to taste

1½ large white onions, diced

4 tablespoons butter

1 cup white wine

1 orange, juiced

1 lemon, juiced

1 lime, juiced

10 scallions, diced

1½ to 2 pieces of large fresh ginger root, peeled and sliced

2 cups chicken stock

French Onion Soup

FLORENCE FITHIAN STONE WESSBERG

This recipe was handed down by my mother-in-law, Mary Frances Hendrickson Wessberg. The first time I made it, she stopped by. While it was simmering, she picked up the ladle I had too close to the stove and burned her hand. Anyone who knew her could just imagine what she said next!

INSTRUCTIONS: Slowly sauté onions in butter and oil in a covered 4-quart heavy pot. Cook about 15 minutes.

Remove cover. Raise heat to medium. Stir in salt and sugar. The sugar will help the onions to caramelize. Cook 35 to 40 minutes, stirring frequently, until onions are evenly browned.

Sprinkle onions with flour. Stir for 3 minutes. Remove from heat.

In a separate pot, bring stock to a boil. Gradually add stock to onion base. Add wine and season to taste.

Return soup to heat. Simmer, partially covered, for 35 to 40 minutes. Skim occasionally.

To serve, top with freshly grated Parmesan cheese. This soup is especially tasty when prepared a day ahead.

INGREDIENTS:

1½ pounds (5 cups) yellow onions, thinly sliced
2 tablespoons butter
2 tablespoons oil
1 teaspoon salt
¼ teaspoon sugar
3 tablespoons flour
2 quarts brown stock (or 1 quart beef broth and 1 quart water)
½ cup dry white wine
salt and pepper, to taste

GARNISH:
freshly grated Parmesan cheese

POTAGE À LA BRETONNE

MRS. RICHARD B. GORDON

 heart-warming soup on a chilly fall or winter day. Serve with hot crusty French bread and a piece of fruit for a simple lunch. For a fat-free, low calorie version, eliminate the cream and butter at the end. The potage is just as good.

INSTRUCTIONS: Cover beans with water. Soak overnight.

The following day, drain beans. Place beans, water, tomatoes, onions, leeks, and seasonings in a large stock pot. Cover. Bring to a boil. Reduce heat. Uncover and simmer for 1¼ hours, until beans are fork tender. Skim foam as necessary.

Remove bay leaves. Purée potage in batches, using a food processor or a blender. Return potage to pot. Add butter and cream. Heat gently. Correct seasonings, if needed.

INGREDIENTS FOR 12 SERVINGS:

2 pounds dry white beans

12 cups water

2 cups canned whole tomatoes, chopped

2 large onions, thinly sliced

2 leeks, chopped

4 bay leaves

2 tablespoons fresh thyme (or 2 teaspoons dried thyme)

salt and pepper, to taste

¼ cup butter

¼ cup heavy cream

POTATO SOUP

JOAN BRILL

 received this recipe from August "Gussie" Brill, a wonderful cook, in 1961.

INSTRUCTIONS: In a 2-quart saucepan, sauté onion in butter until soft, about 5 minutes. Sprinkle the onion with flour. Stir and cook slowly until the mixture turns golden.

Remove saucepan from heat. Gradually whisk in chicken broth. Return to heat.

Add potatoes and celery. Simmer on low heat 20 to 30 minutes until potatoes are tender. Stir in parsley.

To thicken the soup, mash lightly. Season to taste.

INGREDIENTS FOR 4 SERVINGS:

1 onion, finely chopped
2 tablespoons butter
2 tablespoons flour
4 cups chicken broth
2 cups potatoes, peeled and cut into ½-inch dice
1 cup celery (including leaves), chopped
½ cup chopped parsley
dash turmeric
salt and pepper, to taste

Lentil Soup Rosner

Raising two vegetarian daughters forced me to stuff as many proteins and vitamins as possible into each and every meal I prepared. I knew that outside the house there were few healthy choices available. Here is a particular favorite.

INSTRUCTIONS: Combine all ingredients in a large, heavy saucepan. Bring soup to a boil. Reduce heat. Cover and simmer 45 minutes, stirring occasionally. If adding optional vegetables, add them to soup during the last 15 minutes of cooking time.

Serve with wedges of Vermont cheddar and a 7-grain or dark rye bread.

INGREDIENTS FOR 8 TO 10 SERVINGS:

1 ½ cups lentils
1 cup brown or white rice
4 cups vegetable broth
2 cups water
1 (28 ounce) can whole tomatoes, chopped
1 large onion, coarsely chopped
1 cup celery, coarsely chopped
3 cloves garlic, pressed
½ cup fresh parsley, finely chopped
½ teaspoon dried basil
½ teaspoon dried thyme
salt and freshly ground black pepper, to taste

OPTIONAL INGREDIENTS:

1 cup cooked broccoli, chopped
1 cup cooked cauliflower, chopped

Minestrone Soup

BABE BISTRIAN

INSTRUCTIONS: Sauté the garlic and onion in oil for 5 minutes. Add chicken broth and tomato paste. Bring to a boil. Add the remaining ingredients, except the beans. Return to a boil. Reduce heat and simmer until vegetables are tender and the macaroni is cooked. Stir in garbanzo beans.

Serve with freshly grated Parmesan cheese. If soup becomes too thick, add more chicken broth. This soup freezes well.

INGREDIENTS FOR 8 SERVINGS:

1 clove garlic, minced

1 medium onion, chopped

2 tablespoons olive oil

6 cups chicken broth

¼ cup tomato paste

2 cups cabbage, shredded

2 cups zucchini, diced

1 cup celery, diced

1 cup fresh spinach, shredded

2 carrots, diced

2 tablespoons snipped parsley

1 tablespoon dried basil

⅛ teaspoon black pepper

½ cup tubettini macaroni

1 (16 ounce) can garbanzo beans, drained

GARNISH:

freshly grated Parmesan cheese

Pasta e Fagioli con Pollo

RUTH SPEAR

This warming, satisfying one-dish dinner was born one cold winter Sunday when I was trying to figure out how to turn a small amount of leftover chicken into a hearty meal. Without the chicken, you have an exceptionally tasty version of the classic Italian soup.

INSTRUCTIONS: In a large pot, sauté garlic in oil until soft. Add onion, carrot, celery, and parsley. Continue to sauté for 10 minutes, stirring occasionally.

Add tomatoes and their juice. Reduce heat. Simmer 20 minutes.

Add beans; simmer 5 minutes. Add broth and water. Bring to a moderate boil.

Scoop out about 1 cup of solids. Purée. Return to pot. Add salt and pepper, to taste. Stir in hot peppers.

Check soup for consistency. If too thick, add more broth. Stir in chicken. Bring soup to a steady boil. Add pasta. Cook al dente.

Let soup "rest" 20 minutes. Discard hot peppers. Before serving, swirl in Parmesan cheese.

INGREDIENTS FOR 6 SERVINGS:

1 teaspoon chopped garlic

¼ cup olive oil

1 medium onion, coarsely chopped

1 carrot, coarsely chopped

1 stalk celery, coarsely chopped

2 tablespoons chopped parsley

3 to 4 canned Italian plum tomatoes, chopped, plus their juice

1 (20 ounce) can cannellini beans, drained

2 cups canned or homemade chicken broth

2 cups water

salt and pepper, to taste

2 small, dried, hot red peppers, broken in half

1 to 1½ cups cooked chicken

6 ounces orrechiette, tubettini, or other small pasta

2 tablespoons freshly grated Parmesan cheese

Split Pea Soup

INA GARTEN, THE BAREFOOT CONTESSA

INSTRUCTIONS: Sauté onions, ham, garlic, and oregano in oil.

Add 1½ pounds split peas, stock, salt, and pepper. Cook until peas are soft, approximately 1 hour.

Add additional ½ pound split peas; cook 30 minutes more.

Add carrots and potatoes. Cook until al dente. Adjust liquid to correct consistency. Season to taste.

INGREDIENTS FOR 5 QUARTS:
1 pound onions, diced
¼ pound ham, diced
1 tablespoon garlic, minced
1 tablespoon dried oregano
½ cup soy oil
2 pounds split peas
18 cups chicken stock
salt and pepper, to taste
1 pound carrots, diced
1 pound potatoes, peeled and diced

Long Island Style Clam Chowder

MRS. ARNOLD E. RATTRAY, 1939 L.V.I.S. COOKBOOK

Two quarts hard clams, 1 dozen large potatoes, diced, salt pork, about 3 good slices, 2 or 3 onions, good sized ones, 1 can tomato, parsley, carrots, celery, green pepper if desired. Fry salt pork in kettle; take out slices and dice. Cut up onions and brown in pork fat. Put in potatoes, with rather more than enough water to cover. Cook slowly, not to burn, about ½ hour. When cooked, take large can tomato, cutting up large pieces, cook with potatoes a few minutes, making altogether about 2 quarts of liquid. Put clams through grinder, saving juice. Add clam juice to mixture, let it boil up once or twice. Put in chopped clam last of all; let simmer. This is even better the second day. The parsley, carrots, celery, and green pepper (just a little of each) are optional but very good. They would be put in with the potatoes.

Nora Bennett's Clam Chowder

NORA BENNETT

e sure to use a grinder, not a blender or a food processor, as the results will be too mushy.

INSTRUCTIONS: Rinse clams, grind, and set aside. Put clam juice and water in a large kettle and bring to a simmer.

Grind celery, carrots, onions, and potatoes. Add to the kettle. Add half of the clams and refrigerate the other half. Add the tomatoes, butter, salt, and pepper. Bring to a boil, partially cover, lower heat and simmer for 7 hours, adding the milk after 3 hours.

Do not let the chowder boil. Stir from time to time. If the chowder seems to thick, thin it with water.

Cool and refrigerate overnight. Before serving, add reserved clams and heavy cream. Heat about 15 minutes. Do not boil. This chowder freezes well.

INGREDIENTS FOR 8 SERVINGS:

1½ quarts fresh chowder clams, measured without liquid

3 cups fresh clam juice, reserved

3 cups water

4 to 5 stalks celery

3 to 4 carrots

4 to 5 medium onions

6 medium potatoes, peeled

1 (16 ounce) can tomatoes

6 tablespoons butter

salt and freshly ground pepper, to taste

1¼ cups milk

3 tablespoons heavy cream

Oyster Artichoke Soup

LENORE PICARD

Instructions: Sauté onion in butter until soft. Add flour. Stir until smooth. Whisk in broth, oyster liquid, and spices. Cook for 10 minutes.

Add artichokes. Cook 5 minutes. Add oysters. Heat only until oysters curl. Overcooking will cause oysters to toughen.

Add cream. Heat gently. To serve, garnish with parsley.

INGREDIENTS FOR 4 SERVINGS:

1 medium onion, chopped

6 tablespoons butter

6 tablespoons flour

1 (13¾ ounce) can chicken broth

2 cups liquid (reserved oyster liquid plus water)

1 bay leaf

pinch thyme

¼ teaspoon cayenne

1 (8½ ounce) can artichoke hearts, drained and chopped

1 pint oysters, drained

½ cup heavy cream

GARNISH:

fresh Italian parsley, chopped

Spicy Lobster and Sweet Corn Bisque

NANCY NEWMAN, CHEF, DEVON YACHT CLUB

This is a great recipe for using the best local East End specialties: Lobster, corn, and tomatoes.

INSTRUCTIONS: Remove lobster meat from the shell. Chop coarsely. Break the shells into small pieces, using either a food processor or a hammer.

In a soup pot, sauté the shells in oil until they are lightly browned. Add leeks, onion, and fennel. Sauté 5 minutes more.

Add cognac and wine. Simmer 3 minutes. Add herbs, tomatoes, and tomato paste. Add enough cold water to cover by one inch. Simmer gently for 45 minutes. Remove from heat and strain.

In a second pot, make a roux from the butter and flour. Add strained liquid and bring to a boil. Add heavy cream. Season to taste.

Ladle bisque into bowls. Garnish with corn, tomato, chives, and jalapeño.

INGREDIENTS FOR 8 SERVINGS:

4 (1 pound) lobsters, boiled 8 minutes to partially cook meat

4 tablespoons olive oil

1 bunch leeks, sliced thin

1 large onion, sliced thin

2 pieces fennel, sliced thin

½ cup cognac

2 cups white wine

1 bouquet garni (made with a handful of parsley stems, 2 bay leaves, and ¼ bunch fresh thyme)

4 ripe, fresh tomatoes, coarsely chopped or 1 (16 ounce) can whole plum tomatoes

1 tablespoon tomato paste

8 cups water

3 tablespoons butter

3 tablespoons flour

salt, pepper, and cayenne, to taste

GARNISH:

2 cups lightly cooked sweet corn

1 tomato, peeled, sliced, diced

1 bunch chives, finely sliced

½ jalapeño pepper, minced

Tomatoes at local farmstand.

SALADS

Cauliflower and Radish Salad

WITH BLACK OLIVE DRESSING AND FRIED ANCHOVIES

DENNIS MACNEIL, CHEF DE CUISINE, THE LAUNDRY

INSTRUCTIONS: Bring head of cauliflower to a boil in salted water. Remove pot from heat; allow to cool in the liquid. Remove cauliflower and wrap tightly in plastic. Refrigerate just long enough to firm it up. When cool, separate into bite-sized florets.

Meanwhile, roast red peppers over flame. Peel and julienne. Marinate peppers in some oil and vinegar. Finely shred radishes. If you have one, use a mandoline to finely julienne celery, making sure to remove all fibrous strings.

Combine prepared vegetables in a large bowl. Season to taste with black pepper. Toss with dressing. Chill.

FOR FRIED ANCHOVIES: Cut whole anchovies down the middle lengthwise into 4 strips each. If using canned anchovies, be sure to soak them in 3 changes of water; pat dry. Dip each anchovy strip or filet in milk or cream. Coat with flour. Fry in oil until crisp.

FOR BLACK OLIVE DRESSING: Process olives, tuna, anchovy fillets, garlic, and capers until a smooth paste is formed. Whisk in oil, vinegar, and lemon juice. Add basil and parsley.

TO ASSEMBLE: Place dressed vegetables on bed of prepared lettuce. Top each salad with 4 fried anchovy strips or fillets. If desired, garnish with poached baby leeks.

INGREDIENTS FOR 6 TO 8 SERVINGS:

1 large head cauliflower

2 large red peppers, roasted and marinated in oil and vinegar

2 bunches radishes

¾ cup finely julienned celery

freshly ground black pepper, to taste

lettuce, washed, dried and torn into pieces

FRIED ANCHOVIES:

6 to 8 salted anchovies, boned or 1 can anchovies

milk or cream

flour for coating

oil for frying

BLACK OLIVE DRESSING:

½ cup oil-cured black olives, pitted

1 tablespoon canned tuna

4 anchovy fillets

1 garlic clove

1½ tablespoons capers, rinsed

½ cup olive oil

2 tablespoons red wine vinegar

juice of 1 lemon

2 tablespoons chopped fresh basil

2 tablespoons chopped parsley

GARNISH:

poached baby leeks

Dottie's Green Pea Salad

MRS. KENNELL SCHENCK

INSTRUCTIONS: Discard outer lettuce leaves. Tear lettuce leaves into bite-sized pieces; place them in a large, deep glass dish. Spread frozen peas evenly over the lettuce. Layer water chestnuts over peas. Next, create a layer of onions over the water chestnuts.

Combine sugar and mayonnaise together in a small bowl. Spread mixture over the onion layer to seal. Sprinkle generously with Parmesan cheese. Cover tightly with plastic wrap. Refrigerate for 24 hours before serving. When ready to serve, toss.

INGREDIENTS FOR 10 TO 12 SERVINGS:
1 head iceberg lettuce
1 (10 ounce) package frozen peas, unthawed
1 (8 ounce) can sliced water chestnuts, drained
1 red onion, thinly sliced
1 cup mayonnaise
2 teaspoons sugar
Parmesan cheese, grated

German Potato Salad

MRS. HAROLD THAYER, 1965 L.V.I.S. COOKBOOK

Cook potatoes in jackets. Peel, slice thin. Put on spices. Cube bacon. Fry crisp. Put in onion. Add sugar and flour - make paste. Slowly add the vinegar and water. Pour on potatoes. Mix. Serve hot.

INGREDIENTS FOR 6 TO 8 SERVINGS:
12 small potatoes
1¼ teaspoons salt
⅛ teaspoon pepper
8 slices bacon
1 onion
1 tablespoon sugar
2 tablespoons flour
1 cup vinegar and water

Oriental Mushroom Salad

LANCE ROLL, CHEF, RED HORSE MARKET

 his salad attempts to mimic a salad I ate at a small but excellent Japanese restaurant in San Diego called Sushi Ota. For a nice touch, add enoki mushrooms and serve cold over mixed organic greens.

INSTRUCTIONS: Prepare all ingredients. Heat oils in a large skillet. When oil is hot, add garlic. When garlic is brown, add 2 ounces of ginger and 2 ounces of sesame seeds. Then, add all of the mushrooms. Season with salt and pepper. When mushrooms have become soft, add soy sauce and vinegar. Continue to cook for 3 to 4 minutes.

Remove from pan to serving dish. When mushrooms have cooled, add scallions. Serve at room temperature and garnish with remaining sesame seeds. Add more sesame oil to taste, if desired.

INGREDIENTS:

4 ounces sesame oil
4 ounces extra virgin olive oil
6 cloves of garlic, sliced
4 ounces crushed fresh ginger
4 ounces black sesame seeds
1 pound fresh shiitake mushrooms, stemmed and
    sliced
1 pound oyster mushrooms, stems partially removed
1 pound cremini mushrooms, sliced
salt and pepper
2 ounces soy sauce
4 ounces rice wine vinegar
8 scallions, sliced

RED CABBAGE SLAW WITH POPPY SEED DRESSING

ELIZABETH J. MAGILL

This is an excellent, colorful slaw. It keeps well as it does not wilt or get watery.

INSTRUCTIONS: Finely shred or grate red cabbage. A food processor is great for this. Dip avocado slices in lemon juice to prevent discoloration. Combine cabbage with avocado slices and grapes.

FOR DRESSING: In a blender or food processor, mix together vinegar, sugar, mustard, and onion. Slowly incorporate oil. Stir in poppy seeds by hand.

Combine dressing with slaw mixture. Chill until ready to serve.

INGREDIENTS:

1 medium red cabbage

1 avocado, peeled and thinly sliced

1 to 2 teaspoons lemon juice

¼ pound green seedless grapes, cut in half lengthwise

DRESSING:

⅓ cup vinegar

¾ cup sugar

1 teaspoon dry mustard

1 ½ tablespoons freshly grated onion

1 cup salad oil

1 ½ tablespoons poppy seeds

ROMAINE SALAD WITH GARLIC DRESSING

KIM HOVEY

ur favorite recipe! Purchase pignoli nuts and Parmesan cheese at a good Italian store or deli.

INSTRUCTIONS: Remove centers of lettuce leaves. Slice leaves crosswise into very thin strips (chiffonade). Place in a large bowl. Season with pepper to taste. Refrigerate.

Boil garlic (with skins on) in water for 10 minutes. Run under cold water, rubbing skins to remove them. Mash garlic and salt together in a small metal bowl with a fork. Whisk in mustard and vinegar. While whisking constantly, slowly add olive oil.

Toss chilled greens with dressing. Add Parmesan cheese and warm toasted pignoli nuts. Mix well. Serve on chilled plates.

INGREDIENTS FOR 4 TO 6 SERVINGS:
1 head Romaine lettuce
freshly grated pepper
½ cup freshly grated Parmesan cheese
¼ cup pignoli nuts, lightly toasted

DRESSING:
½ to 1 head of garlic
¼ teaspoon salt
1 teaspoon Dijon mustard
2 tablespoons white wine vinegar
½ cup olive oil

Spinach Strawberry Salad

SUSAN VAUGHAN

This is a great salad to make all year long. It's perfect for company. You can double the salad ingredients, but do not double the dressing.

INSTRUCTIONS: Wash and dry spinach. Arrange in a pretty bowl with sliced strawberries and orange sections. Chill until ready to serve.

FOR DRESSING: Shake all ingredients together in a jar. Just prior to serving, pour dressing over salad ingredients and toss.

INGREDIENTS FOR 4 TO 6 SERVINGS:
1 (10 ounce) bag fresh spinach
1 pint fresh strawberries, hulled and sliced
1 (11 ounce) can mandarin oranges, drained

DRESSING:
½ cup olive oil
¼ cup balsamic vinegar
⅓ cup sugar
2 teaspoons minced Bermuda onion
¼ teaspoon Worcestershire sauce
¼ teaspoon paprika
2 teaspoons poppy seeds
2 teaspoons sesame seeds, toasted brown

Chicken Breast Salad

ANNE TREGELLAS

INSTRUCTIONS: Poach the chicken breasts until tender. Chill. Remove skin and pat dry. Thoroughly combine the cream cheese, mayonnaise, lemon juice, lemon peel, scallion, and salt. Coat rounded side of each chicken breast with dressing.

Arrange lettuce leaves on 8 dinner plates. Top with thick tomato slices seasoned with salt and pepper. Place a coated chicken breast on each plate. Sprinkle with toasted almonds and olives. Garnish with avocado.

INGREDIENTS FOR 8 SERVINGS:
8 boned chicken breasts
3 ounces cream cheese
¼ cup mayonnaise
2 teaspoons lemon juice
¼ teaspoon grated lemon peel
1 scallion, chopped
salt, to taste
lettuce leaves, washed and dried
2 to 3 large, ripe tomatoes, peeled
½ cup slivered almonds, toasted
¼ cup pitted ripe olives, drained and chopped
2 large ripe avocados, peeled and cut into 8 slices each

Curried Chicken Salad

CLAIRE MC CREA

Raisins can be substituted for the grapes; try water chestnuts instead of the celery. Cooked rice can also be added.

INSTRUCTIONS: Combine chicken, celery, grapes, and almonds in a bowl. In a separate bowl, whisk together dressing ingredients. Pour dressing over chicken mixture. Toss well to coat. Chill before serving.

INGREDIENTS FOR 4 SERVINGS:
3 cups cooked chicken, cubed
1½ cups chopped celery
1 pound grapes, cut in half lengthwise
½ cup sliced almonds

DRESSING:
⅔ cup sour cream
⅓ cup Italian salad dressing
1 teaspoon curry powder
1 teaspoon salt

Virginia Briggs' Chinese Chicken Salad

VIRGINIA BRIGGS

I learned this recipe from Aunt Basie's Japanese hairdresser in Bel Air. You may substitute crab, Chinese pork, or roast beef for the chicken.

INSTRUCTIONS: Deep fry mai fuu noodles in 3 inches of very hot oil. The noodles will puff up immediately. Turn over, puff the other side, and remove at once to drain on paper toweling.

Place cooked noodles in a serving bowl. Combine with chicken, lettuce, and scallions. Toss with dressing. Top with toasted sesame seeds.

FOR DRESSING: Combine all ingredients. Blend well. Refrigerate until ready to serve.

INGREDIENTS FOR 4 SERVINGS:

2 ounces mai fuu noodles

oil for frying

½ pound cooked chicken breast, shredded

½ head iceberg lettuce, shredded

4 scallions, thinly sliced

4 teaspoons sesame seeds, toasted

DRESSING:

¼ cup sesame oil

3 tablespoons rice wine vinegar

2 teaspoons sugar

2 teaspoons salt (or to taste)

½ teaspoon cracked pepper

Cold Rice and Lobster Salad

MRS. LAWRENCE CLARKE

 delicious and slightly different summer lunch.

INSTRUCTIONS FOR RICE MOLD: Combine all ingredients. Press into an oiled 4-cup ring mold. Cover. Chill for 3 to 4 hours.

FOR LOBSTER SALAD: Combine all ingredients. Chill for 2 to 3 hours to allow flavor to develop.

TO SERVE: Unmold rice ring on platter. Place lobster salad in center of ring. Garnish with watercress, hard-cooked eggs, cherry tomatoes, and lemon slices.

INGREDIENTS FOR 8 SERVINGS:
RICE MOLD:
2 cups cooked rice, prepared with chicken broth
¼ cup diced green pepper
¼ cup chopped onion
¼ cup chopped celery
¼ cup chopped sweet pickles
½ cup chopped chutney
½ cup mayonnaise
1 tablespoon Dijon mustard
1 tablespoon curry powder
dash Tabasco sauce
dash garlic powder
salt and freshly ground pepper, to taste
LOBSTER SALAD:
1 pound cooked lobster meat, diced
1 cup crabmeat, flaked
1 cup cooked small shrimp
1 cup mayonnaise
3 tablespoons minced chives
3 tablespoons chopped parsley
juice of 1 lemon
splash of brandy
dash Tabasco sauce
2 teaspoons dry mustard
dash garlic powder
salt and freshly ground pepper, to taste
GARNISH:
watercress
hard-cooked eggs
cherry tomatoes
lemon slices, cut in half

Lobster and Mixed Grain Salad

NANCY NEWMAN, CHEF, DEVON YACHT CLUB

This salad has the distinction of being high in protein but low in fat — a perfect seasonal combination. Wheatberries come from organically grown wheat and are high in protein, amino acids, and vitamin B, while brown rice is a great source of natural fiber.

INSTRUCTIONS: Steam the lobsters, 10 to 12 minutes to cook the meat. Let cool. Remove the meat from the shell, leaving the tail and claws intact. Cut in half lengthwise. Chill.

Cook the grains together in 6 cups of boiling water for 45 minutes to 1 hour. Even after this time, they will have a nut-like consistency. Chill.

Combine vinegars with mustard in a small stainless bowl. Slowly whisk in oil to make a vinaigrette. Season with salt and pepper.

In a bowl, combine grains, vinaigrette, herbs, fennel, and tomatoes. Add small pieces of lobster and asparagus to the bowl. Toss with greens. Arrange on plates. Garnish each serving with half a lobster tail and one claw.

INGREDIENTS FOR 8 SERVINGS:

4 (1 pound) lobsters or 2 pounds fresh lobster meat
1 cup brown rice
1 cup wheatberries, soaked overnight before cooking
2 tablespoons sherry wine vinegar
2 tablespoons white wine vinegar
1 tablespoon Dijon mustard
½ cup canola or safflower oil
salt and freshly ground pepper, to taste
2 tablespoons chopped chives
2 tablespoons chopped fresh tarragon
2 tablespoons chopped parsley
2 small fennel bulbs, finely diced
2 ripe tomatoes, peeled, seeded and diced
1 bunch asparagus, trimmed, blanched, refreshed, and cut into ½-inch pieces
⅓ pound mixed organic greens, such as mesclun

Herring Salad

MRS. GEORGE B. HAND

Two very important customs to follow on New Year's Day: 1) The first person to enter the house must be a dark man. 2) You must eat some herring.

Every year Mr. Alfred Scheffer, the architect of many fine houses in this area, would look forward to receiving a jar of this salad to be enjoyed on New Year's Day.

INSTRUCTIONS: Drain beets; reserve ¼ cup of the liquid. Dice beets and put in a bowl. Add herring, potato, apple, pickle, and onion. Mix well.

Combine reserved beet juice, mayonnaise, sugar, and pepper. Add to beet mixture and blend.

Press into 6-cup mold or put into sterilized jars and refrigerate.

INGREDIENTS:

1 (16 ounce) can sliced, pickled beets
1 (12 ounce) jar herring in wine sauce
1½ cups diced, cooked potato
½ cup diced apple
⅓ cup diced dill pickle
¼ cup finely chopped onion
¼ cup mayonnaise
2 tablespoons sugar
dash white pepper

Tasty Bluefish Salad

ROSITA MEDLER

INSTRUCTIONS FOR POACHING FISH: Combine ingredients. Simmer for 15 minutes to develop flavor. Add fillets. Poach gently until fish flakes and turns opaque. Remove fillets from poaching liquid and let cool. If desired, remove black meat which is strong in flavor.

FOR SALAD: Flake cooked fish into a bowl. Add celery. In a separate bowl, whisk together remaining ingredients. Depending on the amount of fish you prepare, you may need to increase the mayonnaise and sour cream. Mix dressing with bluefish and celery. Chill. Serve on a bed of lettuce or use as a filling for whole wheat pita sandwiches.

INGREDIENTS:

POACHING LIQUID:
water or white wine, enough to cover fish fillets
skins from bluefish
juice of 2 lemons
2 tablespoons oil
1 small bay leaf
salt, to taste

SALAD:
bluefish fillets
½ cup finely chopped celery
2 tablespoons mayonnaise
2 tablespoons sour cream
½ teaspoon lemon juice
½ teaspoon garlic powder
salt and pepper, to taste

Tuna Macaroni Supper Salad

MRS. EDWARD H. JEWETT, JR.

INSTRUCTIONS: Prepare macaroni according to package directions. Drain and rinse with cold water. Set aside.

In a large bowl, whisk together mayonnaise, Italian dressing, and mustard. Stir in remaining ingredients, including cooked macaroni. Mix well. Cover and chill for at least 4 hours.

To serve, place salad on a bed of chicory. Sprinkle with chopped eggs and parsley.

INGREDIENTS FOR 8 SERVINGS:

1 (8 ounce) package elbow macaroni
1 cup mayonnaise
½ cup Italian style dressing
1 tablespoon mustard
2 cups pared cucumber, thinly sliced
1½ cups diced tomatoes
½ cup diced green pepper
¼ cup chopped green onion
1 teaspoon salt
⅛ teaspoon pepper
2 (7 ounce) cans solid white tuna, drained and
   flaked in large pieces

GARNISH:

chicory
2 hard-cooked eggs, chopped
chopped parsley

Warm Bay Scallop Salad with Balsamic Vinaigrette

MARGE BRINKLEY

This is a light, elegant, uniquely tasty salad. If you wish, you can substitute shrimp, veal, lamb, or lobster for the bay scallops. There are no secrets or tricks to making this. Just don't overcook the scallops. Cook them until they are medium rare. Your guests will love it!

INSTRUCTIONS: In a large skillet, sauté garlic and shallots in hot oil for 10 seconds. Add scallops; sauté for 2 to 3 minutes. Add wine and butter, sautéing 2 to 3 minutes longer, or until scallops just turn opaque. Set aside and keep warm.

Place romaine lettuce and spinach leaves in a medium bowl. Toss well with ¾ cup balsamic vinaigrette.

Arrange salad greens on 8 individual serving plates. Top with sautéed scallops. Sprinkle with feta cheese and pine nuts. Encircle with tomato wedges. And voila! You have a salad that looks beautiful and tastes delicious!

FOR BALSAMIC VINAIGRETTE: Whisk together mustard and vinegar in a medium bowl. Very slowly, while whisking constantly, dribble in the oil. When incorporated, mix in remaining ingredients. Reserve extra dressing for another use.

INGREDIENTS FOR 8 SERVINGS:

2 tablespoons olive oil
3 cloves garlic, finely chopped
1 tablespoon shallots, finely chopped
2 pounds bay scallops
½ cup white wine
⅓ cup unsalted butter
2 heads romaine lettuce, washed, torn, and dried
4 bunches spinach, stems removed, washed, and dried
¾ cup balsamic vinaigrette
½ cup feta cheese, crumbled
½ cup pine nuts, toasted
2 cups tomatoes, peeled, and cut in wedges

3 CUPS BALSAMIC VINAIGRETTE:

2 tablespoons Dijon mustard
1 cup balsamic vinegar
2 cups vegetable oil
1 tablespoon shallots, minced
1 teaspoon lemon juice, freshly squeezed
salt, to taste
white pepper, to taste

Orzo and Artichoke Salad

Mrs. Connie Lefler

INSTRUCTIONS: In a pot of boiling, salted water, cook the orzo until it is just al dente. Drain and refresh under cold water. Drain well. In a bowl, toss orzo with ¼ cup olive oil.

In a small saucepan, simmer artichokes in broth until tender, about 6 to 7 minutes. Drain well; add to orzo. Toss orzo and artichokes with dressing. Add remaining ingredients. Toss again. Garnish with tomato wedges and basil leaves or parsley sprigs.

FOR DRESSING: In a small bowl, whisk together egg yolk, vinegar, mustard, salt and pepper. Add olive oil in a slow, steady stream, whisking until dressing emulsifies. Whisk in basil.

INGREDIENTS:

1½ cups orzo

¼ cup extra-virgin olive oil

2 (9 ounce) packages frozen artichoke hearts, thawed, halved if large

½ cup chicken broth

2 ounces prosciutto, diced

2 ounces freshly grated Parmesan cheese

2 tablespoons fresh lemon juice

¼ cup chopped fresh parsley

2 tablespoons chopped chives

DRESSING:

1 large egg yolk

2 tablespoons white wine vinegar

1 teaspoon Dijon mustard

salt and pepper, to taste

½ cup extra-virgin olive oil

2 tablespoons minced fresh basil

GARNISH:

tomato wedges

basil leaves or parsley sprigs

Apple Crunch Molded Salad

MRS. URBAN S. REININGER, III

INSTRUCTIONS: Dissolve gelatin in boiling water. Add cold water or apple juice. Chill until thickened but not firm. Fold in apples, celery, and nuts. Spoon into 8x4-inch loaf pan. Chill until firm, about 4 hours.

INGREDIENTS FOR 8 SERVINGS:
2 (3 ounce) packages of strawberry Jello
2 cups boiling water
1½ cups cold water or apple juice
1 cup diced, peeled apples
½ cup diced celery
¼ cup chopped nuts

Cranberry Mold

JEANNE C. OWEN

This recipe was given to me by Eileen Jacobs. It is delicious served with chicken salad or in place of cranberry sauce at Thanksgiving.

INSTRUCTIONS: Drain pineapple, reserving juice. Add enough boiling water to juice to make 2 cups. Dissolve Jello in boiling liquid. Stir in remaining ingredients. Chill in a ring mold until set. Serve with a sauce made from mayonnaise, plain yogurt, and any fruit juice.

INGREDIENTS:
1 (16 ounce) can crushed pineapple
boiling water
2 (3 ounce) packages raspberry Jello
1 cup port wine
1 (16 ounce) can whole cranberry sauce
½ cup chopped walnuts

Tomato Aspic

MAURIE BLEE

Delicious served on watercress with mayonnaise.

INSTRUCTIONS: Dissolve gelatin in water. Set aside.

Boil tomato juice with sugar and seasonings for 7 minutes. Discard bay leaves. Combine mixture with dissolved gelatin and vinegar. Chill in a 2-quart mold for at least 6 hours.

INGREDIENTS:

2 envelopes gelatin

½ cup water

4 cups tomato juice

pinch of sugar

1 tablespoon onion, finely minced

1 tablespoon parsley, finely minced

1 teaspoon oregano

1 teaspoon pepper

2 tablespoons vinegar

Honey Mustard Dressing

PHYLLIS FRENKEL

Great with all kinds of salads and cold pasta!

INSTRUCTIONS: Heat vinegar and honey in a small heavy saucepan over low heat, stirring until honey dissolves. Pour into a bowl and cool. Whisk in mayonnaise, mustard, onion, parsley, and salt. Gradually whisk in oil. Cover and refrigerate. May be prepared 3 days ahead. Bring to room temperature before using.

INGREDIENTS:
3 tablespoons cider vinegar
3 tablespoons honey
6 tablespoons mayonnaise
1 tablespoon Dijon mustard
1 ½ tablespoons onion, finely minced
2 tablespoons chopped fresh parsley
pinch of salt
¾ cup vegetable oil

Vinaigrette Dressing

RUTH MC CREA LIZARS

A great standby when you need a simple but elegant dressing.

INSTRUCTIONS: Combine all ingredients and blend thoroughly. Remove garlic before serving. Makes about ½ cup of dressing.

INGREDIENTS:
6 tablespoons olive oil
2 tablespoons lemon juice
1 teaspoon Dijon mustard
½ teaspoon sugar
1 garlic clove, halved
1 teaspoon salt
freshly ground pepper

This bakery was built in 1893, and was near the methodist church on what is now the Memorial Green

Breads

BUCKWHEAT PANCAKES

GEORGE STARKE, 1965 L.V.I.S. COOKBOOK

Mr. Starke is carrying on an old East Hampton tradition. The first L.V.I.S. Cook Book contained no "receipt" for making raised buckwheat griddlecakes because everybody knew how to make them at that time. They were a matter of course, every winter morning, accompanied by homemade sausage, home-cured ham or bacon. One-half to two-thirds cup of batter was saved every morning to leaven tomorrow's batch. Cold water was poured over to keep it moist. This could be kept up for many weeks, before fresh yeast had to be used. But when warm weather came, the mixture would get sour. So, during the summer, cornmeal or flour-and-egg griddlecakes were used. These were made with cream of tartar or saleratus (baking soda).

A good many farm people found a griddle or a frying pan too small for the quantity needed. They would grease the top of the cast iron kitchen range and bake the griddlecakes right there.

INSTRUCTIONS: At night: Dissolve yeast in a little water then add remaining water and salt. Beat in the flour until smooth. Cover with clean towel and let stand in warm place over night.

Morning: Dissolve ¼ teaspoon baking soda in ¼ to ½ cup lukewarm water, add 2 large mixing spoons Sagaponack molasses (or equal) and stir into batter. Batter should not be too thick. Bake on well greased medium to hot griddle, turning cake when bubbles are spread over entire surface. Save 1 cup of seed, cover, and stand in cool place and the next night proceed as described, omitting the yeast.

INGREDIENTS:

1 package dry yeast (new)
2 large mixing spoons molasses
¼ teaspoon baking soda
water
2 cups lukewarm water
½ cup white flour
1 ½ cups buckwheat
1 teaspoon salt

Note: As the sourness increases after days of use, increase the soda to ½ teaspoon.

Gardiner's Island Rice Griddle Cakes

MRS. J. ALEXANDER TYLER. 1965 L.V.I.S. COOKBOOK

Mrs. Frank Dayton discovered in the East Hampton Library's Long Island Collection, Mrs. Tyler's "Receipt Book", from Gardiner's Island and from old families along Main Street. Mrs. Tyler was born Sarah Griswold Gardiner, daughter of Samuel Buell Gardiner, 10th Proprietor of Gardiner's Island. She married the son of President John Tyler and of his wife, Julia Gardiner, who was also born on the historic island. Mrs. J. Alexander Tyler lived on Main Street in the house now owned by Mrs. Edward S. Mills.

INSTRUCTIONS: Mix boiled rice and sweet milk; then put in a separate dish the flour, buttermilk, dissolved saleratus and salt. Drop in yolks of 3 eggs and stir well. Then add rice and milk and beaten whites of 3 eggs. Bake on very hot greased griddle or iron skillet.

INGREDIENTS:

1 pint of cold boiled rice

1 pint of sweet milk

1 pint of flour

1 even teaspoon saleratus, dissolved in 1 tablespoon of water

1 pint of buttermilk

1 teaspoon salt

3 eggs, separated

PUMPKIN PANCAKES

BARBARA FLYNN, MILL HOUSE INN

We serve these pancakes for breakfast in the fall and winter months.

INSTRUCTIONS: In a large bowl, stir together flour, baking powder, brown sugar, salt, cinnamon, and allspice. Stir in milk, pumpkin, eggs, vanilla, and bacon drippings. Stir until batter is combined well.

Heat a greased griddle over moderate heat until drops of water scatter over surface. Working in batches, pour batter onto griddle by ¼ cup measures. Cook pancakes for 2 minutes on each side, or until golden and cooked through. Transfer to heated platter.

Serve with maple syrup, honey, or fruit.

INGREDIENTS FOR 16 PANCAKES:

1½ cups unbleached all-purpose flour

2 tablespoons double-acting baking powder

2 tablespoons light brown sugar, firmly packed

1 teaspoon salt

2 teaspoons cinnamon

1 teaspoon ground allspice

1½ cups canned evaporated milk (not condensed)

1 cup solid-pack canned pumpkin

2 large eggs, beaten lightly

1½ teaspoons vanilla

¼ cup bacon drippings

maple syrup, honey, or fresh fruit as accompaniment

WAFFLES

HARRIETT WAGMAN

INSTRUCTIONS: Sift together dry ingredients into a large bowl. In a small bowl, whisk together the eggs and melted butter. Pour egg-butter mixture and seltzer into dry ingredients. Blend just until combined.

Heat waffle iron; brush grids lightly with oil. Use approximately ¼ cup of batter for each waffle, following the directions given with your waffle iron.

INGREDIENTS FOR 4 SERVINGS:

1½ cups all-purpose flour

2 tablespoons sugar

4 teaspoons double-acting baking powder

½ teaspoon salt

2 large eggs, lightly beaten

4 tablespoons unsalted butter, melted and cooled

1½ cups very fresh seltzer or club soda

Wholesome Pancakes

KEN FERRIN

INSTRUCTIONS: In a large bowl, mix together all dry ingredients. Set aside. In a small bowl, beat egg lightly; add buttermilk and oil. Add liquid mixture to dry ingredients. Cook on hot griddle. For a variation, add fresh blueberries to batter.

INGREDIENTS FOR 6 PANCAKES:
1 tablespoon buckwheat flour
4 tablespoons whole wheat flour
½ teaspoon baking powder
½ teaspoon baking soda
1 tablespoon flax seeds, optional
1 tablespoon wheat germ
1 egg
1 cup buttermilk
1 tablespoon vegetable oil

Potato Split Biscuit

GRANDMA GLOVER. 1901 L.V.I.S. COOKBOOK

Boil two or three medium-sized potatoes; when thoroughly cooked, and while hot, mash and stir into them 1 cup butter and lard mixed; salt to taste; to this add 1 cup milk, in which is dissolved ½ yeast cake; 1 tablespoon sugar, 2 eggs, well beaten; stir into mixture 1 quart sifted flour. Mix at 9 a.m. Mould again at noon and set away for second rising; at 5 p.m. turn the dough out on board with sufficient flour to handle. Roll and cut with biscuit cutter; let them rise and bake for tea.

Best-of-Bran Muffins

PATRICIA AND KEN FERRIN

*I*NSTRUCTIONS: In a large bowl, combine cereal, oil, and raisins. Pour the boiling water over mixture and set aside to cool slightly.

In a small bowl, combine eggs, buttermilk, and molasses. Add to the partially cooled cereal mixture.

In another small bowl, combine flour, sugar, baking soda, and salt. Add the flour mixture to the cereal mixture, stirring just enough to moisten the dry ingredients. Cover the batter with plastic wrap, waxed paper, or a damp towel, and let stand for at least 15 minutes, preferably for 1 hour.

Bake at 400° for 20 to 25 minutes in greased muffin tins, each cup filled about three-fourths of the way with batter. Remove from oven and cool slightly in tins; then remove from tins and cool completely on rack.

INGREDIENTS FOR 24 MUFFINS:

3 cups bran cereal, shredded

½ cup vegetable oil

1 cup raisins

1 cup boiling water

2 eggs, lightly beaten

2 cups buttermilk

¼ cup molasses

2¼ cups whole-wheat flour

4 teaspoons sugar

2½ teaspoons baking soda

½ teaspoon salt, if desired

Scones

DEBBIE CLEMENCE

INSTRUCTIONS: In a large bowl, whisk together flour, sugar, baking powder, baking soda, and salt. Using a pastry blender, cut in butter until mixture resembles coarse crumbs.

In a small bowl, blend together buttermilk and egg. Pour into dry ingredient mixture. Stir with fork until mixture comes together.

Knead dough 5 or 6 times. Transfer onto a greased cookie sheet. With floured hands, pat into an 8-inch circle. Cut into 8 wedges with a long, sharp, floured knife. Do not separate.

Bake at 425° for 14 to 16 minutes until golden.

VARIATIONS:

Parmesan: Reduce sugar to 1 tablespoon. Stir in ½ cup freshly grated Parmesan cheese and ¼ teaspoon freshly ground pepper.

Cheddar-Chive: Reduce sugar to 1 tablespoon. Stir in ½ cup shredded sharp Cheddar and 1 tablespoon chopped chives.

Cherry-Toasted Almond: After cutting in butter, stir in ⅓ cup chopped dried cherries and ¼ cup toasted almonds. Increase buttermilk to ¾ cup and add ⅛ teaspoon almond extract.

INGREDIENTS FOR 8 SCONES:

2 cups all-purpose flour

2 tablespoons sugar

2 teaspoons baking powder

½ teaspoon baking soda

½ teaspoon salt

¼ cup butter or margarine, cut up

⅔ cup buttermilk

1 large egg

Cinnamon Rolls

MARY LAWRENCE-ROBERTS

These cinnamon rolls are a family favorite that were passed down from my grandmother, to my mom, and finally to me. My grandmother lived with our family. I remember as a young girl that Friday was her baking day. She made wonderful breads, cross buns, and pizza dough. Returning home from school on Fridays with my sisters and brother, I would usually find these rolls. This past summer I started my own catering business in East Hampton. Leasing a kitchen from a local tennis club, I provided breakfast and lunch for members and used the kitchen for catering local functions. When I got spread a little too thin, I would ask my mom to help. Whether it was her Apple Butter Cake or these Cinnamon Rolls, they were always the first to go.

INSTRUCTIONS: Sift together flour, Bisquick, baking powder, and salt. Cut ½ cup well-chilled butter into tablespoon pieces. Work into flour mixture with fingertips, until mixture resembles coarse crumbs, and remains light and dry. Soak raisins in warm water for 5 minutes. Drain and add to dough, mixing lightly.

With fork, whisk milk and egg. Pour into mixture and blend lightly with a spatula just until moist. Turn onto lightly floured surface. Sprinkle small amount of flour on dough and rolling pin. Roll dough into rectangle, approximately 24x10-inches.

Spread ½ cup room-temperature butter over dough. Mix together brown sugar and cinnamon and sprinkle over dough. Gently roll dough lengthwise into a cylinder. Slice into 2-inch thick circles and place in buttered baking dish. Bake at 350° for 40 minutes until lightly browned. Cool 15 minutes. Whisk together confectioners' sugar and water. Drizzle over rolls.

INGREDIENTS FOR 1 DOZEN ROLLS:

- 2 cups all-purpose flour
- 2 cups Bisquick
- 1 tablespoon baking powder
- 1 teaspoon salt
- 1 cup unsalted butter (half at room temperature)
- 1 cup raisins
- 1 cup milk
- 1 egg
- ¾ cup dark brown sugar
- 1½ tablespoons cinnamon
- ½ cup confectioners' sugar
- 1 tablespoon water

Casatella (Easter Sweet Bread)

MRS. JO D'AURIA

This started out as an Easter only recipe, but waiting a whole year was too long. INSTRUCTIONS: In a large bowl, beat eggs. Gradually beat in sugar until light and fluffy. Add cooled, melted butter a little at a time. Combine 1¾ cups flour with baking powder. Stir in, mixing well. Add orange juice, vanilla, and cinnamon. Gradually incorporate remaining 1¾ cups flour until a soft dough is formed.

Turn dough onto a lightly floured board. Knead until smooth, adding additional flour if necessary. Let rest about 20 minutes.

Shape dough into a ball and cut in four pieces. Roll each piece into a smooth ball. Flatten each ball, making a hole in the center to hold hard-cooked egg. Bake on a greased and floured cookie sheet at 375° for 25 to 30 minutes until golden brown.

INGREDIENTS:

6 eggs
1 cup plus 2 tablespoons sugar
¾ pound melted sweet butter, cooled
3½ cups flour
4 teaspoons baking powder
juice of 1 medium orange
2 teaspoons vanilla
½ teaspoon cinnamon
4 hard-cooked eggs

Corn Bread

MRS. JOHN D. HEDGES. 1896 L.V.I.S. COOKBOOK

Two cups Indian, one cup wheat;
One cup sour milk, one cup sweet;
One good egg that well you beat;
Half cup molasses, too;
Half cup sugar add thereto;
With one spoon butter new;
Salt and soda each a spoon;
Mix up quick and bake it soon.
Then you'll have corn bread complete,
Best of all corn bread you meet.
If you have a dozen boys
To increase your household joys,
Double then this rule, I should,
And you'll have two corn cakes good.
When you've nothing in for tea
This the very thing will be.
All the men that I have seen
Say it is of all cakes queen —
Good enough for any king
That a husband home may bring;
Warming up the human stove,
Cheering up the hearts you love;
And only Tyndall can explain
The links between corn and brain.
Get a husband what he likes
And save a hundred household strikes.

Indian Loaf

MRS. EVERETT J. EDWARDS. 1955 L.V.I.S. COOKBOOK

This is the same recipe used for the "Rye 'n Injun" loaf baked in the brick ovens beside the fireplace, or in slow wood-stove ovens in the old days; but instead of the ⅓ white flour they used rye flour or canaille and did not steam it, but baked it in an iron basin for 4 or 5 hours. The crust would be ½ or ¾ of an inch thick.

2 cups cornmeal, 1 cup flour, 1 cup molasses, 1 cup milk, 1 even teaspoon soda, 1 tablespoon melted butter, 1 teaspoon salt. Steam 2½ hours; take off cover of steamer and bake in slow oven (about 325°) for 1 hour.

Irish Bread

JEAN RICKENBACH

My mother learned to make this bread as a young girl in Ireland and continued to do so for her children and grandchildren in East Hampton. Everyone loved Mary Smith's Irish Bread!

INSTRUCTIONS: Mix together flour, sugar, powder, soda, salt, and caraway seeds. Slowly add buttermilk, mixing batter by hand. Batter will be thick. Add raisins and mix thoroughly.

Using 2 greased 9-inch round pans or 2 greased loaf pans, fill halfway with batter. Bake at 375° for 30 minutes. Let bread stand in pan for a few minutes before removing to wire rack.

If desired, glaze bread while hot. Brush with milk and sprinkle with sugar.

INGREDIENTS:
4 cups white flour
¼ cup white sugar
1 teaspoon baking powder
1 teaspoon baking soda
½ teaspoon salt
2 tablespoons caraway seeds
2 cups buttermilk
1 ½ cups dark raisins

GLAZE:
milk
sugar

Traditional Italian Holiday Stuffing

MRS. JO D'AURIA

 We have enjoyed this recipe for many years, and now you can too.

INSTRUCTIONS: In a large bowl, mix together bread crumbs, eggs, and Parmesan cheese. Add prosciutto. Mix well. Lastly add ricotta, salt, and pepper.

Lightly grease a glass pan that will give the stuffing about 3 inches in height. Bake at 400° for 10 minutes. Reduce heat, and continue to bake at 325° for 30 to 35 minutes until golden brown.

INGREDIENTS FOR 6 TO 8 SERVINGS:

6 cups coarsely ground Italian bread crumbs, toasted
3 large eggs
¼ cup Parmesan cheese
½ pound thinly sliced prosciutto or salami, julienned
¾ pound of fresh ricotta cheese
pinch of salt and pepper

Carrot Tea Cake with Cream Cheese Frosting

CLAIRE MC CREA

his cake can be served plain as a breakfast or snack cake, or with the cream cheese icing as a tea cake. Wonderful either way!

INSTRUCTIONS: In large bowl, mix together dry ingredients. Add oil to dry mixture. Stir in grated carrots. Add eggs, one at a time, beating after each addition. Mix in nuts and vanilla.

Bake in a greased and floured 9x13-inch pan at 350° for 50 to 60 minutes. Cool in pan. Frost, if desired.

FOR CREAM CHEESE FROSTING: Beat cream cheese and butter until light and fluffy. Gradually add sugar and mix well.

INGREDIENTS:

2 cups flour

2 cups sugar

2 teaspoons baking powder

2 teaspoons baking soda

1 teaspoon salt

2 teaspoons cinnamon

1¼ cups vegetable oil

4 large carrots, peeled and grated

4 eggs

½ cup chopped walnuts

2 teaspoons vanilla

CREAM CHEESE FROSTING:

4 ounces cream cheese, softened

¼ cup butter, softened

2 cups confectioners' sugar

Nut Bread

DEBORAH WALTER

INSTRUCTIONS: In a large bowl, sift together flour, sugar, baking powder, and salt. Add shortening and mix with fork until batter has appearance of coarse cornmeal.

Add milk and egg; mix lightly. Fold in nuts. Pour into greased 9x5-inch loaf pan and let stand for 20 minutes. Sprinkle a little warm water on loaf before baking. Bake at 350° for 60 minutes.

INGREDIENTS FOR I LOAF:

3 cups flour

1 cup sugar

4 teaspoons baking powder

1 teaspoon salt

¼ cup shortening

1 ¼ cups milk

1 egg, slightly beaten

1 cup chopped walnuts

Zucchini Bread

GAYLE E. RATCLIFFE

This recipe was baked and served for our friends' outdoor wedding. Newsday highlighted it and provided instructions in a Sunday magazine section. The bread works well with small or large zucchini and freezes well.

INSTRUCTIONS: In a large bowl, blend zucchini, eggs, sugar, and oil. Sift all dry ingredients together and add to zucchini mixture. Beat well.

Bake at 350° for about 1 hour in greased and floured Bundt pan or 2 loaf pans.

INGREDIENTS:

3 cups shredded zucchini, blotted dry

4 eggs

2 cups sugar

1 cup oil

3 cups flour

1 ½ teaspoons baking soda

1 ½ teaspoons baking powder

1 teaspoon salt

1 teaspoon cinnamon

¼ teaspoon ground cloves

Crumb Cake

DOROTHY ARMBRUSTER

INSTRUCTIONS: Mix together dry ingredients in a large bowl. Cut in shortening. Combine milk, egg, and vanilla. Add to bowl, and mix gently until blended. Spread batter in a greased and floured 9x13-inch pan. Top with crumbs. Bake at 350° for 25 to 30 minutes. If desired, sprinkle with confectioners' sugar when cool.

FOR CRUMBS: Mix together flour, sugar, salt, and cinnamon. Pour melted butter over dry ingredients. Mix with fork, then crumble with hands to form crumbs.

INGREDIENTS:
1¾ cups flour
¾ cup sugar
2½ teaspoons baking powder
½ teaspoon salt
⅓ cup shortening
¾ cup milk
1 unbeaten egg
1½ teaspoons vanilla

CRUMBS:
2 cups flour
1 cup sugar
dash salt
1½ teaspoons cinnamon
¾ cup butter or margarine, melted

Kaffeeklatsch Cake

MRS. L.R. VETAULT. 1939 L.V.I.S. COOKBOOK

Sift measure and sift three times 3¼ cupfuls of cake flour, adding 3½ teaspoons of baking powder and ¼ teaspoon of salt. Cream thoroughly ¾ cupful of butter or other shortening with 2 cupfuls of granulated sugar; add 4 well-beaten eggs, 1½ teaspoons of lemon and vanilla; fold in the flour and baking powder alternately with 1 cupful of milk. Melt 3 tablespoons of butter in a large, round, heavy, pan; sprinkle with 6 tablespoons of light brown sugar and stir till melted; then arrange ½ cupful each of candied cherries and halved pecan meats over the bottom of the pan, pour in the batter and bake in a moderate oven 350° for fifty to sixty minutes. Loosen the cake gently from the pan and turn upside down on a round platter and leave until the cake drops from the pan.

Marble Coffee Cake

MRS. DAVID DAKERS. JR., 1965 L.V.I.S. COOKBOOK

INSTRUCTIONS: Heat oven to 350°. Grease a 9-inch angel food pan. Sift dry ingredients. Cream shortening with sugar and eggs. Alternately add dry ingredients and sour cream then add vanilla. Put half of batter in pan then half of last four ingredients (mixed well) then remaining batter and then rest of last four ingredients. Bake for 45 minutes.

INGREDIENTS:

1½ teaspoons double acting baking powder
1¾ cups sifted cake flour
1½ teaspoons baking soda
½ cup shortening (Crisco)
¾ cup granulated sugar
2 eggs (unbeaten)
½ pint sour cream
1 teaspoon vanilla
¼ cup granulated sugar
2 teaspoons cinnamon
½ cup raisins
½ cup chopped walnuts

Old-Fashioned Raised Doughnuts

MRS. JEREMIAH HUNTTING. 1948 L.V.I.S. COOKBOOK

Doughnuts and crullers, in East Hampton, are two quite different things. The doughnut is made from raised bread dough, with spice and egg added it is big and round, and crisp without, pale beige and soft within; wonderful warmed up for breakfast, or cold with a glass of milk between meals. Doughnuts are almost a lost art today; Miss Mary Ruppel of Bridgehampton still makes them occasionally, on special order. The cruller, ring-shaped, baking-powder raised, has been commercialized until everybody is familiar with it, but few know how good the home-made product can be. Deep-fat frying of doughnuts or crullers makes the price almost prohibitive, for family use.

2 yeast cakes, ¼ cup warm water, 1 tablespoon sugar, ⅓ cup lard, ½ teaspoon salt, ½ cup sugar, 1 beaten egg, 1 teaspoon cloves, 2 teaspoons cinnamon, ½ teaspoon nutmeg, 1¾ cups scalded milk, 5½ cups sifted flour. Dissolve yeast in warm water in small bowl; add 1 tablespoon sugar and set in warm place until light and spongy (about 15 minutes). Combine lard, salt, and sugar in large bowl and add scalded milk; cool to lukewarm. Add yeast mixture and egg, flour and spice, mixing well. Cover, let rise until double in bulk. Pat on board, cut with biscuit cutter, let rise again on waxed paper and fry in hot deep lard.

An old cook book suggests: "Just before putting your doughnuts into the fat, plump them into a well-beaten egg. This will keep out the grease effectually."

Chicken Coop at local Poultry Farm.

Pasta

Grains

Eggs

Cheese

Capellini with Pesto and Scallops

PATRICIA AND KEN FERRIN

INSTRUCTIONS: In a blender or food processor, combine basil, garlic, ½ teaspoon salt, and nuts. With the motor running, gradually add the oil until a smooth paste is formed. Add Parmesan, and process a few seconds more to combine all ingredients thoroughly. Transfer to a large bowl.

In a small saucepan, bring wine, lemon juice, salt, and pepper to a boil. Add scallops, cooking only 2 to 3 minutes. Drain them, reserving the cooking liquid.

In a large pot of boiling, salted water, cook capellini al dente. Drain and place it in the bowl with the pesto. Toss to coat. Gradually add reserved cooking liquid. Add scallops, tossing to mix ingredients well. Refrigerate for at least one hour before serving.

INGREDIENTS FOR 4 SERVINGS:

1 cup fresh basil leaves, washed and dried
2 large cloves of garlic, crushed
½ teaspoon salt
2 tablespoons pine nuts or walnuts
¼ cup olive oil
¼ cup grated Parmesan cheese
½ cup dry white wine
2 tablespoons fresh lemon juice
salt and pepper, to taste
1 pound bay scallops
12 ounces capellini

Linguini with Fresh Clam Sauce

DEBBIE CLEMENCE

There's nothing better than digging fresh clams in my backyard on Napeague Harbor, and then having them for dinner!

INSTRUCTIONS: In a medium saucepan, sauté garlic over medium low flame until golden. Do not brown. Add anchovy paste, stirring until well combined. Stir in parsley, red pepper, and then tomatoes. Simmer for 5 minutes, stirring occasionally.

Add wine. Bring to a boil and reduce mixture by ⅓. Rinse clams in their own juice. Chop coarsely. Strain juice though a sieve lined with a double thickness of cheesecloth. Reserve 1 cup. If you have less, add enough water to make the required amount. Add clam juice to sauce. Bring to a boil and reduce by ⅓.

Add clams. Simmer for just 5 minutes or clams will become tough and rubbery.

Add pasta to rapidly boiling water. Fresh pasta cooks in 30 seconds. Cook commercial dry pasta al dente. Drain well. Transfer pasta to a large serving bowl. Toss with clam sauce, and season with pepper. This dish may or may not need salt, depending upon the saltiness of the clams.

INGREDIENTS FOR 4 SERVINGS:

½ cup olive oil

2 cloves garlic, finely chopped

1 teaspoon anchovy paste or finely chopped anchovies

1 tablespoon finely chopped parsley

⅛ teaspoon crushed red pepper

2 small tomatoes (fresh or canned), peeled, seeded, and chopped

¼ cup dry white wine

2 dozen little neck clams, shucked and juice reserved

1 pound linguini, preferably fresh

freshly ground black pepper, to taste

Spaghetti à la Vongole con Crema

PRISCILLA RATTAZZI WHITTLE

This is an Italian recipe adapted to the Hamptons. In Italy, they keep the clams in their shells. I think this way is tastier. DeCecco spaghetti is recommended.

INSTRUCTIONS: Chop clams and set aside. Strain clam juice through double lined cheesecloth. Do not use more than 1 cup of juice. Reserve.

In a large skillet, sauté the shallots in butter and oil until golden. Add reserved clam juice, wine, and half and half. Cook to reduce by ⅓. Stir in clams. Cook only until clams are just tender, about 5 minutes. If necessary, lighten sauce with 2 tablespoons of the pasta cooking water.

Combine sauce with cooked spaghetti in a large bowl. Toss with parsley.

INGREDIENTS FOR 4 SERVINGS:

3 dozen littleneck clams, shucked and juice reserved
4 shallots, finely chopped
2 tablespoons light olive oil
2 tablespoons butter
¼ cup dry white wine
½ cup half and half
½ cup chopped parsley
1 (12 ounce) box spaghetti, cooked al dente

Spaghetti with Sautéed Scallops and Toasted Bread Crumbs

JAMES D'AURIA

ad's favorite food was fried scallops, but recent health problems banned it from his diet. He was convinced that there was no other way to eat them until we created this delicious recipe.

INSTRUCTIONS: In a heavy covered saucepan, sauté garlic cloves in olive oil and butter until translucent. Do not allow to brown. Add wine. Bring to boil and reduce to half. Add stock and reduce slightly. Add salt and red pepper flakes. Remove garlic cloves.

Add scallops, cooking 4 to 5 minutes until the scallops turn opaque. Stir in parsley. Cover and reduce heat to low. Cook briefly.

Cook pasta for 8 to 10 minutes in boiling, salted water. Drain. Combine with scallops in a large bowl and toss. Divide into individual serving plates. Top each plate with 1½ tablespoons of toasted bread crumbs*. Garnish with additional parsley, if desired.

*Note: To toast bread crumbs, spread on a flat cookie sheet. Cook at 450° for 5 to 8 minutes.

INGREDIENTS FOR 4 SERVINGS:

6 cloves garlic, peeled
3 tablespoons olive oil
1 tablespoon butter
½ cup white wine
1 ½ cups home-made chicken stock (or low-sodium canned chicken broth)
salt, to taste
pinch crushed red pepper flakes
¾ pound bay or sea scallops, rinsed and dried
3 tablespoons chopped parsley
1 pound spaghetti
¾ cup plain bread crumbs, toasted*

Gnocchi

ROBERT FARRAR CAPON

INSTRUCTIONS: Boil the first 3 ingredients. Remove from heat and add the flour all at once. Beat vigorously with a wooden spoon. Return to low heat and cook for a minute or so, stirring vigorously till it forms a stiff ball of dough. Put the dough into a food processor and add the eggs one at a time, pulsing after each addition until the egg is incorporated. Add the cheeses, pulsing until incorporated. Let stand at least 10 minutes.

Boil 4 quarts of water with 2 tablespoons of salt. Put the dough into a pastry bag fitted with a large plain tip. Butter a large deep baking pan generously. Pipe the gnocchi dough the entire length of the pan in close rows. Put the pan over low heat (over two burners, if possible) and immediately add boiling water to cover generously, breaking the fall of the water with a small frying pan. Using a pancake turner, cut the strips of dough in the water into ½-inch lengths. Raise or lower the heat to keep the water at a simmer and cook the gnocchi for 10 to 15 minutes, stirring them often but gently to keep the water temperature evenly distributed.

Drain, reserving a bit of the liquid. Put the gnocchi in a serving dish, top with butter and some of the reserved liquid, and serve with any suitable sauce.

INGREDIENTS:
1 cup water
½ cup (1 stick) butter
¼ teaspoon salt
1 cup all-purpose flour
4 large eggs
½ cup grated Parmesan cheese
½ cup grated Gruyère cheese
butter for the pan

Soba Noodles Vinaigrette

JOHN SHERWOOD JEWETT

This goes well with cold champagne.

INSTRUCTIONS: Cook noodles in salted water according to directions. Drain well. Toss with 1 teaspoon of oil. Chill.

Whisk together vinaigrette ingredients. Reserve 1 teaspoon of the caviar for garnish.

Just before serving, toss cold noodles, carrot, radish, and scallions with vinaigrette. Garnish with reserved caviar.

INGREDIENTS:
6 ounces dry soba noodles
1 teaspoon canola oil
¼ cup finely julienned carrot
¼ cup finely julienned daikon radish
4 scallions, finely shredded

VINAIGRETTE:
½ cup canola oil
¼ cup rice wine vinegar
1 teaspoon grated fresh ginger root
1 teaspoon finely chopped shallots
4 ounces fresh caviar

GARNISH:
1 teaspoon reserved caviar

Sesame Chicken Pasta

JOHNNA ANDERSON, JENNIFER BLUME, JENNIFER BOEREM, PAT COYLE

This recipe, conceived by some students in East Hampton High School's Gourmet Food class, received the highest marks for taste in the "Create an Original Pasta Dish" contest.

INSTRUCTIONS: In a large skillet, sauté garlic in oil until soft. Add chicken; sauté until golden. Stir in soy sauce and sesame oil. Add tomatoes, parsley and sesame seeds, heating slightly. Stir in snow peas. Place cooked pasta in a large bowl. Pour on sauce. Toss to coat.

INGREDIENTS FOR 4 SERVINGS:

¼ cup vegetable oil

2 cloves garlic, minced

2 whole chicken breasts, boned, skinned, and julienned

¼ cup soy sauce

¼ cup sesame oil

6 plum tomatoes, seeded and diced

1 tablespoon fresh parsley, minced

2 tablespoons sesame seeds, toasted

3 ounces whole snow peas, trimmed and blanched

1 pound rotelle or fusilli, cooked al dente

Debbie's Greek Pasta

DEBBIE CLEMENCE

INSTRUCTIONS: In large skillet, melt butter and oil. Sauté garlic, shallots, and scallions until translucent. Add white wine, cooking to reduce slightly. Season to taste with pepper. In a separate bowl, gently combine feta cheese, tomatoes, olives, and basil.

Add cooked pasta to skillet. Toss well to coat. Add remaining ingredients. Heat on low just until feta cheese softens.

INGREDIENTS FOR 6 TO 8 SERVINGS:

6 tablespoons sweet butter
3 tablespoons olive oil
3 cloves garlic, minced
4 shallots, minced
6 scallions, diced
½ cup white wine
freshly ground pepper, to taste
12 ounces feta cheese diced
10 to 12 ripe plum tomatoes, seeded and diced
16 pitted black olives, rinsed and sliced in half
¼ cup fresh basil leaves, julienned
1½ pounds rotelle, cooked al dente

One Pan Spaghetti

ELIZABETH J. MAGILL

Years ago, this recipe appeared on a Sacramento tomato juice can. While real Italians and purists may faint, it really is delicious and very, very easy.

INSTRUCTIONS: In a 4-quart heavy pot, brown beef, onions, and garlic in oil. Add juice, celery, spaghetti, and seasonings. Cover and simmer on low heat for 30 to 35 minutes. Serve with Parmesan cheese.

INGREDIENTS FOR 6 SERVINGS:

1 tablespoon oil
1 pound chopped beef
1 cup chopped onions
3 cloves of garlic, minced
1 (46 ounce) can tomato juice
1 cup chopped celery
6 ounces thin spaghetti
2 teaspoons oregano
¼ teaspoon pepper
salt, to taste
Parmesan cheese

Pasta Cruda

JAMES D'AURIA

 his is the simplest recipe I know, but one we all enjoy frequently, especially towards the end of the summer when nothing can equal the taste of a ripe Hampton tomato.

INSTRUCTIONS: Combine tomatoes and basil in a bowl. Sprinkle with salt. Set aside to let the tomatoes weep.

Sauté garlic cloves in oil until pale yellow. Do not brown. Turn off heat and let sit for 30 minutes. Discard garlic, and add red pepper flakes.

Cook pasta in rapidly boiling water to which 1 tablespoon of salt has been added. Cook approximately 10 minutes. Drain.

Return flavored oil to heat. Stir in tomatoes. Heat for a maximum of 1 minute. Turn off heat. Combine mixture with cooked pasta.

INGREDIENTS FOR 4 SERVINGS:

5 ripe tomatoes, chopped

3 tablespoons fresh basil

2 teaspoons coarse salt

4 cloves of garlic

4 tablespoons extra virgin olive oil

¼ teaspoon red pepper flakes

1 pound penne, tubettini, or small farfalle

Pasta Primavera

DEBORAH WALTER

A wonderful way to use fresh vegetables! INSTRUCTIONS: Cook pasta according to directions on package. In about the last 3 minutes of cooking, cut off the very tips of the broccoli into small florets, and add to the cooking pasta. Cook for 3 minutes. Drain well in colander.

In large skillet, heat oil and margarine. Sauté onion, peppers, garlic and parsley until onions are soft. Add zucchini and mushrooms; sauté for 3 more minutes.

Put pasta in serving dish. Pour vegetables over top and toss gently. Serve with grated Parmesan cheese.

OPTIONAL:

Slice 2 boneless chicken breasts into finger-sized pieces and brown in 1 tablespoon olive oil. Also is very tasty with slices of sweet and hot sausage, browned thoroughly before adding.

INGREDIENTS FOR 4 SERVINGS:

1 pound thin spaghetti or linguini
1 stalk fresh broccoli
¼ cup olive oil
3 tablespoons margarine
1 small onion, chopped
½ red bell pepper, chopped
½ green bell pepper, chopped
3 cloves garlic, minced
1 tablespoon parsley
2 small green zucchini, quartered and sliced
½ cup sliced mushrooms
Parmesan cheese

Pasta with Cauliflower and Pesto Sauce

ANDREE DAVIS

Instructions for pesto sauce: Blend basil, oil, pine nuts, garlic, and salt in a blender or food processor. Transfer mixture to small bowl. Stir in cheese and softened butter.

For cauliflower and pasta: Cook cauliflower florets for 2 to 3 minutes in boiling, salted water for pasta. Add pasta; cook al dente. Cauliflower should be fork tender. Drain, reserving 1 to 2 tablespoons of cooking water. Place cauliflower and pasta in a large bowl.

To lighten pesto sauce, stir in reserved cooking water. Toss cauliflower and pasta with pesto sauce, olives, and pepper flakes (if desired). Pass extra Parmesan cheese at the table.

Ingredients for 4 servings:

Pesto Sauce:

2 cups fresh basil leaves, washed and dried
½ cup olive oil
2 tablespoons pine nuts
2 cloves garlic, lightly crushed
1 teaspoon salt
¾ cup freshly grated Parmesan cheese
2 tablespoons butter, softened

Cauliflower and Pasta:

1 large head cauliflower, separated into small florets
1 pound fusilli or shells
salt
1 to 2 tablespoons reserved cooking water
1 cup pimento-stuffed olives, finely chopped
red pepper flakes (optional)

Penne Puttanesca

PAT TRAMA, DELLA FEMINA RESTAURANT

INSTRUCTIONS: In a large skillet, heat olive oil over high heat. Add shallots and garlic. Sauté until translucent. Add capers, anchovies, olives, and parsley. Deglaze pan with the wine. Heat to reduce the wine by half. Stir in the milled tomatoes and butter. Simmer until thickened.

Drain the cooked pasta and add it to the sauce. Cook the pasta in the sauce for 1 minute. Serve in warm bowls.

INGREDIENTS FOR 2 SERVINGS:

2 ounces extra virgin olive oil
2 tablespoons minced shallots
2 tablespoons minced garlic
2 tablespoons capers, rinsed well
2 tablespoons coarsely chopped anchovy filets
¼ cup Kalamata olives, pitted
2 tablespoons minced Italian parsley
¼ cup dry white wine
16 ounces milled plum tomatoes
2 tablespoons butter
6 ounces penne, cooked al dente in boiling salted water

PENNE WITH ARTICHOKES AND SHRIMP

INSTRUCTIONS: In a large saucepan, sauté white onions in olive oil until tender. Add carrots, wine, and 2 cups of the vegetable stock. Cook for approximately 15 minutes until volume is reduced to half.

Add prosciutto, sweated onions, orange zest, tomatoes, tomato paste, and artichokes. Cook sauce for 30 minutes.

In a large skillet, quickly sauté shrimp in olive oil. Add tomato sauce. Adjust thickness with balance of vegetable stock.

Add pasta and toss quickly. Season to taste with salt and pepper. Plate, garnishing with fresh chopped parsley.

INGREDIENTS:

2 white onions, diced

olive oil

1 pound carrots, peeled, sliced into thin diamond-shaped strips and blanched

½ cup white wine

3 cups vegetable stock

1 cup prosciutto, diced

4 cups onion, diced and sweated in butter

2 oranges, zest only from peel

3 pounds plum tomatoes, blanched and peeled, quartered and sautéed in olive oil

2 tablespoons tomato paste

1 pound baby artichokes, trimmed and blanched in court bouillon with 1 tablespoon flour to keep artichokes from turning dark

1 pound fresh small shrimp, peeled and deveined

1 pound penne, cooked al dente

salt and pepper, to taste

3 sprigs fresh parsley, chopped

Penne with Artichokes, Sun-dried Tomatoes, and Basil

MARY LAWRENCE-ROBERTS

Enjoy this at lunch time with a simple salad. For dinner, let it accompany a roast chicken for a delicious meal.

INSTRUCTIONS: Arrange artichoke hearts and whole garlic cloves separately in a small baking dish. Drizzle with 2 tablespoons oil and a pinch of salt. Bake at 350° for 25 minutes until garlic is slightly browned. In a food processor, process sun-dried tomatoes with roasted garlic, and remaining 2 tablespoons of oil.

Cook penne in 5 quarts of rapidly boiling water to which 1 teaspoon of salt is added. Cook al dente, approximately 10 to 12 minutes. Drain.

Toss pasta with sun-dried tomato purée, artichokes, and basil. Season to taste.

INGREDIENTS FOR 4 SERVINGS:

1 (14 ounce) can artichoke hearts, drained and sliced
5 cloves garlic, peeled
4 tablespoons olive oil
pinch of salt
½ cup sun-dried tomatoes, packed in oil
1 pound penne
1 cup chopped fresh basil
salt and pepper, to taste

Summer Delight

I had eight people over for lunch one August day after tennis. It was impromptu, so I used only what I had and what was in the garden. This has been requested ever since! It's low-calorie and low-fat.

INSTRUCTIONS: Simmer onions, garlic, salt, and pepper in water and wine over moderate heat for 20 minutes until onions are soft.

Add oil, tomatoes, and peppers. Simmer on low heat until peppers are tender.

Meanwhile cook pasta al dente.

To serve, top drained pasta with vegetable sauce. Garnish with basil and Parmesan cheese.

INGREDIENTS FOR 6 TO 8 SERVINGS:

2 cups water
1 cup white wine
2 small white onions, finely chopped
2 cloves garlic, minced
salt and pepper, to taste
2 tablespoons olive oil
6 large ripe tomatoes, peeled and each cut into eight wedges
2 yellow peppers, sliced
fresh basil, chopped
Parmesan cheese, freshly grated
1 ½ pounds linguini

Stuffed Pasta Roll with Tomato Cream Sauce

JOEL ANDERSON, KATIE ANDERSON, MARCY GROSS, JESSE ROTHWELL

Each year, the Gourmet Foods class at East Hampton High School holds a "Create an Original Pasta Dish" contest. This is 1994's winner! It's a very impressive dish!

INSTRUCTIONS FOR PASTA: Place flour on a board and form a well. Put eggs, oil, and salt in the center of the well. With a fork, carefully beat the liquids, gradually incorporating flour from the interior walls of the well. Continue stirring, until a ball of dough that can be kneaded is formed. Knead dough by hand until almost all of the flour is absorbed, then knead an additional 10 minutes. Cover dough with plastic wrap. Let it rest for about 10 minutes. If making ahead, dough can be refrigerated.

FOR FILLING: Melt butter in skillet. Add chicken. Season with salt and pepper. Sauté until lightly browned on all sides, about 2 to 3 minutes. Set aside to cool. When cool, chop chicken as fine as possible. Combine with remaining ingredients. Mix thoroughly.

FOR BÉCHAMEL SAUCE: Melt butter in sauce pan over medium heat. Add flour. Stir well until roux is free of lumps and begins to foam. Gradually add milk. Stir constantly over low heat until mixture thickens. Season with nutmeg, salt, and pepper. Reserve ½ cup sauce for filling. Cover remaining sauce with a buttered round of waxed paper. Set aside.

INGREDIENTS FOR 4 SERVINGS:

PASTA:
2 cups flour
2 extra-large eggs
2 teaspoons olive oil
pinch of salt

FILLING:
3 tablespoons butter
1½ cups chicken breast, cut in ½-inch cubes
salt and pepper, to taste
1 cup broccoli florets, steamed and coarsely chopped
1½ cups ricotta cheese
⅔ cup mozzarella cheese, shredded
2 egg yolks
½ cup béchamel sauce
1 teaspoon fresh basil, chopped

BÉCHAMEL SAUCE:
3 tablespoons butter
3 tablespoons flour
2 cups milk
nutmeg, freshly grated
salt and pepper, to taste

Continued on next page

FOR TOMATO CREAM SAUCE: In a medium saucepan, sauté onion and garlic in oil until translucent. Add purée, oregano, basil, and cheeses. Simmer 20 minutes. Add cream. Heat on low until sauce reduces slightly.

TO ASSEMBLE: Roll out pasta into a large circle on a lightly floured surface. Turn pasta at quarter intervals. When pasta is rolled to a uniform thickness of 1/16 of an inch, let dry for 10 minutes.

Bring a large pot of salted water to a boil. Arrange a large damp towel open flat on work surface. Have a large bowl of cold water to which 1 tablespoon of oil has been added set close to your sink.

Carefully place the pasta round in the boiling water. Cook for 30 seconds. Drain in a colander and quickly transfer to bowl of cold water. Let cool. Remove and arrange on damp towel. Let dry 15 minutes.

Place filling on pasta circle, leaving a 1/2-inch border all around. Roll up jelly roll fashion, using the towel as an aid. Place stuffed roll in buttered baking pan. Coat with remaining béchamel sauce. Bake at 375° for 20 to 25 minutes.

TO SERVE: Pool tomato cream sauce on large serving platter. Carefully transfer pasta roll to platter. If desired, drizzle with some sauce. Slice to serve.

TOMATO CREAM SAUCE:
2 tablespoons olive oil
1 small onion, finely chopped
2 cloves garlic, minced
2 cups tomato purée
1 teaspoon oregano
1 tablespoon fresh basil, chopped
2 tablespoons Romano cheese
2 tablespoons Parmesan cheese
1/4 cup heavy cream

Vegetable Lasagne

JAYNI AND CHEVY CHASE

INSTRUCTIONS: Cook lasagne noodles according to package directions. Set aside.

FOR VEGETABLE FILLING: Sauté the onion, garlic, zucchini, broccoli, and tomatoes in oil over high heat for 5 minutes. Season to taste.

FOR CHEESE FILLING: In a large bowl, combine all ingredients.

TO ASSEMBLE: Spread half of the spaghetti sauce in the bottom of a 9x13x2-inch pan. Add a layer of lasagne noodles. Spread with half of the vegetable filling; then add half of the cheese filling. Top with another layer of lasagne noodles. Repeat layers, ending with lasagne noodles. Top with remaining spaghetti sauce. Bake at 350° for 45 minutes.

INGREDIENTS FOR 8 SERVINGS:
1 (16 ounce) box curly edge lasagne noodles
1 (16 ounce) jar spaghetti sauce

VEGETABLE FILLING:
2 teaspoons oil
1 medium onion, chopped
2 cloves garlic, minced
4 medium zucchini, chopped
2 pounds broccoli, pared, chopped, and steamed for 2 minutes
1 (28 ounce) can whole tomatoes
salt, to taste

CHEESE FILLING:
3 cups (24 ounces) skim milk ricotta cheese
12 ounces mozzarella cheese
½ cup Parmesan cheese
1 teaspoon oregano

Noodle Pudding

ANDREA COOPER

INSTRUCTIONS: Cook noodles according to package directions. Drain well and set aside.

Combine all ingredients except egg whites in a large bowl. Mix well. Stir in noodles.

In a separate bowl, beat egg whites until stiff peaks form. Fold into mixture. Pour into greased 9x13-inch baking pan.

To make topping, combine all ingredients. Sprinkle evenly over pudding. Bake at 350° for 1 hour. Do not overbake.

INGREDIENTS:
1 pound medium egg noodles
½ cup margarine, softened and cut into thin slices
1 pound cottage cheese
1 cup sour cream
1 cup milk
1 cup sugar
1 teaspoon vanilla
1 teaspoon orange or lemon zest
1 cup white raisins (optional)
6 egg whites

TOPPING:
1 ½ cups Special K cereal, crushed
¼ cup sugar
3 tablespoons margarine, melted
¼ teaspoon cinnamon

Fresh Tomato Sauce

JANET SCHWITTER

My mother gave me this recipe which she said was from her mother, who was born in Italy. This is the tomato sauce that I donate to the L.V.I.S. Fair.

INSTRUCTIONS: Blanch tomatoes in boiling water. Peel. Purée tomatoes in blender or food processor.

In a large sauce pot, sauté garlic in olive oil until clear. Add puréed tomatoes, basil, oregano, sugar, and pepper. Simmer on low heat for only 1 hour.

You may wish to increase the amounts of fresh herbs used. This sauce freezes well.

INGREDIENTS:

4 pounds fresh plum tomatoes
4 cloves garlic, minced
1 tablespoon olive oil
1 tablespoon fresh basil, chopped
1 tablespoon fresh oregano, chopped
1 tablespoon sugar
1 teaspoon pepper

Marinara Sauce

ELEANORE KENNEDY

 Instructions: In a large saucepan, sauté onions, carrots, and garlic in olive oil until brown. Add purée, wine, salt, pepper. Partially cover and simmer 15 minutes. Purée sauce in food processor or blender. Return to saucepan and add remaining ingredients. Partially cover, and simmer 30 minutes longer.

Ingredients:
½ cup olive oil
2 cups coarsely chopped onion
½ cup sliced carrots
4 cloves garlic, finely minced
3 cups tomato purée
1 cup red wine
salt and freshly ground pepper, to taste
4 tablespoons butter
1 tablespoon fresh basil, chopped
1 teaspoon oregano
pinch of sugar

Tomato-Meat Sauce

MRS. JOHN T. ALLEN

This is the result of several trials in cooking this sauce. It's the final best. Imported Italian tomato products are recommended.

INSTRUCTIONS: Sauté onion, celery, green pepper, and garlic in oil until limp. Add tomatoes, tomato paste, wine, and Worcestershire sauce. Simmer 30 minutes.

Shape ground beef and sausage into small balls. Brown in a separate pan until any accumulated liquid evaporates. Drain excess fat, if necessary. Add meat to sauce. Simmer an additional 30 minutes.

INGREDIENTS:
½ cup sliced onion
½ cup diced celery
½ cup diced green pepper
2 cloves garlic, finely chopped
1½ tablespoons olive oil
1 (28 ounce) can tomatoes
2 (6 ounce) cans tomato paste
½ cup dry red wine
2 teaspoons Worcestershire sauce
1 bay leaf
1 pound ground beef
½ pound sausage meat
salt and pepper, to taste

Baked Cheese Grits

QUEEN DAVIS-PARKS

INSTRUCTIONS: Bring water to a rapid boil. Stir in grits and salt. Reduce heat to medium-low and cover. Cook 5 to 7 minutes until thickened, stirring occasionally. Remove from heat.

Add small amount of grits to beaten egg. Return grits mixture to pan. Add remaining ingredients. Cover and cook over low heat, about one minute, until cheese is melted.

Pour into a greased 1½-quart casserole dish. Bake at 350° for 30 to 40 minutes, until top is set and lightly puffed. Let stand 5 minutes before serving.

INGREDIENTS FOR 4 TO 6 SERVINGS:
- 3 cups water
- ¾ cups quick (not instant) grits
- ¼ teaspoon salt
- 1 egg, beaten
- 4 ounces Cheddar cheese, shredded
- 2 tablespoons margarine
- ⅛ teaspoon garlic powder
- dash red pepper sauce or cayenne

Baked Creamy Grits

PEG D'ANDREA

Grits are wonderful to use instead of mashed potatoes. We especially like them with leg of lamb.

INSTRUCTIONS: Butter a 1½- to 2-quart casserole dish. In a saucepan, bring 2 cups of milk, broth, and salt to a boil. Add grits. Cook, stirring, for 4 minutes. Remove from heat.

Stir in butter, remaining ½ cup of milk, and eggs. Pour into casserole. Bake at 350° for 50 to 55 minutes until golden brown and puffed.

INGREDIENTS FOR 6 SERVINGS:
- 2½ cups milk
- 2 cups chicken broth
- ½ teaspoon salt
- 1 cup quick (not instant) grits
- 4 tablespoons unsalted butter
- 2 eggs, beaten

Christie's Couscous

CHRISTIE BRINKLEY

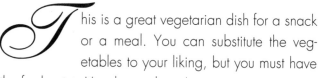his is a great vegetarian dish for a snack or a meal. You can substitute the vegetables to your liking, but you must have the fresh mint. It's what makes it!

INSTRUCTIONS: In large saucepan, bring broth, butter, and salt to a boil. Stir in couscous; cover. Remove from heat. Let stand 5 minutes until all liquid is absorbed.

Fluff couscous lightly with a fork, and transfer to a large mixing bowl. Stir in remaining ingredients.

Whisk together vinaigrette ingredients. Pour over couscous. Serve warm or cool.

INGREDIENTS:

2¼ cups couscous
3¼ cups vegetable broth
3 tablespoons butter
½ teaspoon salt
2 cups corn kernels
1 cup fresh garden peas
6 sticks hearts of palm, sliced into ¼-inch pieces
1 small red pepper, diced
1 (19 ounce) can garbanzo beans, drained
15 to 20 fresh mint leaves

VINAIGRETTE:

⅓ cup extra virgin olive oil
4 tablespoons balsamic vinegar
juice of 1 large lemon
1½ teaspoons dry mustard
salt and freshly ground pepper, to taste

COUSCOUS WITH RED PEPPERS, ALMONDS, AND RAISINS

DEBBIE CLEMENCE

INSTRUCTIONS: In medium saucepan, sauté onion and red pepper in butter until onion is translucent. Add broth and salt. Bring to a boil. Stir in couscous. Cover. Remove from heat, and let stand for 5 minutes until liquid is absorbed.

Add raisins and almonds. Fluff couscous lightly with a fork before serving. If desired, sprinkle with Parmesan cheese.

INGREDIENTS FOR 6 SERVINGS:

2 tablespoons butter

1 small onion, diced

1 red pepper, diced

1 ½ cups chicken broth

½ teaspoon salt

1 cup couscous

3 tablespoons raisins

2 tablespoons sliced almonds, lightly toasted

Parmesan cheese (optional)

GRANOLA

PAM CATALETTO

INSTRUCTIONS: In a large bowl, mix together first 6 ingredients. Set aside. Blend oil and honey; heat in microwave or on top of stove until very warm. Pour over dry ingredients and mix until moist. Spread in large oven pan. Bake at 250° for 1 hour or at 300° for ½ hour, stirring during baking. When brown, remove and add seeds, nuts, and/or raisins. Cool and store in air-tight container.

INGREDIENTS:

4 cups uncooked oatmeal

1 ½ cups wheat germ

¼ cup powdered dry milk

1 tablespoon brown sugar

1 to 2 tablespoons cinnamon

1 cup grated coconut

⅓ cup vegetable oil

½ cup honey

½ cup sesame seeds

½ cup nuts

½ cup raisins

*S*AMP

*C*orn kept the Pilgrims alive in Plymouth, Massachusetts, those first few hard winters. The Indians showed them how to plant it; and our forefathers who came here from Maidstone, Kent, England, via New England depended on it too. Cornmeal was still called "Injun meal" within living memory here. Samp (whole corn, its outer husk removed, and cooked) was the most typical Long Island dish, up to forty or fifty years ago. It was served for dinner on Sundays, when cooking was not considered proper. The method:

One quart samp (or big hominy) was put to soak overnight, with 1 cup white beans. The next morning it was put on the back of the range to simmer all day, with 2 pounds salt pork, mixed fat and lean (sometimes a pig's foot, a piece of corned beef, or a ham bone was used.) When done, the beans have gone to pieces and the porridge is thick. It is served very hot, with a pitcher of cold milk. That, with a slab of pie baked on Saturday, was Sunday dinner; and the same, with the addition of a few potatoes, also served for dinner on Monday which was washday.

When the 1939 L.V.I.S. cook book came out, with its recipe for samp, East Hampton people had homesick letters from exiles, asking where dry samp could be bought nowadays. It is very hard to find. It was prepared at home, in the old days. Older men here still remember their Saturday morning stint at the samp-mortar, pounding off the outer covering of corn kernels. Most stores now carry only big hominy, slightly cooked in cans; this must be simmered for ten or twelve hours if it is expected to taste anything like the real thing. Samp is a cheap and satisfying dish.

Nineteen Ninety One Samp

HELEN S. RATTRAY

Instructions: Search out old-fashioned dried big hominy - corn kernels from which the husks have been removed. Local gourmet food shops may have it. This makes a huge quantity, and is good served with a holiday meal or buffet.

Sauté vegetables just until soft in oil and butter.

Combine sautéed vegetables, samp, broth*, and bay leaf in a large stock pot or Dutch oven. Simmer on stove or cook in very low oven all day. Add more liquid as needed.

Add bits of ham and seasonings 2 hours before done.

Ingredients:

3 tablespoons olive oil

3 tablespoons unsalted butter

3 cups yellow onion, finely diced

1 ½ cups celery, finely diced

1 red pepper, finely diced

1 green pepper, finely diced

1 quart dried samp, soaked overnight

1 bay leaf

2 quarts broth*, or more as needed

bits and pieces of ham

salt, to taste

1 teaspoon dried thyme

1 teaspoon ground coriander seed

*Note: Ideally, use broth in which a meaty ham bone has been braised. If not available, substitute chicken or beef broth.

Risotto with Dried Wild Mushrooms

MARY ANN BOZZI

My husband's grandmother, Mary, would visit her hometown in Bogotaro, Italy, every year and return with a bag of these valuable mushrooms pinned to her brassière to get through customs. Of course, we would all cringe that she did this. But, she shared the wealth, and her daughter, daughter-in-law, and granddaughters loved using them in the risotto she taught them how to make.

INSTRUCTIONS: Soak mushrooms in 2 cups lukewarm water for at least 30 minutes. When liquid turns brown, strain through sieve lined with paper towels. Reserve liquid. Chop mushrooms very fine. Bring broth to a steady simmer.

In a heavy casserole, sauté onion and garlic in 2 tablespoons of butter and all of the oil until golden. Add rice. Stir until coated; sauté several minutes longer.

Add ½ cup of heated broth. Slowly stir. As rice dries out, continue to add more broth. When rice has cooked for 10 to 12 minutes, add mushrooms. Then add ½ cup reserved mushroom liquid. Continue cooking in same manner until all mushroom liquid is used. Cook until rice is tender and creamy, stirring in additional broth as needed.

Turn off heat. Stir in remaining 2 tablespoons of butter and Parmesan cheese. Season to taste. Serve with additional cheese on the side. Perfect with veal cutlet Milanese!

INGREDIENTS FOR 6 SERVINGS:

1 ounce dried wild mushrooms

1 quart homemade chicken broth (or 1 cup canned broth combined with 3 cups water)

2 tablespoons chopped onion

1 clove garlic, minced

4 tablespoons butter

3 tablespoons olive oil

2 cups Arborio rice

¼ cup freshly grated Parmesan cheese

salt and pepper, to taste

Risotto with Lemon and Braised Shrimps

ANGELO SESSA, CHEF, CESARINA RISTORANTE

INSTRUCTIONS FOR LEMON SAUCE: Bring rinds, lemons, and water to a boil. Reduce heat. Simmer for 20 to 30 minutes until rinds are soft. Combine all in blender, then strain through a fine sieve. Set aside.

FOR SHRIMP: Braise shrimp in oil and wine just until tender. Set aside.

FOR RICE: In large skillet, sauté rice and shallots in butter for 3 minutes. Add wine. When wine evaporates, gradually add the heated stock, stirring constantly. After 10 minutes of cooking, add 2 tablespoons of lemon sauce. Cook an additional 10 minutes. Stir in 1 tablespoon of butter and Parmesan cheese. Cook until rice is tender and liquid is absorbed. Transfer cooked risotto to a large shallow serving bowl. Top with braised shrimp and serve.

INGREDIENTS FOR 4 SERVINGS:

LEMON SAUCE:
rinds (yellow part only) of 5 lemons
5 lemons, peeled
½ cup cold water

SHRIMP:
12 jumbo shrimp, peeled and deveined
2 tablespoons olive oil
¼ cup white wine

RICE:
1 ½ cups Arborio rice
2 shallots
4 tablespoons butter
1 cup white wine
4 ½ cups chicken stock, heated
1 tablespoon butter
2 ½ ounces grated Parmesan cheese

RISOTTO WITH SPINACH AND PINE NUTS

JUDY LICHT AND JERRY DELLA FEMINA

*I*NSTRUCTIONS: Sauté spinach in 3 tablespoons of olive oil; chop and set aside. Toast pine nuts; set aside.

In a medium saucepan, sauté onion in 2 tablespoons of olive oil and 2 tablespoons of butter. Add risotto rice and cook over high heat for 2 minutes.

Mix stock and water in a large pot and bring to a boil. Add a ladle full of hot liquid to the rice mixture and stir. Keep stirring constantly. When liquid has been absorbed, add more liquid and continue to stir. After 25 minutes, the rice will have absorbed most of the liquid. It will be fluffy, cooked. Any remaining liquid can be reserved for another use.

Add cooked spinach and pine nuts. Stir in remaining 2 tablespoons of butter and Parmesan cheese.

INGREDIENTS FOR 4 SERVINGS:
½ pound fresh spinach
5 tablespoons olive oil
4 ounces pine nuts
½ small onion, chopped
4 tablespoons butter
1 cup Arborio rice for risotto
6 cups chicken stock
6 cups water
½ cup Parmesan cheese

Wild Rice with Fresh Roasted Turkey and Corn

LANCE ROLL, CHEF, THE RED HORSE MARKET

This dish will adapt easily with snow peas or broccoli florets. A good substitute for hazelnuts would be walnuts or pecans. Serve hot as a side dish or entrée, or serve as a cold salad.

INSTRUCTIONS: In a large saucepan, heat olive oil. Add garlic and brown. Add carrot, celery, and onions; sauté 5 minutes. Add rice and stir to coat. Add wine and cook one minute. Add stock and cook rice until the hull has released. Meanwhile, sauté corn kernels in a separate small skillet and set aside. Drain rice and discard extra liquid. Leave all of the cooked vegetables in the rice. Add turkey, tarragon leaves, and scallions. Garnish dish with roasted hazelnuts and drizzle on hazelnut oil just before serving.

INGREDIENTS:
¼ cup extra virgin olive oil
4 cloves garlic, sliced
1 carrot, cut on bias
3 stalks celery, cut on bias
1½ red onions, sliced
1 pound wild rice
¾ cup white wine
4 quarts chicken or turkey stock
2 cups fresh corn kernels, cut from the cob
1 pound roasted turkey, cut into large cubes
2 tablespoons fresh tarragon leaves
6 scallions, chopped

GARNISH:
¼ cup hazelnut oil
¾ cup roasted hazelnuts

Breakfast Casserole

ANN KIRK WILLARD

INSTRUCTIONS: Cover bottom of a greased 7x11-inch baking pan with bread. Brown sausage and sprinkle over bread. Top with mushrooms and cheeses. In a bowl, beat eggs slightly. Add milk and seasonings, stirring well. Pour over ingredients in pan. Cover and refrigerate overnight. Bake at 350° for 35 to 40 minutes in the morning.

INGREDIENTS FOR 4 TO 6 SERVINGS:

6 to 8 slices white bread, crusts removed, cubed

1 pound bulk sausage

1 (4 ounce) can sliced mushrooms, drained

½ cup Swiss cheese, shredded

½ cup sharp Cheddar cheese, shredded

5 eggs

2 cups milk

1 teaspoon mustard

1 teaspoon Worcestershire sauce

salt and pepper, to taste

Cheese Shrimp Strata

RUTH MC CREA LIZARS

Instructions: Cut each slice of bread in half diagonally. Brush each side of pieces with melted butter. Arrange half of the slices in an 8x8-inch baking dish.

Sprinkle with half the cheese, shrimp, scallions, and parsley. Top with remaining bread slices. Repeat process.

In a separate bowl, whisk together remaining ingredients. Pour evenly into casserole. Cover and chill overnight.

Before serving, bake at 350° for 30 to 40 minutes, until golden and puffed. Cut into squares.

INGREDIENTS FOR 6 TO 8 SERVINGS:

6 slices firm white bread, crusts removed
4 tablespoons butter, melted
1 cup Swiss cheese, grated
½ pound tiny cooked shrimp
2 scallions, minced
2 tablespoons chopped parsley
3 eggs
1 ½ cups milk
½ cup sour cream
½ teaspoon Dijon mustard
½ teaspoon salt

Creole Eggs

MRS. GREYDON A. RHODES, 1948 L.V.I.S. COOKBOOK

Two tablespoons fat, 2 tablespoons flour, 1 cup milk, 2 tablespoons chopped onions, 2 tablespoons green pepper, 1 ¼ cups canned tomatoes, 1 clove garlic, mashed, ¼ teaspoon chili powder, 4 hard-cooked eggs, sliced, ½ cup buttered cracker or bread crumbs, ½ cup grated American cheese. Make a white sauce of the fat, flour, and milk, add pepper and salt to taste. Sauté onion and pepper in 2 tablespoons fat until tender but not brown. Add tomatoes, garlic, and chili powder. Cook until thick. Add to white sauce. Place alternately in greased casserole the sauce and a layer of eggs, top with crumbs and cheese. Bake in a moderate oven (350°) for 15 minutes or until heated through. Serves 6-8.

Spanakopita

ISABEL (SUE) SHOUKAS

Spanakopita has been a family favorite for many generations. This recipe originally was made with homemade phyllo and fresh spinach. It has been modified to reflect today's busier lifestyles.

INSTRUCTIONS: Thaw spinach. Press out excess moisture thoroughly.

Sauté scallions in 1 tablespoon of butter until soft.

Combine drained spinach, scallions, cheeses, and eggs. Season with salt and pepper. Set mixture aside.

Brush a 9x13-inch pan with some melted butter. Line bottom of pan with one sheet of phyllo. Brush with melted butter. Repeat this process until there are 8 sheets of buttered phyllo.

Spread mixture evenly over phyllo layers. Top with 8 more sheets of phyllo, brushing each sheet with melted butter. Trim edges if necessary. With a sharp knife, cut through top layers of phyllo to indicate desired serving pieces.

Bake at 375° for about 40 to 45 minutes until golden brown. Serve immediately or refrigerate and reheat.

INGREDIENTS:

4 (10 ounce) packages frozen chopped spinach
1 bunch scallions, chopped
1 tablespoon butter
1 pound cottage cheese
1 pound feta cheese, crumbled
6 eggs, lightly beaten
salt and pepper, to taste

16 sheets phyllo dough
¼ pound butter, melted

Scotch Chinese Eggs

JOHN M. WILLARD

INSTRUCTIONS: One day in advance, place hard-cooked eggs in marinade in a medium saucepan. Simmer, uncovered, for 25 minutes. Let stand overnight.

The following day, peel eggs and prepare for coating. In a bowl, combine sausage, ginger root, and garlic. Carefully encase each egg in a thin layer of sausage mixture, using moistened hands.

In another bowl, beat together raw eggs and mustard. In a separate bowl, combine bread crumbs and sesame seeds. Dip encased eggs first in egg mixture, then in crumb mixture. Set on a plate. Refrigerate 3 hours or overnight.

Heat 2 inches of vegetable oil to 375°. Fry 2 to 3 eggs at a time, turning carefully, until well browned. If sausage does not look cooked all the way, pop them into a 350° oven for 10 minutes more. Drain well on paper towels. Let rest 5 minutes before serving. Use a sharp, thin knife dipped into water to slice each egg into quarters.

INGREDIENTS:

8 hard-cooked eggs, unpeeled but cracked all over

MARINADE:

3 teaspoons soy sauce
2 whole star anise
2 bags Chinese black tea
water to cover

1 pound bulk country sausage
2 teaspoons chopped fresh ginger root
2 teaspoons chopped garlic
2 raw eggs
1 tablespoon sesame mustard
2 cups bread crumbs
2 tablespoons sesame seeds
vegetable oil, for frying

Mrs. S. Kip Farrington, a long standing L.V.I.S. Member, and Dr. Arthur Terry.

SEAFOOD

Basque 'n Blue

ROSITA MEDLER

This sauce recipe came from the Basque area of Spain. We had it on baccala (salted cod). It's very tasty with bluefish.

INSTRUCTIONS: Place sauce ingredients in food processor. Blend until smooth.

Arrange washed and dried fillets in glass or ceramic dish. Cover evenly with sauce. Bake at 350° until fish flakes easily.

INGREDIENTS FOR 4 SERVINGS:
4 medium bluefish fillets

SAUCE:
2 plum tomatoes, seeded
1 (7 ounce) jar pimentos, drained
2 medium garlic cloves, peeled
1 small chili pepper, seeded
3 tablespoons olive oil
3 tablespoons red wine vinegar.

Broiled Bluefish

BETTY MARMON

INSTRUCTIONS: Preheat broiler. Make a mixture of oil, lemon juice, herbs, and pepper. Line a broiler pan with aluminum foil. Cover the foil with a thin layer of milk. Arrange the fillets on foil. Brush oil mixture generously over the fish.

Broil fish for 6 minutes, 2 minutes longer if fillets are thick. Turning the fillets is not necessary.

INGREDIENTS FOR 4 SERVINGS:
2 pounds bluefish fillets
½ cup oil
1 tablespoon lemon juice
fresh herbs, chopped
1 teaspoon pepper
milk

Bluefish Roquefort

MARJORIE CHESTER

In the summer of 1975, on the way back from a camp visiting weekend in Maine, we got off the Shelter Island Ferry and stopped for dinner at the American Hotel, dead tired. There on the menu was Bluefish Roquefort — a dish we'd never encountered — and it was heavenly. From the chef via our waiter came the instructions, more or less, and we've been making it ever since.

INSTRUCTIONS: Cream the butter well. Beat in the shallots, garlic, and parsley. Then mash in the Roquefort cheese. Season to taste with pepper.

Rub olive oil on each fillet. Season with freshly ground pepper and lemon juice. Place the fillets skin side down on a well-greased rack of a broiler pan. This will catch the excess drippings and keep the skin from getting soggy. Place under a preheated broiler long enough to partially cook the fish, 2 to 5 minutes, depending mainly on whether you have an electric or gas broiler. Remove from broiler.

Mound the cheese mixture over the entire top of each fillet. Next, coat evenly with bread crumbs. Top with Parmesan cheese. Each layer should cover the one beneath.

Place the fish under the broiler again for approximately 3 to 5 minutes, long enough to give each fillet a delicately browned crust. Serve with lemon slices.

INGREDIENTS FOR 6 SERVINGS:
6 bluefish fillets, ½ pound each
¾ cup butter
¼ cup minced shallots
1 to 3 cloves garlic, mashed
2 tablespoons parsley
¾ cup Roquefort cheese
freshly ground pepper, to taste
¼ cup olive oil
juice of 1 lemon
½ cup bread crumbs
½ cup grated Parmesan cheese
lemon slices

BROILED WEAKFISH

MRS. CONDIE LAMB, 1965 L.V.I.S. COOKBOOK

Weakfish is so delicate in flavor that it needs to be fresh, fresh, fresh. Have fish split for broiling. Dribble white wine over it and let stand for an hour. Spread the fish with anchovy butter, freshly ground pepper, fresh grated nutmeg, and broil gently for about 12 to 15 minutes. Do not overcook. Put aside on hot platter. Add more anchovy butter to pan together with thinly sliced cucumbers. Heat through until cucumbers are just limp. Pour over fish. Garnish with parsley and lemon.

CREAMED COD WITH EGG SAUCE

HELEN VORPAHL

This dish is of Swedish origin and was always served Christmas Eve. Dried salt cod may be used, if freshened. Finnan haddie, which is smoked haddock, is also excellent.

INSTRUCTIONS: Poach or steam fish about 10 minutes per one-inch thickness of fish. Fish is done when it is opaque.

Melt butter in saucepan. Add flour and whisk together. Gradually add milk and continue to whisk over medium heat until it thickens. Stir in egg, mustard, salt, and pepper. Pour sauce over fish.

Serve fish with boiled or baked potatoes. A nice accompaniment would be green peas or beet salad.

INGREDIENTS FOR 3 TO 4 SERVINGS:
1 pound cod or haddock
1 tablespoon butter
1 tablespoon flour
1 cup milk
1 hard-cooked egg, chopped
pinch dry mustard
salt and pepper, to taste

152

Baked Flounder with Spinach and Mushrooms

ELISE RAYMOND

INSTRUCTIONS: Sauté onion in butter and oil. In a medium bowl, combine sautéed onion, sour cream, lemon juice, flour, and salt. Mix well.

Par-boil cleaned spinach. Drain well. Combine with half the sour cream mixture.

Cover the bottom of a baking dish with spinach mixture. Arrange fillets on top. Cover with mushrooms. Spread with remaining sour cream mixture. Sprinkle with paprika. Bake at 375° for 20 minutes.

INGREDIENTS FOR 4 TO 6 SERVINGS:

2 pounds flounder fillets
1 medium onion, chopped
1 teaspoon butter
1 teaspoon olive oil
1 cup sour cream
2 tablespoons lemon juice
½ teaspoon flour
salt to taste
fresh spinach
¼ pound mushrooms, thinly sliced
paprika

Corn Bread and Crab Stuffed Flounder with Hollandaise

ROBERT THIXTON

My Grandmother originally came from Massachusetts, and this recipe was one her mother taught her. It was originally made with simple white bread and crab stuffing and topped with a white sauce. I added the corn bread and Hollandaise changes some years ago. If you decide to use prepared corn muffins, they give the stuffing a sweet flavor which I prefer with the tartness of the Hollandaise.

INSTRUCTIONS FOR STUFFING: Sauté celery and leek in butter until crisp tender. Break corn bread or muffins into coarse crumbs. Combine sautéed vegetables and crab with corn bread crumbs. Gently mix in beaten egg. Do not overmix.

TO ASSEMBLE: Rinse fillets and pat dry. Place equal amounts of the stuffing in the center of each fillet. Place a teaspoon of butter on top of each mound of stuffing. Starting at the wide end of the fillet, gently roll up. Place into a buttered baking dish tail-side down. Place an additional teaspoon of butter on top of each fillet. Recipe may be prepared ahead up to this point. If you prepare this earlier, bring fish up to room temperature before baking. Bake at 350°, covered, for 30 minutes.

FOR HOLLANDAISE: Prepare sauce 5 minutes before the fish is expected to be done. Melt butter in saucepan. Pour hot butter into a blender along with the lemon juice. Blend, gradually adding the egg yolks. Season with cayenne pepper. Blend only until slightly thickened.

TO SERVE: Top each stuffed fillet with a dollop of Hollandaise. Sprinkle lightly with paprika for color.

INGREDIENTS FOR 6 SERVINGS:
6 medium flounder fillets
4 tablespoons sweet butter, cut into 12 slices (1 teaspoon each)

STUFFING:
½ cup butter
3 large stalks of celery, diced
1 large leek, rinsed and diced
1 pan of corn bread, or 6 large corn muffins
1 pound lump crab meat, slightly shredded or cooked shrimp or lobster meat
1 egg, lightly beaten

HOLLANDAISE:
½ pound sweet butter
juice of 1 large lemon
4 egg yolks
cayenne or ground red pepper
paprika

FLOUNDER BUNDLES

I devised this method to have the fish retain its natural juices. It is virtually fat-free, attractive, and can be prepared ahead and baked just before serving.

INSTRUCTIONS: Drop lettuce leaves into boiling water. Simmer until soft, about 1 minute. Drain and cool. Line a baking pan with foil. With a small sharp knife, slice fillets in half lengthwise. Place fillets skinned side up on the foil.

In a small bowl, mix together remaining ingredients. Spoon mixture along each fillet. Roll up fillets, placing each one in the center of a lettuce leaf. Fold leaf neatly around the fish, tucking ends underneath.

Arrange bundles in rows on foil-lined baking pan. Drizzle with any excess liquid from soy mixture. Fold foil up around bundles to cover, crimping edges. Bake at 375° for 20 minutes. Serve on a bed of rice.

INGREDIENTS FOR 4 SERVINGS:

4 skinless flounder fillets, of uniform size
8 large romaine lettuce leaves
2 tablespoons tamari or soy sauce
1 tablespoon dry white wine or vermouth
8 to 10 scallions, thinly sliced, some green included
1 tablespoon grated ginger root
1 tablespoon parsley or cilantro, minced

Flounder Stuffed with Shrimp and Crab

This dish can be made a day ahead. Complete all steps except the final cooking.

INSTRUCTIONS FOR STUFFING:
Melt ¼ cup butter in large skillet. Sauté all the vegetables until just tender. Add flour and stir until free of lumps. Add wine and milk. Stir until thickened. Remove from heat. Add remaining filling ingredients.

TO ASSEMBLE: Brush fillets and baking pan lightly with melted butter. Divide filling into 6 equal portions. Place each portion across the wide end of each fillet. Gently roll up and secure with 2 toothpicks. Slice roll in half crosswise with a sharp knife. Readjust toothpicks so that each piece will hold together.

Arrange fillet rolls in baking dish, cut end facing up. Sprinkle with paprika. Cover and bake at 375° for 25 minutes. Uncover and bake an additional 5 minutes. Serve with rice.

INGREDIENTS FOR 6 SERVINGS:
6 whole flounder fillets
¼ cup butter, melted
paprika

STUFFING:
¼ cup butter
½ cup white onion, chopped
½ cup celery, chopped
½ cup shallots, chopped
¼ cup green pepper, chopped
1 garlic clove, minced
1 tablespoon flour
½ cup dry white wine
½ cup milk
½ cup cooked shrimp, chopped
½ pound lump crabmeat, shredded
½ cup bread crumbs
2 tablespoons fresh parsley, chopped
1 egg, lightly beaten
salt, pepper, and cayenne, to taste

Baked Salmon with Dill

BRUCE. WAINSCOTT SEAFOOD SHOP

Instructions: Sauté onion and red pepper slices in butter over medium heat until they soften. Cover the bottom of a small baking dish evenly with the sautéed vegetables. Place salmon, skinned side down, on top of the vegetables. Completely blanket with fresh dill. Place lemon slices side by side on top of dill and salmon. Sprinkle with garlic. Pour Italian dressing over dish until lightly saturated (like mist on grass).

Bake at 350° for 30 minutes. Serve hot. Any leftover salmon can be served cold sprinkled over a fresh garden salad the next day.

INGREDIENTS FOR 2 TO 3 SERVINGS:

1 pound salmon fillet, with skin removed

1 medium onion, cut into ⅛-inch slices

1 fresh red pepper, cleaned and cut in ⅛-inch slices

2 tablespoons butter

1 cup minced fresh dill (no stems)

2 slices of lemon, ¼-inch thick

1 teaspoon chopped garlic

4 to 6 ounces Italian dressing

Salmon and Cream Sauce

ANNE TREGELLAS

Instructions: Cut salmon into 2-inch wide pieces. Sauté salmon in very hot butter for about 3 minutes on each side. Remove to a warm platter; keep warm in oven. Deglaze pan with wine. Add tomato and anchovies. Bring to a boil and reduce slightly. Add the cream. Return to a boil and reduce it until it is the right consistency for a sauce. Pour sauce over salmon. Sprinkle with parsley and serve.

INGREDIENTS FOR 6 SERVINGS:

3 pounds salmon, boned and skin removed

½ cup unsalted butter

¼ cup white wine

1 tomato, peeled, seeded, and minced

1 (2 ounce) tin anchovies, minced

1 cup cream

parsley, minced

Salmon Cakes

DENNIS MACNEIL, CHEF DE CUISINE, THE LAUNDRY

INSTRUCTIONS: Prepare béchamel sauce. Melt butter in a medium saucepan. Blend in flour, cooking slowly over low heat for about 2 minutes, to create a roux. Remove from heat. Gradually stir in milk; add remaining ingredients. Return to low heat, stirring constantly until very thick. Strain sauce, discarding solids. Measure 8 ounces of sauce and add to salmon mix.

Gently combine all ingredients for the salmon mix. Form into 3-inch cakes; you should be able to make about 10 to 12 cakes. This recipe is also adaptable to making 1½-inch cakes for appetizers.

Prepare the cakes for coating; coat first with flour, then eggs, and finally bread crumbs.

Heat a small amount of vegetable oil in a heavy skillet. Fry salmon cakes on each side until lightly golden. Drain on paper towels.

INGREDIENTS FOR 5 SERVINGS:

SALMON MIX:

2 pounds salmon scraps (⅓ smoked and ⅔ fresh)
2 stalks celery, cut in ⅛-inch cubes
4 shallots, minced and sweated in butter
1 egg
1 egg yolk
8 ounces thick béchamel sauce
1 ounce Dijon mustard
¼ cup fresh lemon juice
6 ounces bread crumbs
½ cup mixed chopped fresh herbs
½ teaspoon spiced salt
freshly ground pepper, to taste

BÉCHAMEL SAUCE:

2 tablespoons butter
3 tablespoons flour
1 cup milk
¼ onion wedge stuck with 1 clove
1 garlic clove, crushed
1 sprig thyme
1 bay leaf
small grating of nutmeg
salt and freshly ground pepper, to taste

flour, egg, and bread crumbs for coating
oil for frying

Salmon Steaks with Caper Sauce

MARLENE DION

lways use fresh salmon and never overcook it. The fish should flake away easily to ensure if it is moist.

INSTRUCTIONS: Melt butter in saucepan. Blend in flour and make a smooth paste. Add milk and wine. Stir until thickened. Add hard-cooked eggs, capers, basil, salt, and pepper.

Place salmon in shallow, greased pan. Pour sauce over fish. Bake at 350° for 20 minutes, or until fish flakes easily.

INGREDIENTS FOR 4 SERVINGS:

1 ½ pounds salmon steaks

2 tablespoons butter

2 tablespoons flour

½ cup milk or cream

½ cup white wine

2 hard-cooked eggs, peeled and chopped

1 teaspoon capers

¼ teaspoon basil or dill

salt and pepper, to taste

Fresh Tuna with Tartar Sauce

BETTY CAFISO

INSTRUCTIONS: Place tuna in a bowl. Cover with olive oil. Marinate for one hour. Drain and reserve oil.

Coat tuna chunks with flour. Dip in egg, then roll in bread crumbs. Fry coated tuna in some of the olive oil used for marinating. Brown on both sides. Take care not to overcook.

FOR TARTAR SAUCE: Combine all ingredients. Chill for at least 2 hours before serving.

INGREDIENTS FOR 4 SERVINGS:

1 ½ pounds fresh tuna, cut into 2-inch chunks

olive oil to cover tuna

flour

1 egg, lightly beaten

bread crumbs

TARTAR SAUCE:

2 cups mayonnaise

3 tablespoons chopped onion

2 teaspoons fresh lemon juice

3 tablespoons chopped fresh dill

2 tablespoons chopped fresh parsley

Swedish Fish Mousse with Lobster Sauce

MARY BRETT

Instructions: Remove skin and bones from raw fish. Cut into pieces. Blend first 8 ingredients in food processor until fairly smooth. Add butter and blend some more.

Transfer mixture to a bowl. Fold in beaten egg whites and whipped cream. Butter a 2-quart casserole dish and dust with bread crumbs. Spoon fish mixture into casserole. Cover tightly with buttered foil and lid.

Place casserole dish in a large pan. Fill pan with hot water until level is halfway up the casserole dish. Bake at 350° for 1½ to 2 hours. Unmold on hot platter. To serve, cover with lobster sauce.

For Lobster Sauce: Heat bisque, cream, sherry, and brandy in a medium saucepan. Add cooked lobster or shrimp, if desired.

Ingredients for 8 servings:

1 to 1½ pounds haddock, halibut, or flounder
1 cup milk
4 egg yolks
3 tablespoons flour
4 to 6 anchovy fillets
1 teaspoon salt
¼ teaspoon pepper
dash cayenne
1 cup butter, softened
4 egg whites, beaten stiff
1 cup cream, whipped
bread crumbs

Lobster Sauce:

1 can lobster or shrimp bisque
½ cup light cream
1 tablespoon sherry
1 tablespoon brandy
pieces of lobster or shrimp, cooked (optional)

Pan-Fried Whiting with Jalapeño Mayonnaise

FLORENCE FABRICANT

On chilly winter weekends, when the crowds have disappeared, we welcome the chance to enjoy quiet lunches. This is one of our favorites. In summer, substitute baby "snapper" blues.

INSTRUCTIONS: Rinse and dry the fish. Rub the fish inside and out with one garlic clove and season with salt and pepper.

Combine flour and cornmeal. Season to taste with salt and pepper. Dip the fish in the milk, then roll in the cornmeal mixture.

In a large, heavy skillet, melt the butter over medium-high heat. Add the garlic to the melting butter, then remove it before it has a chance to brown. Add the fish to the pan and sauté until golden brown, about 3 to 5 minutes on each side.

Transfer the fish to a serving platter, garnish with the lemon and parsley, and serve with Jalapeño Mayonnaise.

FOR JALAPEÑO MAYONNAISE: Mix the mayonnaise and yogurt in a bowl. Add the remaining ingredients and stir well.

INGREDIENTS FOR 2 SERVINGS:
2 whole whiting, cleaned (about 2½ pounds)
2 garlic cloves, lightly mashed
salt and freshly ground black pepper
¼ cup all-purpose flour
¼ cup white cornmeal
½ cup milk
2 tablespoons unsalted butter
lemon wedges and parsley for garnish

JALAPEÑO MAYONNAISE:
3 tablespoons mayonnaise
1 tablespoon plain yogurt
1 jalapeño pepper, seeded and finely diced
1 scallion, trimmed and minced
½ tablespoon ground cumin
1 tablespoon minced fresh coriander

Seared Tuna Tarts with Citrus and Fennel Salad

GERARD HAYDEN, CHEF, EAST HAMPTON POINT RESTAURANT

t is recommended that you use a small coffee grinder for the spices.

INSTRUCTIONS FOR TUNA AND TARTARE: Portion tuna into 2x5-inch rectangular blocks. Take excess tuna and dice for tartare.

Grind 1 tablespoon coriander seed. Combine with rosemary, chives, lemon zest, and diced tuna (tartare). Add olive oil and salt. Refrigerate.

Grind remaining coriander seed, fennel seed, and peppercorns semi-fine. Beat egg whites slightly to foam. Roll the tuna loins first in the egg whites, then in the spiced mixture. Refrigerate 10 minutes.

Add canola oil to sauté pan. Heat over medium high flame. Place tuna loins in pan and sear until golden, making sure to cook all sides (about 20 seconds on each side). The idea is to cook the outside, but leave the inside raw. Remove from the oil and refrigerate.

FOR CITRUS AND FENNEL SALAD: Section grapefruit and orange. Set sections aside. Reserve juice and combine with lemon juice in a stainless steel bowl. Add salt. Whisk in grapeseed oil to make a citrus vinaigrette.

Slice fennel very thin on a mandoline. Place in a bowl, salt slightly, and sprinkle with 2 tablespoons of citrus vinaigrette.

INGREDIENTS FOR 4 SERVINGS:

TUNA AND TARTARE:
¾ to 1 pound yellowfin tuna, sushi quality
1 bunch rosemary, chopped
1 bunch chives, chopped
zest of 1 lemon, chopped
1 tablespoon coriander seed
2 tablespoons extra virgin olive oil (Colavita)
dash kosher salt
1 tablespoon fennel seed
¼ cup black peppercorns
2 egg whites
3 tablespoons canola oil

CITRUS AND FENNEL SALAD:
1 navel orange
1 ruby red grapefruit
juice of 1 lemon
pinch of salt
⅓ cup grapeseed oil
1 piece fennel

Continued on next page

FOR PARSLEY OIL: Pick parsley leaves and discard the stems. Blanch the leaves in boiling water. Place blanched leaves in the blender. Turn on high. Slowly pour in olive oil until the parsley is puréed. Set aside.

FOR CROUTONS: Cut bread in ⅛-inch thick slices. Cut out croutons with a 3-inch cookie cutter. Sauté one side of each crouton in oil until golden. Remove and cool.

TO ASSEMBLE TARTS AND SERVE: Spread 1½ to 2 ounces of tartare mixture over the sautéed side of each crouton. For each tart, cut 2 pieces ¼-inch thick from the tuna loin. Fan and place on top of the tartare. Arrange the fruit segments and fennel on four serving plates.

Brown the bottoms of the assembled tuna tarts in a sauté pan. Do not cook the tuna. Remove, and place atop fennel and fruit segments. Drizzle parsley oil and citrus vinaigrette around the plate.

PARSLEY OIL:
1 bunch Italian parsley
8 to 9 tablespoons extra virgin olive oil

CROUTONS:
¼ loaf Pullman white bread
1 tablespoon canola oil

Charlie's Accabonac Creek Surprise Clams

LUCRETIA SIMPSON JUCKETT

INSTRUCTIONS: Sauté onions in 2 tablespoons of butter until translucent. Combine with chopped clams in a bowl. In a medium saucepan, gently heat 1 tablespoon of butter, bread crumbs, Swiss cheese, parsley, and milk with enough reserved clam liquid to moisten. Combine with clam mixture.

Mound stuffing in shells. Bake at 375° for 20 minutes until lightly browned. If freezing, only bake partially.

INGREDIENTS:
1 dozen medium clams, coarsely chopped and liquid reserved
3 medium onions, chopped
3 tablespoons butter
1½ cups seasoned bread crumbs
½ pound Swiss cheese, coarsely chopped
1 tablespoon parsley
1 tablespoon milk

Clam Pie

ROBIN NEIMARK-SEEGAL

My husband and I had the best clam pie at a fair in Springs the summer of 1990. When we couldn't purchase the pies locally, we spent the next 6 months experimenting until we came up with this recipe.

INSTRUCTIONS: Sprinkle pie shells with clams, onion, potato, and bacon. In a bowl, beat together eggs, cream, and poultry seasoning. Pour over mixture in pie shells. Bake at 375° for 30 to 40 minutes until golden brown.

INGREDIENTS FOR 2 PIES:
2 (9-inch) unbaked pie shells
2 cups clams (about 35 littlenecks), chopped and drained
1 medium onion, chopped
1 small potato, chopped
4 strips bacon, cooked until crisp and crumbled
3 eggs
1 cup heavy cream
¾ teaspoon poultry seasoning

Clam Pie

MRS. KENNELL SCHENCK

INSTRUCTIONS: For filling, sauté onions in butter in a skillet until translucent. Add remaining ingredients. Bring to a boil. Reduce heat. Simmer 15 minutes.

Pour into a pie tin lined with a bottom crust. Cover with top crust. Cut vents. Seal edges. Bake at 400° for 20 to 25 minutes.

INGREDIENTS FOR 1 PIE:
pastry for 2-crust pie

FILLING:
1 tablespoon butter
1 onion, chopped
2 cups hard clams, chopped
¼ cup strained clam juice
1 medium potato, peeled, parboiled, and diced
1 cup milk
1 egg, well beaten
½ cup cracker crumbs
pinch of thyme
salt and pepper, to taste

EVILED CLAMS

MRS. N.H. DAYTON. 1939 L.V.I.S. COOKBOOK

One dozen fairly large hard shelled clams washed thoroughly. Place in pan in oven until opened; take from shell and chop fine; use about one-third as many bread crumbs as you have clams, 1 teaspoon butter. Add 1 teaspoon mustard (scant), dash of pepper, 1½ teaspoons chopped parsley and equal parts milk and clam broth, usually about one cup. Let stand for bread crumbs to absorb liquid. Wants to be quite moist. Fill the half shells. Sprinkle each with bread crumbs and dot with butter. Bake twenty minutes in moderate oven and serve in shells.

RABMEAT AU GRATIN

MRS. URBAN S. REININGER. III

This can be made early in the day and heated just before serving.

INSTRUCTIONS: Prepare white sauce. In a medium saucepan, melt butter over low heat. Blend in flour and salt. Add milk all at once. Whisk until sauce thickens and starts to bubble.

Stir in grated cheese until it melts. Add lemon juice, Worcestershire sauce, pepper, and crabmeat; blend well.

Spoon into lightly buttered pie plate. Sprinkle with cracker crumbs. Bake at 300° until bubbly. Serve over toast points.

INGREDIENTS FOR 4 SERVINGS:
1 cup medium white sauce
1½ cups Jarlsberg cheese, grated
2 tablespoons lemon juice
2 tablespoons Worcestershire sauce
½ teaspoon white pepper
2 cups fresh crabmeat, picked over carefully
¼ cup cracker crumbs

MEDIUM WHITE SAUCE:
2 tablespoons butter
2 tablespoons flour
pinch of salt, if desired
1 cup milk

CRAB SHRIMP CASSEROLE

This is a recipe from Wilmington, North Carolina. It is absolutely delightful.

INSTRUCTIONS: Mix all the ingredients together. Put them into a greased 2-quart casserole dish. Cover with cracker crumbs. Bake at 450° for 20 minutes.

INGREDIENTS FOR 15 SERVINGS:

2 pounds shrimp, cooked, peeled, and deveined
2 pounds crabmeat
2 onions, chopped fine
2 large green peppers, chopped fine
1 large stalk celery, chopped fine
3 cups mayonnaise
1 (10 ounce) bottle Durkee's dressing
dash of Tabasco sauce
salt and pepper, to taste
cracker crumbs

FATHER-SON GRILLED LOBSTER

ROBERT AND NICHOLAS STERN

Baseball & apple pie. Rock & roll. Sun & surf. Son & Father, both over the age of 25, sharing a weekend house. Whoa! Surely a crazy match destined for a bizarre and grisly ending the likes of which only Long Island residents could envisage! Not necessarily. Father-Son Grilled Lobster is a recipe/activity designed to create culinary joy and social pleasure within the most stressful summer shares and shocks. Perfected by years of weekend test trials by two of the most stubborn New Yorkers, Robert and Nicholas Stern, this meal will occupy, satisfy, and fortify (with ample protein) the most trying of two day transient relationships.

SERVES FOUR IRASCIBLE VACATIONERS.
Send financially stable half of relationship (deciding this is a potential source of first weekend skirmish) to perform the most straining portion of the recipe:

1. THE PURCHASE. Avoid grimacing as you spend your dwindling pay-check, Social Security, dowry, or inheritance (whichever may apply) on four 1¼ to 1¾ pound lobsters (heavier is O.K. but more difficult to cook evenly over a grill) as well as 8-10 ears of corn, 1 stick of butter, and some fine lager. You may also wish to purchase vegetables for a green salad depending upon whether or not "balanced," "healthy," and "Surgeon

General" are words relevant to your life.

2. THE RAW DEAL. The purchaser now has earned his God-given right to retire to seclusion with a good book and a plentiful portion of the lager while the thrifty chef prepares a charcoal grill (allow ½-¾ hour for coals to burn to a very hot white). Use this time to prepare the salad and boil a large pot of water for the corn (if your grill is extremely large you may wish to cook the corn by wrapping the ears in aluminum foil and placing them directly on the coals for 3-5 minutes). In a small saucepan, melt ½-¾ of the stick of butter (you may wish to use the remainder at the table).

3. THE KILLING. Herein lies an opportunity to torture the squeamish, enter into an argument about capital punishment, and otherwise wreak havoc on the collective morality of the dinner company. When the coals are ready, remove the lobsters from the refrigerator and place them belly-up on a large cutting board. Set the point of a sharp heavy knife between the eyes of the lobster and slice downward towards the tail. Do not cut through the shell. This is a brutal, but quick, death. P.C. pseudo-humanitarians may wish to drop the lobsters into a pot of boiling water for 1 minute, let them die an equally awful death and then remove them and cut them open. Either way, these critters were once alive and

Continued on next page

now they are dead. Intellectually minded chefs may wish to supply company with Kierkegaard, Kafka, and other such appropriate reading material.

4. THE GRILLING. Place the lobsters belly-up on the grill and lightly baste the tail with the melted butter. Immediately turn the lobsters over and allow them to cook for a total of 7-14 minutes depending on their size and heat of the fire. Repeat the basting process 2-3 times during cooking. When grilling, it is critical that you place the claws of the lobsters in the middle (hottest) part of the grill with the tails facing outward to the cooler areas. The tails will cook VERY quickly while the claws require more time to allow the heat to penetrate the thick shells.

Remove the lobsters when the tails are white and tender. Crack a claw open to check whether the meat inside has been cooked to a tender, but solid, pinkish red. If not, baste the tail again and place the lobsters back on the grill. If the tails are cooked and the claws are not, place the lobsters on the grill belly-up. The shell will insulate the sensitive tail meat (but only for a few more minutes). Remember, unlike jaded New York human flesh, lobster is a sensitive meat. It is better to undercook the lobsters and return them to the grill than to overcook and spoil an expensive treat.

5. YE OLDE DON'T FORGET. Immediately after you remove the lobsters from the grill, drop the corn in boiling water for two minutes. A short cooking time will bring out the corn's sweetness while retaining its natural crispness.

6. THE CLOSEST THING TO A SANCTIONED FOOD FIGHT. Make a mess of yourself and others as you crack open the shells and dribble the succulent meat all over your only weekend shirt. You will find that the basting and grilling process has given the lobster a subtle flavor of its own eliminating the need for butter at the table.

Gastronomical ecstasy guaranteed. Peace, harmony, and household love may vary with individual usage. Offer void where crustacean murder prohibited.

Lobster Fra Diavolo

HELENE SILVERBLANK-FORST

Instructions: Prepare sauce. In a large saucepan, sauté onions in 2 to 3 tablespoons of oil until clear. Add remaining ingredients. Simmer on low heat for 1 hour. While sauce is cooking, wash lobsters. Cut them into pieces. Heat ¾ cup oil in deep skillet. Cook lobsters in the oil for approximately 4 minutes on each side, or until shells turn red. Add lobster pieces to simmered sauce. Cook an additional 10 minutes over low heat. Serve over spaghetti or linguini.

INGREDIENTS FOR 4 SERVINGS:

3 live lobsters, (1½ pounds each)

¾ cup olive oil

SAUCE:

2 to 3 tablespoons olive oil

⅓ cup chopped onions

1½ pounds tomatoes, peeled and chopped

3 tablespoons tomato paste

1 cup dry white wine

2 tablespoons chopped parsley

1 teaspoon oregano

½ teaspoon dried, ground red peppers

salt, to taste

Nick and Toni's Oven-Roasted Lobster

NICK & TONI'S RESTAURANT

Instructions: Blanch lobsters in boiling water for 1 minute. Split lobsters in half lengthwise. Simmer balsamic vinegar over a high heat until it glazes. Spread hot vinegar on split lobster. Season with salt and pepper. Lay lobsters in baking pan. Roast in 500° oven for about 7 minutes until lobster is glazed. Garnish with fresh herbs. Serve with corn on the cob.

INGREDIENTS FOR 2 SERVINGS:

2 lobsters (1½ pounds each)

balsamic vinegar

salt and pepper, to taste

fresh herbs, such as rosemary, thyme, or parsley, chopped

Greenport Scalloped Oysters

ANNE THEODORE BLUEDORN

This was one of my mother's favorite recipes. It went with us to France, where for 10 years it was the highlight of our expatriot Thanksgiving dinners. Our French friends all loved these "Huitres à la façon de Greenport."

INSTRUCTIONS: Arrange half the oysters in the bottom of a well buttered, shallow baking dish.

Combine the crackers, salt, pepper, melted butter, and chives. Toss lightly to mix. Sprinkle half the mixture over the oysters. Spread the remaining oysters over the cracker mixture.

Combine the oyster liquor, milk, Worcestershire sauce, and Tabasco sauce. Pour over oysters in dish. Top with remaining cracker mixture. Bake at 400° for 25 minutes.

INGREDIENTS FOR 6 SERVINGS:
1 quart shucked oysters, and their liquor
2 cups saltine crackers, crushed
salt and pepper
½ cup sweet butter, melted
2 tablespoons chopped chives
¼ teaspoon Worcestershire sauce
dash Tabasco sauce
1¾ cups scalded milk

Oyster Stew

MRS. GEORGE B. HAND

INSTRUCTIONS: Heat milk and cream in double boiler. Meanwhile, in a separate saucepan, heat oysters in their liquor until just the edges curl. Add oysters to the milk and cream. Season with salt and pepper. Let sit in the double boiler for a few minutes to blend flavors. When ready, add the butter and serve stew steaming hot.

INGREDIENTS:
2 dozen shucked oysters, and liquor
3 cups milk
1 cup cream
½ teaspoon salt
¼ teaspoon white pepper
2 tablespoons butter

East Hampton Bay Scallops with Fresh Garlic

EDWARD GORMAN

This is probably the simplest and possibly the most delicious recipe in this entire cookbook. That is because the local bay scallops are so good that the less done to them the better. It is important that scallops be fresh so get them from a seafood store you have confidence in. Bay scallop season in East Hampton usually opens about October 15. Peel and mince garlic first so that it will be ready alongside stove at the moment you will need it. Scallops should be draining while garlic is being prepped.

INSTRUCTIONS: Heat butter in a large skillet, preferably non-stick, until bubbling hot but not yet brown. Pan and butter should be hot so scallops will cook quickly, probably two or three minutes, depending on size of scallops. Move scallops around in pan to brown all over as much as possible. Grind some pepper onto scallops as they cook. Sprinkle on salt if you like salt. When scallops are cooked — do not overcook — turn off flame and quickly sprinkle minced garlic over scallops mixing them together with a wooden spatula. The idea is to not cook the garlic. Spoon neatly onto individual plates.

INGREDIENTS FOR 6 SERVINGS:

1 quart bay scallops, fresh, not frozen
¼ cup butter
3 to 4 garlic cloves
salt and freshly ground pepper, to taste

Sautéed Local Bay Scallops

BRUCE. WAINSCOTT SEAFOOD SHOP

Serve scallops over a bed of white rice or rice pilaf. Have a lightly toasted baguette on hand for dipping in pan juices.

INSTRUCTIONS: Sauté shallots, garlic, parsley, and tarragon in butter until shallots are soft. Add scallops, and cook on medium heat for 4 to 6 minutes until scallops turn white. Sprinkle with wine. Cook for 1 additional minute.

INGREDIENTS FOR 4 SERVINGS:
1 pound local bay scallops, fresh or frozen
6 tablespoons butter
2 tablespoons chopped shallots
1 teaspoon chopped garlic
1 tablespoon fresh chopped parsley
1 teaspoon fresh chopped tarragon (or ½ teaspoon dried tarragon)
2 tablespoons white cooking wine

Scallops on Toast

ED GIFFORD

INSTRUCTIONS: Sauté shallots in butter in hot heavy skillet. When shallots have softened, about 3 minutes, add the wine. Cook over high heat to reduce the wine by half.
Toast the bread. Cut off crusts and cut each slice in half to form triangles. Arrange them on two dinner plates. When wine is reduced and almost syrupy, stir in the scallops. Cook 1 to 2 minutes, stirring often and watching carefully so they do not overcook. They are ready when they have just turned white. Add Worcestershire, salt if needed, and pepper. Spoon with all the juices over the toast and serve.

INGREDIENTS FOR 2 SERVINGS:
1 ½ ounces shallots, minced
1 ½ teaspoons butter
1 cup dry white wine
4 slices thin white bread
10 ounces bay scallops, with their juices
3 generous dashes of Worcestershire sauce
⅛ teaspoon salt, if desired
freshly ground pepper, to taste

South Fork Scallops Royale

EUNICE JUCKETT MEEKER

This is an excellent recipe to make expensive bay scallops go further. It's quite rich.

INSTRUCTIONS: Dust scallops with flour. Sauté scallops and garlic in butter until scallops turn opaque. Remove scallops from pan and set aside. Sauté onion until translucent. Add mushrooms, continuing to sauté several minutes longer. Stir in white wine and mustard, cooking to reduce slightly. Reduce heat. Gently blend in sour cream, tomatoes, and parsley. Return sautéed scallops to pan. Heat through. Serve over rice or pasta.

INGREDIENTS FOR 6 SERVINGS:

1 quart bay scallops

½ cup flour

3 tablespoons butter or margarine

2 cloves garlic, minced

1 onion, chopped

1 ½ cups mushrooms, sliced

1 cup white wine

1 tablespoon Dijon mustard

1 cup sour cream

2 medium tomatoes, cut into 8 wedges each

1 tablespoon fresh chopped parsley

Hot Peppered Shrimp

ROBERT A. DURKIN, KAREN LEE'S RESTAURANT

*M*others in the South used to give Hot Peppered Shrimp to their children while they were playing before dinner. It kept them quiet and busy!

INSTRUCTIONS: Combine the dry ingredients and reserve. Melt the butter in a large skillet. Add a tablespoon of the spice mixture. Stir constantly. Cook for 30 seconds and immediately add the lemon juice, stock or wine, and shrimp. Cook furiously. Stir and stir again. Serve the shrimp in their shells.

The object is to produce neither a soup nor a paste, but rather a spicy gloss that coats each shrimp. Serve with crusty bread accompanied by many napkins. Provide cider or lemonade.

INGREDIENTS:

2 crumbled bay leaves
2 teaspoons rosemary
½ teaspoon basil
½ teaspoon oregano
½ teaspoon cayenne pepper
½ teaspoon nutmeg
½ teaspoon salt
½ tablespoon paprika
¼ cup black pepper
6 ounces butter
¼ cup lemon juice
½ cup fish stock or white wine
shrimp in their shells

Shrimp Amandine Casserole

GRETCHEN MUNSON

This dish is just great for special company. My theory is to cook everything before the guests arrive so you will be free to enjoy them.

INSTRUCTIONS: Shell and devein shrimp. Boil in salted water for 1 minute; drain. Split shrimp down the back, reserving a few for garnish.

Prepare rice according to package directions. Set aside. In a large skillet, sauté green pepper and onion in butter for 5 minutes. Add remaining ingredients. Heat through. Combine mixture with cooked rice and shrimp in a buttered 2- or 3-quart casserole dish. Garnish with almonds and paprika. Bake at 350° for 30 minutes. Top with reserved shrimp. Bake an additional 10 minutes, or until casserole bubbles.

INGREDIENTS FOR 4 TO 5 SERVINGS:
2 pounds shrimp
¾ cup raw white rice
2 tablespoons butter or margarine
¼ cup chopped green pepper
¼ cup chopped onion
1 (10½ ounce) can condensed tomato soup
1 cup light cream
½ cup sherry
¼ cup sliced blanched almonds
⅛ teaspoon mace
salt, to taste
⅛ teaspoon pepper

GARNISH:
¼ cup sliced blanched almonds
paprika
reserved cooked shrimp

Shrimp Creole

ANNE WRIGHT WILLIAMS

This recipe is from one of my mother's cookbooks. My mother, Mrs. John H. Wright (Ann), first started coming to East Hampton in 1920 and always worked hard for The L.V.I.S. Fairs.

INSTRUCTIONS: Slowly sauté all of the vegetables in the butter until tender. Stir in the tomato paste and the meat glaze. The recipe can be prepared ahead up to this point.

Before serving, gently whisk in sour cream and cream. Heat briefly over a low flame. Season to taste with cayenne pepper, chili powder, and salt. If more liquid is needed, stir in a little bit of stock. Add cooked shrimps. Heat through. Serve over rice.

INGREDIENTS FOR 15 SERVINGS:

¾ cup butter
½ pound mushrooms, thinly sliced
1 cup finely chopped green pepper
1 cup finely chopped red pepper
1 cup finely chopped carrots
½ cup finely chopped onion
1 teaspoon tomato paste
1 teaspoon meat glaze
1¼ cups sour cream
1 cup cream
cayenne pepper, to taste
chili powder, to taste
salt, to taste
fish or chicken stock, if needed
4½ pounds shrimp, cooked, shelled, and deveined

Shrimp or Lobster Curry

BARBARA DUBITSKY

Instructions: Melt butter and sauté scallions, onion, and garlic until golden. Add apples, chicken broth, tomato paste, and curry. Simmer until apples are tender and liquid volume reduced by half. Stir in cream. Simmer until sauce is slightly thickened. Sauce may be made ahead up to this point.

Stir in cooked shrimp or lobster. Salt to taste. Heat through. Serve on saffron rice along with chutney, raisins, shredded coconut, and peanuts as garnishes.

INGREDIENTS FOR 6 SERVINGS:

1½ pounds shrimp, cooked, shelled, and deveined, or lobster meat, cooked

¼ cup butter

4 scallions, chopped

1 small onion, chopped

1 garlic clove, chopped

3 green apples, peeled, cored, and chopped

2 (13 ounce) cans chicken broth

1 (6 ounce) can tomato paste

1 teaspoon curry, or more to taste

1½ cups cream

salt, to taste

2 packages cooked saffron rice

GARNISHES:

chutney

raisins

chopped peanuts

shredded coconut

STIR-FRIED SHRIMP WITH VEGETABLES

ROSEMARY DOUCETTE

INSTRUCTIONS: Mix cornstarch, water, broth, and soy sauce in bowl until creamy in consistency. Set aside. Heat peanut oil in wok over high heat. Stir-fry garlic and ginger root for 30 seconds. Do not let burn. Drop shrimp in wok. Stir quickly until they turn pink. Remove from pan; set aside.

Add scallions; stir-fry 20 seconds. Add cabbage or celery. Stir-fry 1 minute. Add mushrooms. Stir-fry 1 minute. When vegetables are crisp tender, add water chestnuts. Stir until they are lightly browned. Add snow peas. Stir-fry only 1 minute in order to retain bright green color. Return cooked shrimps to wok. Pour in sauce around the interior rim of the wok. Heat until sauce slightly thickens. Season to taste if necessary. Serve over cooked rice.

INGREDIENTS FOR 4 SERVINGS:

1 pound shrimp, shelled and deveined
1 tablespoon cornstarch
1 tablespoon water
½ cup canned chicken broth
2 tablespoons soy sauce
¼ cup peanut oil
2 cloves garlic, minced
6 paper thin slices of ginger root, peeled and minced
5 or 6 scallions, cut diagonally, in 1-inch slices
1 pound Chinese cabbage, shredded, or 3 stalks celery, sliced
¼ pound fresh mushrooms, sliced
1 (6 ounces) can sliced water chestnuts, rinsed and drained
½ pound snow peas, cleaned and trimmed
salt

Local East Hamptoners displaying their geese.

POULTRY

Chicken Breasts à la Parisienne

PIDDY CLAY

*I*nstructions: Dust chicken breasts lightly with flour. In a large skillet, quickly brown breasts in foaming butter, turning once. Add Marsala wine. Heat gently. Remove breasts to a warm platter.

On a low flame, stir in flour and tomato paste. Stir continuously for 2 minutes. Gradually add broth, stirring until sauce thickens. Gently whisk in sour cream. Do not overheat, as cream may curdle. Whisk in jelly, Parmesan, salt, and pepper. Return breasts to skillet. Cover and simmer for 15 minutes.

Transfer breasts to a baking dish. Cover with the sauce, and sprinkle with Swiss cheese. Bake at 325° for 30 to 40 minutes. Pass baking dish under broiler for 2 minutes to brown Swiss cheese. Garnish with parsley.

INGREDIENTS FOR 4 SERVINGS:
4 whole chicken breasts, halved, boned, and skinned
flour, to coat
2 tablespoons butter
2 tablespoons Marsala wine, warmed
1 tablespoon flour
½ teaspoon tomato paste
½ cup chicken broth or stock
1½ cups sour cream
1 tablespoon red currant jelly
1 heaping tablespoon Parmesan cheese
salt and pepper, to taste
¾ cup grated Swiss cheese
fresh parsley, chopped

Chicken Paprika

ALFRED HOWARTH, 1955 L.V.I.S. COOKBOOK

*O*ne pullet, disjointed; 1 tablespoon butter, 2 medium white onions, chopped fine; 1 tablespoon flour, heaping; 1 pint sour cream, 1 teaspoon Hungarian paprika, fresh, level; salt and pepper to taste. Melt butter in deep skillet, slowly sauté onions until yellow and soft. Arrange chicken over these in even layers. Cover skillet and slowly cook about one hour, or until chicken is done. Remove chicken to serving dish and keep warm. Add flour to gravy in skillet, stirring to keep smooth. Slowly stir in sour cream for sauce of consistency of heavy cream. Add salt and pepper to taste. Add paprika. Pour sauce over chicken. Serve. It is important that the onions not be overdone, and that the paprika not be added until the last minute lest it be bitter.

CHICKEN WITH PRUNES

ELIZABETH J. MAGILL

This recipe can easily be reduced or enlarged. It is very delicious and contains no added fat.

INSTRUCTIONS: Cover the bottom of a large casserole with the onion rings. Add flour and mix well. Layer chicken, lemon zest, and prunes. Top with the tomato sauce. Cover and bake at 350° for 2 hours. Remove cover during the last 10 minutes of baking.

INGREDIENTS FOR 6 SERVINGS:

3 medium onions, sliced into rings

3 tablespoons flour

4 boneless chicken breasts, halved

4 boneless chicken thighs

grated zest of 1 lemon

½ pound (or more) pitted prunes

1 (15 ounce) can tomato sauce

LEMON CHICKEN

BABE BISTRIAN

INSTRUCTIONS: Pound chicken breasts with a mallet to flatten evenly.

In a shallow dish, stir together egg, milk, garlic, salt, and pepper. Dip chicken in egg mixture to coat; then coat with bread crumbs.

In a large skillet, heat olive oil over medium heat. Sauté breasts on each side until golden brown. Drain on paper towels.

Place chicken in a baking dish. Combine broth, wine, and lemon juice. Pour over the chicken. Sprinkle with cheese. Cover and bake at 350° for 25 minutes. Uncover and bake an additional 10 minutes.

INGREDIENTS FOR 6 SERVINGS:

4 boneless chicken breasts, halved and skinned

1 egg

1½ teaspoons milk

clove of garlic, crushed

⅛ teaspoon salt

dash of pepper

seasoned bread crumbs

¼ cup olive oil

⅓ cup chicken broth

2 tablespoons dry white wine

1 to 2 tablespoons fresh lemon juice

¼ cup freshly grated Parmesan cheese

Chicken with Sun-dried Tomatoes

JUDITH SULZBERGER, M.D.

INSTRUCTIONS: Cut each breast half, diagonally, into 6 pieces. In a large skillet, sauté chicken in olive oil over medium heat until no longer pink, about 5 minutes. Season to taste with salt and pepper. Remove chicken with slotted spoon.

Add shallot; sauté until soft. Add remaining ingredients, cooking 5 more minutes until sauce is slightly thickened. Return chicken to skillet. Heat 2 to 3 minutes until warmed thoroughly. Serve with rice.

INGREDIENTS FOR 4 SERVINGS:

4 boneless chicken breast halves, skin removed
3 tablespoons olive oil
salt and freshly ground pepper, to taste
1 shallot, minced
¼ cup sun-dried tomatoes, coarsely chopped
½ cup white wine
⅔ cup heavy cream
⅛ teaspoon marjoram

Grilled Chicken Fajita on Focaccia Bread

GRAND CAFÉ RESTAURANT

Focaccia bread can be found in most specialty gourmet markets.

INSTRUCTIONS: Slice chicken breast and place on bottom piece of focaccia bread that's been cut in half horizontally. Top with bell pepper and onion that have been sautéed in oil until tender. Top with cheese. Cover with top half of bread. Bake at 350° until cheese is fully melted.

INGREDIENTS FOR 2 SERVINGS:

1 large chicken breast, sprinkled with Fajita spices*
    and baked
1 bell pepper, julienned
½ medium Spanish onion, julienned
1 tablespoon oil
2 slices Monterey Jack cheese
focaccia bread for two (Italian pan bread brushed
    with pesto and rosemary)

*FAJITA SPICES:
equal amounts of cilantro, coriander, cumin, and
    white pepper

Grace's Chicken

MRS. STEPHEN G. MARTIN

ears ago, I made up this recipe. It was such a hit with my husband that he usually responded "Grace's Chicken" when asked what he would like for dinner. Serve with some rolls and a salad.

INSTRUCTIONS: Cut each half of the chicken breasts in half, for a total of 8 pieces. Set aside.

In a very large skillet, sauté onion in olive oil until translucent. Add chicken. Season with spices. Brown chicken on both sides.

Add lemon juice, wine, reserved olive juice, and mustard. Cook and simmer for 15 minutes. Add mushrooms, olives, parsley, and capers. Continue to simmer, covered, for 10 minutes more. Serve over rice.

INGREDIENTS FOR 4 SERVINGS:

2 whole chicken breasts, boned and skinned
2 tablespoons olive oil
1 medium onion, diced
1 teaspoon oregano
paprika, to taste
salt and freshly ground pepper, to taste
2 tablespoons lemon juice
2 tablespoons dry white wine
2 tablespoons reserved olive juice
1 tablespoon Dijon mustard
1 cup sliced mushrooms
½ cup green olives stuffed with pimentos, drained
    and juice reserved
¼ cup fresh parsley, chopped
2 tablespoons capers, rinsed and drained

Moroccan Chicken with Vegetables

Alison Elizalde

INSTRUCTIONS: Melt butter in a large saucepan. Add chicken, onions, salt, pepper, and seasonings. Cover and simmer on low heat for 10 minutes. Lift and swirl pan occasionally. Turn over chicken pieces. Add broth and parsley. Cover and simmer for 40 minutes until chicken is just tender.

Remove chicken to a baking pan. Brush surface with honey. Bake at 300° for 10 to 15 minutes.

As chicken bakes, discard cinnamon stick, dried chili, and parsley sprigs. Boil liquid to reduce slightly. Add remaining ingredients to liquid, cooking 10 to 15 minutes until vegetables are tender.

Serve chicken with rice. Vegetables and sauce may be spooned on top of the rice, or served on the side.

INGREDIENTS FOR 4 SERVINGS:

1 3 to 3½ pound chicken, cut up, washed and dried
1 tablespoon butter
2 onions, sliced
1½ teaspoons salt
¼ teaspoon coarse black pepper
¾ teaspoon ground ginger
¾ teaspoon coriander
¾ teaspoon turmeric
1 cinnamon stick
½ dried red chili
2 cups chicken broth
4 sprigs parsley
honey
1 (16 ounce) can garbanzo beans, drained
1 sweet potato, cut into chunks
2 carrots, peeled and cut into chunks
2 zucchini, cut into chunks
2 tablespoons raisins

POACHED CHICKEN BREASTS WITH TUNA BASIL SAUCE

LOUISE KELLY

This recipe is delicious and great to do ahead!

INSTRUCTIONS: In a kettle, combine the chicken breasts with enough cold water to cover them by 1 inch. Remove them. Bring the water to a boil, add salt to taste, and return the chicken to the kettle. Poach the chicken at a bare simmer for 18 minutes, remove the kettle from the heat, and let the chicken cool in the liquid for 30 minutes. Drain the chicken and let it stand until it is cool enough to be handled. Discard the skin and bones from the chicken, removing each breast half carefully from the bone in one piece. Chill the chicken, wrapped well in plastic wrap, for at least 6 hours or overnight.

In a blender or food processor, blend together the tuna, mayonnaise, yogurt, anchovies, 1 tablespoon of the capers, the lemon juice, and salt, and pepper to taste until the sauce is smooth. Transfer the sauce to an airtight container, and chill for at least 6 hours or overnight.

Cut the chicken breasts diagonally into ¼-inch thick slices. Transfer a breast to each of 6 dinner plates. Just before serving, stir the chopped basil into the sauce. Spoon some of the sauce over each breast. Garnish the chicken with the additional capers, basil sprigs, and lemon slices. Serve it with the olives.

INGREDIENTS FOR 6 SERVINGS:

3 large whole chicken breasts with skin and bone (about 1¼ pounds each)
1 (6½ ounce) can tuna packed in olive oil, drained well
½ cup mayonnaise
¼ cup plain yogurt
3 anchovy fillets
1 tablespoon drained bottled capers plus additional for garnish
2 tablespoons fresh lemon juice, or to taste
salt and pepper, to taste
¼ cup finely chopped fresh basil leaves, or to taste, plus, if desired, 6 basil sprigs for garnish
lemon slices for garnish
mixed brine-cured black olives such as Niçoise and Kalamata as an accompaniment

Poached Dijon Chicken Breasts with Tarragon

MRS. ALFRED DEVENDORF

Easy and excellent! This recipe has never failed to get rave reviews!

INSTRUCTIONS: Gently poach chicken breasts in white wine to cover. Drain and cool. Thoroughly combine mustard, mayonnaise, and sour cream until smooth. Coat cooled chicken breasts evenly with this mixture. Garnish with sprigs of tarragon. Serve cold or warm. Provide extra sauce on the side.

INGREDIENTS FOR 6 SERVINGS:
12 boneless chicken breast halves, skin removed
white wine
1 cup Dijon mustard
1 cup Hellmann's mayonnaise
1 cup sour cream
1 bunch fresh tarragon

Fifty Clove Garlic Chicken

NADINE KALACHNIKOFF

INSTRUCTIONS: Salt and pepper the cavity of the chicken. Rub olive oil on chicken and place on roasting pan. Leave skin on garlic cloves. Peel and slice onions. Surround chicken with garlic and onions, drizzling them with ¼ cup olive oil.

Cook at 325° for 45 minutes plus 7 minutes per pound. When chicken is cooked, remove some fat from the pan. Deglaze pan with chicken stock, squeezing a few garlic cloves into the pan juices. To serve, place chicken surrounded by roast garlic cloves on a platter. Serve pan juices on the side.

INGREDIENTS:
1 large free-range chicken
salt
pepper
olive oil
50 cloves of garlic
onions
chicken stock

Stuffed Pine Nut Crusted Chicken Breasts

LANCE ROLL, CHEF, RED HORSE MARKET

I prefer to use a chicken breast with its skin, wings, rib bones, and tenders attached. A skin-on chicken will tend to cook up more moist with more flavor. However, this recipe will adapt to a boneless, skinless chicken breast. Have your butcher cut the chicken the way you prefer.

INSTRUCTIONS: Make an incision in the meat of each breast. Combine basil and tomatoes with goat cheese. Spoon filling (or use a pastry bag) into breast incisions. Season chicken with salt and pepper.

Set up standard breading procedure, beginning to dip chicken first in flour, and then in eggs beaten with water and salt. Combine bread crumbs and pine nuts. Coat breasts. Place crusted breasts on a baking sheet. Cook at 425° until chicken reaches an internal temperature of 165°. Chicken should be a deep brown. Serve whole or sliced.

INGREDIENTS:

8 single Frenched chicken breasts
8 ounces goat cheese, softened
½ ounce fresh basil, julienned
6 ounces sun-dried tomatoes, in oil, julienned
salt and pepper
1 cup flour
4 eggs, lightly beaten
2 tablespoons water
pinch of salt
1 cup bread crumbs
2 cups toasted pine nuts, ground

Brunswick Stew

CAROLYN PREISCHE

INSTRUCTIONS: Combine first 4 ingredients in an 8- to 12-quart stock pot. Bring to a boil. Reduce heat, cover, and simmer for 2 hours. Remove chicken; set in a bowl to cool. Discard celery and onion.

Add potatoes and carrots to broth. Cook until tender, about 30 minutes. Mash potatoes and carrots in the broth.

Remove the meat from the bones; discard skin and bones. Coarsely chop meat. Add meat and remaining ingredients to broth. If necessary, add additional water to create 6 quarts of stew. Bring to a boil. Reduce heat, cover, and simmer 3 hours; stir often. Adjust seasonings to taste. This recipe freezes well.

INGREDIENTS FOR 5 1/2 TO 6 QUARTS:

1 2½ to 3 pound broiler-fryer chicken

2 stalks celery, each cut into 4 segments

1 small onion, quartered

2 quarts water

4 medium potatoes, peeled and quartered

1 pound carrots, peeled and cut into chunks

3 (28 ounce) cans crushed tomatoes

1 cup chopped onion

2 (10 ounce) packages frozen baby lima beans

2 (10 ounce) packages frozen whole kernel corn

2 teaspoons salt

½ to 1 teaspoon red pepper

½ teaspoon black pepper

CREAMY CHICKEN CASSEROLE

HELEN HOIE

INSTRUCTIONS: Prepare rice according to package directions. Set aside.

In medium saucepan, sauté onion in butter until translucent. Remove from heat; stir in flour. Measure reserved liquid from canned mushrooms. Add enough chicken broth to measure 1½ cups. Gradually stir in liquid to roux mixture. Return to heat. Add cream. Stir constantly over medium heat until thickened. Combine cooked rice with remaining ingredients. Gently mix with sauce. Place in greased 2-quart casserole. Garnish with almonds. Bake at 350° for 25 to 30 minutes.

INGREDIENTS FOR 6 SERVINGS:

1 cup wild rice

½ cup chopped onion

½ cup butter or margarine

¼ cup flour

1 (6 ounce) can sliced, broiled mushrooms, drained, with liquid reserved

chicken broth

1½ cups light cream

3 cups diced cooked chicken

¼ cup diced pimento

2 tablespoons snipped fresh parsley

1½ teaspoons salt

¼ teaspoon pepper

GARNISH:

½ cup slivered, blanched almonds

Dutch Oven Chicken

JANE KIRK KIMBRELL

Instructions: In a heavy 4-quart Dutch oven, brown chicken pieces in butter. Season on all sides with salt, pepper, thyme, and tarragon. Set aside.

Deglaze pan with 1 cup vermouth. Stir well. Dissolve cornstarch in remaining ⅓ cup of vermouth. Add to pan, stirring until gravy thickens.

Return chicken to Dutch oven with onions, carrots, celery, and potatoes. Cover and simmer 20 minutes. Add peas and mushrooms. Continue to cook gently until potatoes are tender.

Ingredients for 6 to 8 servings:

3½ pounds chicken pieces, skinned

4 tablespoons butter

salt

pepper

thyme

tarragon

1⅓ cups dry vermouth or white wine

1 heaping tablespoon cornstarch

2 cups chopped onions

2 cups chopped carrots

2 cups chopped celery

3½ cups tiny new potatoes

1 cup frozen green peas

1½ cups sliced mushrooms

Fulling Mill Farm Drunken Chicken

EUNICE JUCKETT MEEKER

I was actually born at Fulling Mill Farm in 1914. Here we grew most of our own fruits, vegetables, and meats. We even had our own smoke house, dairy, 2 orchards, 2 large berry patches (currants, gooseberries, strawberries, raspberries) as well as cattle, pigs, chickens, and sometimes, sheep. It's no longer a farm - but was at one time a showplace for farm activities - including the Suffolk Hunt on occasion. My dad was a Cornell graduate and was one of the earliest in East Hampton to use scientific farming methods.

INSTRUCTIONS: Fry chicken pieces in 3 tablespoons of olive oil in a large heavy skillet until light brown. Transfer chicken pieces to a large, heavy oval baking dish. Combine ½ cup wine, lemon juice, parsley, chives, salt, and pepper. Pour over chicken and let marinate for 1 hour.

Combine water, remaining ½ cup wine, and oil. Pour over chicken pieces. Bake at 300° for 30 minutes, making sure that the chicken does not get too brown.

Combine sauce ingredients and spread over chicken pieces. Raise oven temperature to 400°. Cook briefly, about 5 to 8 minutes, until golden.

Transfer chicken pieces to a warm platter. Whisk sauce in baking dish until smooth. Pour over chicken or put in a special serving bowl.

INGREDIENTS FOR 6 SERVINGS:

16 chicken pieces, skin removed
3 tablespoons olive oil
1 cup white wine
1 tablespoon lemon juice
1 tablespoon fresh chopped parsley
1 tablespoon fresh chopped chives
salt and pepper, to taste
½ cup water
½ cup oil

SAUCE:

¾ cup sour cream
½ cup Bailey's Irish Cream or Frangelico liqueur
1 tablespoon Dijon mustard

Cornish Hens Sauté Provençal

PIERRE L. FRANEY

INSTRUCTIONS: Heat the olive oil in a heavy skillet large enough to hold the pieces of Cornish hens in one layer. Sprinkle the pieces with salt and pepper to taste. When the oil starts to become hot, add the pieces of Cornish hens skin side down. Cook over medium high heat until lightly browned, about 5 minutes. Turn and cook 5 minutes more.

Add onions, leeks, and garlic. Cook, stirring until wilted, about 2 minutes. Add the tomatoes, green olives, thyme, wine, chicken broth, bay leaf, saffron, Tabasco, salt, and pepper to taste. Stir and scrape the bottom to dissolve any brown particles on the bottom of the skillet. Cover closely and simmer for 10 minutes.

Remove the thyme sprigs and the bay leaf. If there is too much liquid, reduce the sauce a bit. Sprinkle with the chopped basil and serve.

INGREDIENTS FOR 4 SERVINGS:

2 Cornish hens, 1½ pounds each, each cut into 8 pieces

salt and freshly ground pepper, to taste

2 tablespoons olive oil

1 cup chopped onions

2 leeks, cut into small pieces, about 1½ cups

1 tablespoon finely chopped garlic

2 cups skinless dry plum tomatoes, cut into ½-inch cubes

24 green olives stuffed with pimentos

4 sprigs fresh thyme, or 1 teaspoon dried

½ cup dry white wine, such as Chardonnay

1 cup fresh or canned chicken broth

1 bay leaf

1 teaspoon saffron threads or turmeric

Tabasco to taste

4 tablespoons freshly chopped basil

Duckling à l'Orange

HENRI SOULE, 1965 L.V.I.S. COOKBOOK

Clean well and season duck with salt. Place in a pan in a 500° oven and let it cook on its side. One hour to an hour and a quarter is required for a duck of about 5 or 6 pounds. It should be well done and very crisp. The gizzard and neck should be roasted along side of the duck in the pan. When done, remove duck from pan and skim the fat from the gravy. Add one cup of canned consomme or stock to gravy. Let boil a few minutes, stirring in crust formed around the pan.

Correct the seasoning with salt if necessary and rub through a fine strainer. Put to one side.

Peel the very top skin of 2 oranges and cut in fine julienne (in long strings). Boil the peel for 2 minutes and strain well. Place 2 tablespoons sugar in saucepan, let it come to a light caramel color. Moisten with the duck gravy which has been thickened by adding 1 tsp. of arrowroot diluted in a little water to the gravy while it is boiling. Put through a fine strainer and add the julienne of orange. When ready to serve, add 1 glass of curaçao liqueur. Garnish duck with sections of orange and pour the sauce over it.

Mr. Soule, proprietor of Le Pavillon in New York, former owner of the Hedges Inn in East Hampton and La Cote Basque in New York, still has a house at Montauk where he often spends weekends. Craig Claiborne, food editor of The New York Times, says that Mr. Soule "has without question been the most towering figure in America where French restaurants are concerned." He came to America in 1939 to manage the French Restaurant at the New York World's Fair.

Long Island Duck with Apple-Raisin Dressing

JOHN B. WESTERHOFF, JOHN DUCK JRS., SOUTHAMPTON

This is the John Duck - Eastport 1900 recipe for duck and stuffing still used by John Duck Jrs. today. In 1900, mashed potatoes, local vegetables in season, and homemade applesauce were served with the duck.

INSTRUCTIONS: Remove end two joints of wings from duck. Remove extra skin from neck end of duck. Rinse with water. Stuff with Apple-Raisin Dressing. Rub skin with salt. Place in a baking pan, breast side up. Cook at 350° for 2 hours. Drain fat from pan every ½ hour. Replace with about 1 cup of water.

For best results, serve duck the next day. After cooking, refrigerate. The next day, remove duck from refrigerator and bring to room temperature. Place in a hot oven, 475° to 500°, for 20 minutes, until crisp.

FOR APPLE- RAISIN DRESSING: Mix all ingredients and stuff into cavity of duck. Close with skewer.

INGREDIENTS:
1 4½ pound Long Island duck
salt

APPLE-RAISIN DRESSING:
12 slices of water-moistened bread
¼ cup seedless black raisins
1 cup peeled and sliced pie (Granny Smith) apples
1 tablespoon sugar
salt to taste

PHEASANT JUBILEE

WHITING HOLLISTER

This recipe works equally well with chicken. INSTRUCTIONS: Quarter pheasants. Wash and dry them with paper towels. Shake a few pieces of pheasant at a time in a plastic bag containing seasoned flour. Brown pieces well in hot oil. Transfer pheasant to an accommodating casserole dish with a cover.

Combine all sauce ingredients in a small bowl. Deglaze the skillet with the sauce, and pour over pheasant in casserole. Cover and bake at 325° for 1½ hours.

Remove cover. Add cherries and sherry. Bake uncovered for an additional 10 minutes. Season to taste with salt and pepper.

INGREDIENTS FOR 6 TO 8 SERVINGS:

2 pheasants
seasoned flour
oil
1 (17 ounce) can Bing cherries, well drained
½ cup sherry
salt and pepper, to taste

SAUCE:

1 clove garlic, minced
1 onion, chopped
½ cup seedless raisins
½ cup chili sauce
½ cup water
¼ cup brown sugar, packed
1 tablespoon Worcestershire sauce

Turkey Cranberry Squares

MRS. DON L. ANDRUS

his recipe is from the Old Dominion State—Danville, Virginia. You may substitute cranberry sauce for the cranberries, reducing sugars to ¼ cup.

INSTRUCTIONS: Melt butter in an 8x8-inch baking dish. Stir in sugar and orange rind, blending well. Spoon cranberries over sugar mixture.

Combine remaining ingredients in a large bowl. Mix well. Pack turkey mixture firmly over cranberries. Bake at 400° for 25 to 30 minutes. Invert immediately onto serving platter. Cut into squares and serve.

INGREDIENTS:
2 tablespoons butter
½ cup granulated sugar
¼ cup brown sugar, packed
1 teaspoon grated orange rind
2 cups fresh cranberries
5 cups diced cooked turkey
1 cup turkey gravy
1 cup milk
2 eggs, lightly beaten
2 cups soft bread crumbs
2 tablespoons minced onion
1 teaspoon salt
¼ teaspoon pepper

Thanksgiving Oyster Stuffing

PATTI WALTON SILVER

This recipe has been in my family for over 60 years; I've just updated it with dill and shiitake mushrooms. The stuffing has been a source of amusement for all of us over the years because of the oysters. Many who have eaten large quantities of it have done so proclaiming they don't like oyster stuffing but love this stuffing! We've never revealed the secret to those oyster haters! Buy the freshest herbs, mushrooms, and oysters for the best results.

INSTRUCTIONS: Cook celery and onion in half of the butter and oil until soft but not brown. Remove from pan and put in large mixing bowl. Add the remaining butter and oil to the pan and sauté the mushrooms until soft.

Prepare the stuffing according to the package directions, reserving ⅓ of the water and butter mixture for the end, if needed.

Add the stuffing mix to the celery and onion and add the sautéed mushrooms. Mix well. Add the chopped oysters and seasonings. Mix well. Add the beaten egg gradually, continually checking the moistness of the stuffing. It should be very moist with no dryness. If necessary, add the remaining butter and water mixture from the package directions (but this probably won't be necessary). It's more delicious to add needed moisture from the remaining oyster liquid and the beaten egg. To be truly decadent, you may even add a bit of half and half. Stuff the turkey with the stuffing and put the remainder in a covered baking dish to cook for 30 minutes at 350 degrees.

INGREDIENTS:
- 1 cup chopped celery
- 1 cup chopped onion
- 4 tablespoons butter
- 4 tablespoons vegetable oil
- 1 package Pepperidge Farm cornbread stuffing mix
- 1 ½ dozen shucked and chopped oysters with their liquid
- ½ pound sliced shiitake mushrooms
- ¼ cup chopped fresh dill
- 2 tablespoons chopped fresh sage leaves
- 2 tablespoons chopped fresh parsley
- 1 beaten egg
- salt and pepper, to taste

Schenck Meat Market on Main Street. Left to right: Charles Tillinghast, Jules King, Christian Schenck, Will Gay, George Schenck, Percy Schenck.

Meats

Canadian Meat Pie

NANCY NAGEL

In the early 1900's, my maternal grandmother's family arrived from D'Ecousse, Cape Breton Island, Nova Scotia, and settled in Montauk. With them, they brought this recipe which is traditionally served after midnight mass on Christmas Eve.

INSTRUCTIONS: On the day before making the pies, salt and pepper the meat. Brown meat well in the oil. Add onion. Continue to stir until all liquid disappears. Add just enough hot water to cover. Simmer on low heat for two hours. Separate the meat from the gravy and refrigerate overnight.

FOR CRUST: The following day, combine flour, salt, baking powder, and baking soda. Mix well. Using an electric mixer, blend flour mixture, shortening, and fat from the top of the refrigerated gravy until there are no lumps. Gradually add some of the cold brown gravy until the dough sticks together and forms a ball.

Divide dough into quarters. On a generously floured surface, roll out the dough to accommodate a 9x13x2-inch Pyrex dish. Roll a bit thicker than regular pie crust. Place dough in dish. Add half of the meat, sprinkle lightly with flour and top with some of the remaining gravy. Tuck in edges of crust. Roll top crust in the same manner. Cut vents. Place over meat. Spread meat gravy on top crust with a pastry brush.

Repeat process for second pie. Bake at 450° for 45 minutes or until golden.

INGREDIENTS FOR 2 PIES:
4 pounds lean beef stew meat, cut into ½-inch cubes
salt and pepper
1 tablespoon oil
1 large onion, finely chopped

CRUST:
4 cups all-purpose flour
1 teaspoon salt
1 teaspoon baking powder
½ teaspoon baking soda
3 heaping tablespoons vegetable shortening

ECLECTIC MEAT LOAF

INSTRUCTIONS: In a large mixing bowl, combine all ingredients by hand, adding the eggs last. Don't overwork the meat or it will produce a meat loaf too tightly packed and dry.

Transfer meat mixture to a baking pan that has been greased or lined with foil. Form into a loaf of desired shape - oval, rectangular, or round. Bake at 350° for 1 hour, possibly a bit longer.

Let stand for a few minutes before slicing. This meat loaf can be served with tomato or mushroom sauce, yet it is delicious just by itself.

INGREDIENTS FOR 4 TO 6 SERVINGS:

2 pounds ground lean meat (preferably half beef and half pork)

1 cup fine bread crumbs or 2 cups seasoned poultry stuffing

½ cup finely chopped shallots or onions, or a mixture of both

2 to 3 minced garlic cloves

1 ½ teaspoons dry mustard

1 ½ teaspoons salt

½ teaspoon freshly ground pepper

½ cup fresh parsley, finely chopped

1 ½ teaspoons dried herbs (thyme, basil, tarragon, etc., or herbes de Provence mixture)

2 tablespoons Worcestershire sauce

¾ cup red wine or sherry or tomato juice or V-8 juice

2 eggs, lightly beaten

OPTIONAL:

1 cup finely diced fresh mushrooms, or 4 ounces dried shiitake mushrooms, moistened, then chopped

Lo-Fat Chili

MARY TURI

I like making this the day before as it keeps well and always tastes better when re-heated. It is also a recipe that can be varied easily depending on individual tastes. I usually make a very hot, spicy version - lots of red pepper, hot salsa, and chili powder.

INSTRUCTIONS: Brown beef and sausage in skillet sprayed with vegetable oil cooking spray. Stir often to break up pieces. Put in colander and rinse with hot water to remove any grease. Let drain.

Respray the same skillet with cooking spray. Sauté peppers, onions, and garlic until soft. Add crushed red pepper and wine. Simmer 5 minutes.

Transfer pepper mixture and ground beef mixture to large saucepan or crock pot. Stir well. Add beans, tomatoes, salsa, and chili powder. Blend well and simmer 45 minutes.

Serve with shredded Cheddar cheese on top if desired.

INGREDIENTS FOR 12 SERVINGS:

2½ pounds lean ground beef
4 Italian sausages, hot or sweet, casings removed
vegetable oil cooking spray
1½ large green peppers, chopped fine
3 large onions, chopped fine
2 cloves garlic, minced
crushed red pepper, to taste
¼ to ½ cup white wine
2 (16 ounce) cans kidney beans, drained
1 (16 ounce) can black beans, drained
1 (28 ounce) can tomato purée
1 (16 ounce) jar salsa (mild, medium, or hot)
chili powder, to taste
Cheddar cheese, shredded

Maple-Orange Pot Roast

BETTY CAFISO

INSTRUCTIONS: Heat olive oil in a heavy pan and brown beef in it.

Mix together and add to the beef: maple syrup, orange juice, orange peel, Grand Marnier, vinegar, Worcestershire sauce, bay leaves, salt, and pepper. Cover and simmer 1¾ hours or until tender.

Add carrots and onions. Simmer about 15 minutes more until carrots are tender.

Remove meat and vegetables to a serving platter. Discard bay leaves.

If juices need thickening for gravy, combine 1 tablespoon of flour with 2 tablespoons of cold water for each cup of pan juice. Make sure mixture is lump-free before adding to pan juices. Stir over medium heat until thickened. Serve gravy on the side, or pour over meat.

INGREDIENTS FOR 4 SERVINGS:
- 1 tablespoon olive oil
- 2 to 3 pounds beef shoulder, chuck, blade, or rump
- ¾ cup maple syrup
- ½ cup orange juice
- 1 tablespoon shredded orange peel
- 1 tablespoon Grand Marnier
- 2 tablespoons white vinegar
- 2 tablespoons Worcestershire sauce
- 4 bay leaves
- ½ teaspoon salt
- ¼ teaspoon pepper
- 5 carrots, peeled and julienned
- 2 small onions, peeled and cut in wedges
- 1 to 2 tablespoons flour

Roast Beef with Yorkshire Pudding

MRS. ROELOF JONKER, 1965 L.V.I.S. COOKBOOK

This recipe, I believe, first appeared in the L.V.I.S. Cook Book for 1916, and was given by the late Mrs. W.B. Robinson. It was repeated in 1948. That Yorkshire Pudding was the best I ever ate. I have copied the recipe for so many friends and would like to see it in the new cook book. The recipe follows:

When roasting a piece of beef set it upon a rack so that the fat will drop into the pan below; if this is inconvenient, remove some of the fat and have it in another pan; the grease should be about ¼ of an inch deep. About three-fourths of an hour before serving pour in a batter made as follows: 1 pint of milk, 4 eggs beaten very light, a pinch of salt, 1 cup of flour. When done, cut in pieces and serve with roast.

Oxtail Stew Tortola

MARY BRETT

We had a lovely kitchen in Tortola, but finding meat was difficult.

They did have frozen oxtails and we enjoyed this stew.

INSTRUCTIONS: Roll oxtail sections in flour seasoned with salt and pepper. Heat oil in Dutch oven; brown oxtails on all sides in several batches. Return browned oxtails to the pot. Add ½ cup chopped onion, tomato juice, beef broth, and wine. Bring to a boil. Reduce heat and simmer 3 hours.

Add remaining onions, celery, carrots, and Worcestershire sauce. Simmer for 45 minutes.

Refrigerate stew until fat rises to the surface. Discard fat. Return pot to heat. To thicken sauce, knead together butter and flour. Add small balls of mixture to hot liquid, stirring until thickened.

INGREDIENTS FOR 4 TO 6 SERVINGS:

5 pounds oxtails, cut into 2-inch pieces

¾ cup flour

1½ teaspoons salt

freshly ground pepper

3 tablespoons olive oil or beef fat

2½ cups onions, chopped

2 cups tomato juice

1½ cups beef broth

1 cup red wine

½ cup celery, diced

1 cup carrots, sliced

1½ teaspoons Worcestershire sauce

3 tablespoons butter

3 tablespoons flour

Spicy Beef Stew with Polenta

Martha S. Murray

Instructions: Heat oil in Dutch oven over high heat and brown beef on all sides, about 5 minutes. This is best done in 3 to 4 batches. Transfer each batch to a bowl with slotted spoon.

Reduce heat to medium. Add onion and parsley; cook until onion is golden, about 10 minutes. Add garlic, bay leaves, cloves, cinnamon, and allspice.

Return beef to Dutch oven and stir until it is coated with spice mixture. Add red wine and simmer 15 minutes. Add beef broth and simmer 10 minutes.

Break up tomatoes and add them with their juices. Mix in rosemary and olives. Cover and cook over low heat 1½ hours, stirring occasionally.

Add peppers and cook, covered, another 15 minutes. Season with salt and pepper and serve over polenta. The polenta soaks up the gravy which is thin.

INGREDIENTS FOR 12 SERVINGS:

4 tablespoons olive oil
6 pounds beef chuck roast, trimmed and cut into 1-inch cubes
1 large onion, chopped
¼ cup fresh parsley, chopped
2 garlic cloves, minced
2 bay leaves
¼ teaspoon ground cloves
¼ teaspoon ground cinnamon
¼ teaspoon ground allspice
1 cup dry red wine
20 ounces beef broth
1 (28 ounce) can whole plum tomatoes
½ cup pitted olives, halved
2 teaspoons dried rosemary, crumbled
2 red bell peppers, cut into strips
salt and pepper

Steak à la Stone

ANTHONY TAMMERO, CHEF, THE PALM AT HUNTTING INN

INSTRUCTIONS: Cook steak on flame broiler at high heat until medium rare.

Sauté onions and pimentos separately in sweet butter. If using peppers, sauté them separately by color. Season to taste with salt and pepper.

Arrange sautéed vegetables on top of toasted white bread. Slice steak on the bias. Cover the entire plate with steak. Garnish with parsley.

INGREDIENTS:

17 to 18 ounces prime aged New York strip steak

4 ounces Spanish onions, sliced

6 ounces pimentos, sliced (or substitute fresh yellow, green, and red peppers, approximately ½ a pepper of each color)

1 ½ tablespoons sweet butter

salt and freshly ground black pepper

1 piece white toast

fresh parsley, chopped

Butterflied Leg of Lamb

BONNIE KRUPINSKI

This recipe has been served at many dinner parties at Breeze Hill.

INSTRUCTIONS: Combine all ingredients to make a marinade for the lamb. Simmer marinade 20 minutes, stirring occasionally.

Two hours before cooking, pour marinade over lamb. Turn frequently.

Cook the meat over charcoal about 40 minutes, basting with marinade and turning often.

INGREDIENTS FOR 10 TO 12 SERVINGS:

2 small legs of lamb, boned and butterflied

MARINADE:

1 cup dry red wine

1 cup beef stock

2 tablespoons wine vinegar

1 tablespoon minced onions

1 tablespoon rosemary

1 tablespoon marjoram

1 large bay leaf, crumbled

1 teaspoon salt

½ teaspoon ginger

Navarin of Lamb

DOLORES FREY

The chef at Le Cirque Restaurant appeared on television one day and gave this recipe. Though the ingredient list seems endless, it really is an easy recipe to prepare. It's great for guests on a cold winter night. I've made it many times, and it is always delicious.

INSTRUCTIONS: Cut lamb into 1½-inch cubes. Season with salt and pepper. In a large heavy casserole, heat the olive oil. Over medium heat, brown the lamb, 1 pound at a time. Add garlic, rosemary, and the rind of 1 orange in one piece. Sprinkle with flour. Stir to coat. Bake at 375° for 10 minutes to brown flour.

Remove from oven. Add tomato paste, wine, and Cointreau. Stir to loosen browned bits. Cover lamb with chicken broth by 1 inch. Add carrots, celery, onions, and turnips. Return to oven and cook for 2 hours, or until lamb and turnips are tender.

Remove from oven. Add blanched haricots verts and green peas that have been microwaved for 1 minute. Garnish with julienned zest of the second orange. Serve with buttered bowtie pasta tossed with chopped fresh basil.

INGREDIENTS FOR 6 SERVINGS:

3 pounds lean lamb, cut from a leg of lamb
salt and pepper
3 tablespoons olive oil
5 cloves garlic, minced
1 fresh rosemary sprig
2 oranges
½ cup flour
2 tablespoons tomato paste
½ cup white wine
2 tablespoons Cointreau
2 cups (or more) chicken broth
1 pound baby carrots, whole
1 cup sliced celery
8 ounces frozen pearl onions
6 white turnips, pared and cut into eighths
½ pound haricots verts (tiny string beans)
1 (10 ounce) box frozen green peas
1 pound bowtie pasta, cooked al dente
2 tablespoons butter
½ cup fresh basil, chopped

Lamb Shanks with White Bean Purée

CALISTA WASHBURN

This recipe seems like a lot of work, but it is all done ahead, thus making it an easy dinner party dish. Prepare one or two days ahead of serving.

INSTRUCTIONS: Heat 1 tablespoon olive oil in a large heavy casserole dish. Add onions, carrots, celery, and garlic. Cook over medium-low heat for 10 to 15 minutes until they soften.

Put flour in brown paper bag; add lamb shanks and shake. Heat 1 tablespoon olive oil in a heavy skillet. Brown the shanks on all sides, adding more oil if needed. Transfer shanks to the casserole with the vegetables. Deglaze the skillet with the wine. Add to casserole. Stir in tomatoes and bouquet garni. Add enough water to barely cover meat. Cover and bring liquid to a boil. Transfer casserole to a preheated 325° oven. Cook for 1½ to 2 hours until meat easily slips off the bone.

Using tongs and a fork, carefully push meat off the bones into a 9x13-inch Pyrex baking dish. Cover and refrigerate. Strain the remaining liquid into a quart size jar. Discard solids. Add additional water to liquid in jar to fill to the top. Cover and refrigerate.

Prior to serving, skim surface fat from liquid. Place liquid in saucepan. Add soy sauce. Bring to a boil; cook until reduced to 2 cups.

Bring meat to room temperature. Bake, uncovered, at 500° until meat sizzles and starts to brown, about 15 minutes. I sometimes add some pre-cooked onions and

INGREDIENTS FOR 4 SERVINGS:

2 tablespoons olive oil

1 cup onions, coarsely chopped

1 cup carrots, coarsely chopped

1 cup celery, coarsely chopped

2 garlic cloves, chopped

2 tablespoons flour

4 lamb shanks

1 cup wine, red or white

2 cups canned Italian plum tomatoes, broken up with a fork

1 bouquet garni (or sprigs of thyme and parsley)

water

2 tablespoons dark soy sauce

GREMOLATA:

2 tablespoons chopped parsley

½ lemon peel, chopped

1 clove garlic, minced

WHITE BEAN PURÉE:

1 pound cannellini beans

water

extra virgin olive oil

salt and pepper, to taste

Continued on next page

baby carrots at this point. Remove from oven. Pour simmering sauce over meat. Combine gremolata ingredients; sprinkle over meat. Serve with white bean purée.

FOR WHITE BEAN PURÉE: Cook cannellini beans according to package directions until they are very soft. Reserve some cooking liquid. Purée beans with a small amount of cooking liquid in a food processor. The desired consistency is that of mashed potatoes. Swirl in some olive oil. Season with salt and pepper.

Mediterranean Leg of Lamb

DIANE DUNST

INSTRUCTIONS: Place lamb skin side up in roasting pan. Add onions and mushrooms. Combine butter with lemon juice, oregano, parsley, garlic, salt, and pepper and mix well. Pour evenly over meat. Add ½ cup water to pan. Roast in 500° oven for 20 minutes.

Add remaining water. Lower oven to 350° and roast to desired doneness: 140° on meat thermometer for rare, 170° for medium. Baste occasionally. If necessary, add more water to pan.

Remove lamb from pan. Let stand 20 minutes before slicing. Serve pan gravy with onions and mushrooms on the side.

INGREDIENTS FOR 6 TO 8 SERVINGS:
1 5 to 6 pound leg of lamb
3 medium onions, chopped
½ cup dried mushrooms, chopped
4 tablespoons butter, melted
juice from 2 lemons
2 tablespoons dried oregano
3 tablespoons dried parsley
2 to 3 large cloves of garlic, crushed
salt and freshly ground pepper
1 cup water, or more as needed

Charcoal Grilled Glazed Spareribs

PETER DOHANOS

INSTRUCTIONS: Place ribs, onion, garlic, and salt in pot and cover with water. Boil for 20 minutes. This may be done in advance of starting the charcoal fire. Drain ribs. Simmer glaze ingredients until thoroughly blended. Cook ribs over a slow charcoal fire, basting frequently with glaze, until all edges are crisp.

INGREDIENTS FOR 6 SERVINGS:
5 to 6 pounds lean spareribs, cut into pairs
1 large onion, chopped
3 cloves garlic, quartered
1 teaspoon salt

GLAZE:
1 cup catsup
⅓ cup red currant or beach plum jelly
3 tablespoons soy sauce
juice of 1 lemon

Fruited Pork Tenderloin

MARTHA S. MURRAY

This is my variation of a recipe from The Silver Palate.

INSTRUCTIONS: Arrange fruit between halves of pork tenderloin. Tie with twine to hold together. Make slits in the roast and insert slivers of garlic. Salt and pepper and smear roast with butter. Sprinkle with thyme

Set roast in shallow baking pan. Mix wine and molasses and pour over meat. Bake in 350° oven for 45 minutes. Cut into thin slices and spoon juices over them.

INGREDIENTS FOR 4 SERVINGS:
1 pork tenderloin, halved horizontally
1 cup mixed dried fruit
1 garlic clove, cut into slivers
salt and pepper to taste
4 tablespoons sweet butter, softened
1 teaspoon dried thyme
⅔ cup Madeira wine
1 tablespoon molasses

Kielbasa and Spinach Casserole

ANN KIRK WILLARD

INSTRUCTIONS: Sauté sausage in a skillet until lightly browned.

Cook spinach according to package directions. Drain and press out excess water. Stir in nutmeg.

Spread sausage in a 9x13-inch baking dish. Top with spinach. Set aside some sliced sausage for garnish.

Put cheese, beer, Worcestershire, flour, and mustard in top of double boiler. Whisk over medium heat until a smooth sauce is created.

Pour sauce over spinach. Garnish with reserved sausage slices. Bake at 350° until heated through, or pass under broiler to brown.

INGREDIENTS FOR 8 SERVINGS:

1 ½ to 2 pounds kielbasa (Polish sausage) cut into ½-inch thick pieces
3 (10 ounce) packages frozen spinach
½ teaspoon nutmeg
3 cups (about 1 pound) Cheddar cheese, grated
1 cup beer
1 teaspoon Worcestershire sauce
2 tablespoons flour
¼ teaspoon dry mustard

Pork Medallions with Mustard Cream Sauce

ANNE TREGELLAS

*I*NSTRUCTIONS: Flatten the medallions to ½-inch thickness. Dust them with flour, salt, and pepper. Sauté in 3 tablespoons of butter for 2 to 3 minutes on each side. Transfer medallions to platter and keep warm.

Add vinegar and peppercorns to pan. Boil mixture. When liquid is reduced by two-thirds, add cream and simmer for 5 minutes until thickened. Remove sauce from heat and stir in mustard and 2 tablespoons of butter. Adjust seasoning if necessary. Pour sauce over warm medallions.

INGREDIENTS FOR 4 TO 6 SERVINGS:
12 medallions of pork tenderloin, 1-inch thick
flour to dust pork
salt and pepper
3 tablespoons butter
⅓ cup vinegar
8 peppercorns, crushed
2 cups heavy cream
⅓ cup Dijon mustard
2 tablespoons butter, cut into pieces

Pork Chops in Sour Cream and Applesauce

ANNE CANNON

*I*NSTRUCTIONS: Dredge pork chops in flour seasoned with salt and pepper. Heat oil in skillet and brown chops on both sides. Place in a baking dish. Heat combined applesauce and sour cream; pour over chops. Bake, covered, at 350° for 1 hour or until tender. Serve with noodles.

INGREDIENTS FOR 4 SERVINGS:
4 (¾- to 1-inch thick) pork chops
flour for dredging
salt and pepper, to taste
2 tablespoons oil
4 ounces applesauce
6 ounces sour cream

Jimmy's Special Kidney Stew

JIMMY G. STIER

This recipe is good for a cool weather lunch or light supper. It's great for Sunday breakfast or brunch. My kids started to like all innards after trying this dish. Beef kidneys can be used if soaked overnight in buttermilk. Madeira or Marsala wine can be substituted for the sherry.

INSTRUCTIONS: Sauté sliced kidneys in butter until done, 2 to 3 minutes. Sprinkle with flour and mix well. Add beef stock to create sauce. Add mushrooms and cook 1 minute longer. Add tongue, sherry, Worcestershire sauce, salt, and pepper. Serve over toast, couscous, rice, or noodles. Garnish with parsley.

INGREDIENTS FOR 4 SERVINGS:

4 veal kidneys or 12 lamb kidneys, sliced
2 tablespoons clarified butter
3 tablespoons flour
1 cup beef stock or bouillon
4 ounces mushrooms, very thinly sliced
¼ cup tongue or flavorful ham, julienned
sherry, to taste
dash Worcestershire sauce
salt and pepper, to taste
fresh Italian parsley, chopped

Osso Bucco

BETTY WHITE

his is delicious served with saffron risotto. INSTRUCTIONS: Wipe shanks with a damp towel. Combine flour with salt and pepper; rub into meat.

Slowly heat oil in a Dutch oven. Cook veal, in batches, until well browned. Remove and set aside.

Add onions, carrots, and garlic. Sauté until onions are soft, about 5 minutes. Add tomato sauce, wine, basil, thyme, and bay leaf. Return veal to the pot. Bring to a boil. Reduce heat, cover, and simmer for 2 hours until veal is tender.

Sprinkle with parsley, lemon peel, and celery. Cook over very low heat, covered, for 5 minutes.

INGREDIENTS FOR 6 SERVINGS:

3 whole shanks of veal, sawed into 3-inch pieces
⅓ cup flour
1½ teaspoons salt
¼ teaspoon ground pepper
½ cup olive oil
1 cup onions, coarsely chopped
1 cup sliced carrots
1 clove garlic, crushed
1 (8 ounce) can tomato sauce
1 cup dry white wine
1 teaspoon dried basil
½ teaspoon dried thyme
1 bay leaf
2 tablespoons parsley, chopped
1 teaspoon grated lemon peel
¼ cup celery, finely chopped

Veal

MRS. J.T. TRIPPE, 1948 L.V.I.S. COOKBOOK

Four thin pieces of veal, dust lightly in flour. Brown quickly each side in hot butter. Pour 2 tablespoons of hot Sherry, remove veal and add 2 sliced mushrooms and cook briskly few minutes and season. Add ½ teaspoon tomato paste, 1 tea-spoon potato flour, ¾ cup soup stock. Stir over slow fire until boiling, add cooked asparagus tips, ¼ cup of cream, freshly chopped tarragon and parsley. Replace veal, cover and cook for 15 minutes. Arrange on platter, pour over sauce and sprinkle with bacon.

Veal in Wine

BARBARA BOLTON DELLO JOIO

A great winter buffet dish served over noodles with crusty French bread and salad. I use Gallo Hearty Burgundy. It's a terrific cooking wine.

INSTRUCTIONS: Coat veal pieces with seasoned flour; dip in eggs, then in bread crumbs. Brown veal pieces quickly in oil and butter.

Arrange meat in casserole. Add wine (enough to cover meat) and herbs. Cook at 350° for at least 30 minutes. This dish can be kept in a warm oven for up to 1 hour. Add more wine if necessary.

INGREDIENTS FOR 4 TO 6 SERVINGS:
2 pounds veal steak, cut into serving portions
flour
salt and pepper
2 eggs, beaten
1 cup bread crumbs
1 tablespoon oil
1 tablespoon butter
1 cup red wine (to cover meat)
¼ teaspoon thyme
¼ teaspoon rosemary
1 bay leaf

Veal Ragout

MRS. MARSHALL CLARK

INSTRUCTIONS: Brown veal in bacon fat or oil. Remove from skillet and set aside. Add peeled onions to the pan and brown well.

Place meat and onions in a 3-quart buttered casserole. Season with salt and pepper. Pour mushroom soup over meat; mix well. Bake, covered, at 300° for 2 hours, or until meat is tender. Recipe can be made ahead to this point. It may also be frozen now. Defrost before continuing.

Remove stems from mushrooms. Reserve for another use. Sauté caps gently in butter for 5 minutes. Set aside.

Prior to serving, gently stir sour cream into casserole. Top with sautéed mushroom caps. Heat at 300° for 25 to 30 minutes.

INGREDIENTS FOR 4 TO 6 SERVINGS:

3 pounds veal (leg or shoulder) cut into 2-inch cubes

3 tablespoons bacon fat or olive oil

12 small white onions, peeled

salt and pepper

2 (10 ounce) cans cream of mushroom soup

1 pound small fresh mushrooms, wiped clean

3 tablespoons butter

1 pint sour cream

Veal with White Beans

PATRICIA AND KEN FERRIN

Instructions: Heat oils in heavy casserole. Add veal and cook over high heat, turning often. When meat begins to brown, add garlic and onion. When onion wilts, add mushrooms, wine, rosemary, bay leaf, salt, and pepper. Reduce heat and simmer about 8 minutes. Add tomatoes, beans, and stock. (*If canned beans are used, do not add them until veal has cooked about 45 minutes.) Cover and simmer over low heat about 1½ hours. Discard garlic.

Garnish with chopped parsley. Serve hot with rice.

INGREDIENTS FOR 6 SERVINGS:

2 tablespoons olive oil
2 tablespoons safflower oil
1 ½ pounds stewing veal, cut into 1-inch cubes
2 cloves garlic, skins on
1 medium onion, finely chopped
10 ounces mushrooms, chopped
½ cup dry white wine
1 teaspoon rosemary
1 bay leaf
salt and pepper, to taste
1 cup tomatoes, chopped
2 cups dried white beans, cooked*
¼ cup chicken stock
fresh parsley, chopped

Local produce at
farm stand.

Vegetables

asparagus

Artichoke Spinach Casserole

SHIRLEY M. COLLINS

This is an easy recipe, ideal for a special luncheon or dinner. It's a nice change of pace from ordinary vegetable casseroles.

INSTRUCTIONS: Drain artichoke hearts slightly. Line bottom of casserole dish with artichokes.

Cook spinach according to package directions. Drain lightly; spread over artichoke hearts.

Cream together cream cheese and butter. Spread mixture over vegetables.

Top with Parmesan. Cover and bake at 350° for 40 minutes. Remove cover during the last 15 minutes of baking time.

INGREDIENTS FOR 6 TO 8 SERVINGS:

2 (6 ounce) jars marinated artichoke hearts

2 (10 ounce) packages frozen chopped spinach

8 ounces cream cheese

5 tablespoons butter

½ to ¾ cup freshly grated Parmesan cheese

Asparagus Custard

CRISTA G. MARTIN

I brought this recipe from my mother's recipe file. She is a fabulous gourmet cook. Now 76, she lives in Palo Alto, California.

INSTRUCTIONS: Combine all ingredients, except the butter. Pour into a buttered 1½-quart casserole dish. Top with melted butter. Bake at 350° for 30 minutes.

INGREDIENTS FOR 6 SERVINGS:

1 pound asparagus, cooked and cut into 1-inch segments

3 eggs, well beaten

1 cup milk

1 cup Cheddar cheese, grated

¾ cup cracker crumbs

1 pimento, diced

1 teaspoon salt

¼ teaspoon pepper

3 tablespoons butter, melted

Sesame Broccoli

CONNIE GRETZ

This is an original recipe. I was looking for a variation to plain steamed "trees" which my children were getting tired of. I searched my cookbooks, yet found nothing of interest. A trip to my pantry inspired the results!

INSTRUCTIONS: Wash broccoli. Separate florets from stems. Cut florets into bite-sized pieces. Trim and pare stems. Angle cut. Steam stems first, then florets until fork tender.

Combine sesame oil, teriyaki sauce, garlic powder, and salt. Drizzle over hot broccoli. Sprinkle with sesame seeds. Serve hot or cold.

INGREDIENTS FOR 4 SERVINGS:
1 head fresh broccoli
3 tablespoons sesame oil
¼ cup teriyaki sauce
½ teaspoon garlic powder
salt, to taste
¼ cup sesame seeds, lightly toasted

Fresh Corn Pudding

MRS. LAWRENCE FLINN, JR.

INSTRUCTIONS: Beat eggs thoroughly in a bowl. Combine flour, salt, and pepper. Stir into eggs. Add corn, cream, and butter. Pour mixture into a 1½-quart casserole. Place in a pan of hot water. Bake at 325° for one hour, or until knife inserted in center comes out clean.

INGREDIENTS FOR 4 TO 6 SERVINGS:
3 eggs
¼ cup flour
1 teaspoon salt
½ teaspoon pepper
2 cups fresh corn kernels, cut from the cob
2 cups light cream
2 tablespoons melted butter

Stir-Fried Broccoli Stems

DOLORES FREY

This is "what to do" with those broccoli stems that are often left over.

INSTRUCTIONS: Heat pan. Add oil. Add onion, ginger root, and garlic. Stir-fry for 30 seconds.

Add broccoli. Stir-fry for 5 minutes. Combine broth, black bean sauce, and lemon juice. Pour around sides of pan. Stir-fry 2 minutes longer. Season to taste with salt and pepper.

One can find black bean sauce in the Chinese food section of your local gourmet market.

INGREDIENTS:
1 tablespoon peanut oil
¼ large onion, sliced
4 thin slices fresh ginger root, finely julienned
1 clove garlic, minced
broccoli stems from 1 head of broccoli, pared and angle cut
½ cup chicken broth
1 ½ teaspoons black bean sauce
juice of ½ lemon
salt and pepper, to taste

Carrot Soufflé

MRS. MALCOLM ALDRICH, 1965 L.V.I.S. COOKBOOK

Put cooked carrots through a sieve. Stir in the salt and honey, the milk (in which has been dissolved the cornstarch), then add the well beaten eggs, and last the melted butter. Pour into a buttered casserole and bake 45 minutes in a 400° oven. An excellent dish, say even non-carrot lovers.

INGREDIENTS FOR 6 TO 8 SERVINGS:
2 cups cooked carrots
3 eggs
4 tablespoons melted butter
1 ¼ cups very rich milk or thin cream
1 teaspoon salt
¼ cup strained honey
3 tablespoons cornstarch

Russian Cabbage Pie

MRS. HAL B. LARY

INSTRUCTIONS FOR PASTRY: Sift together dry ingredients. Cut in shortening and butter until mixture resembles coarse meal. With a fork, stir in egg and enough ice water until a ball forms. Knead briefly. Wrap in plastic wrap and chill.

FOR CABBAGE FILLING: Sauté onion in butter until translucent. Add cabbage; cover and braise on low heat until tender. Stir occasionally. Season to taste with salt.

TO ASSEMBLE: Grease and flour a 9x9-inch pan. Divide pastry in half. Roll each half into a 9x9-inch square. Line pan with one square of pastry. Add cabbage filling. Top evenly with chopped egg. Top with second pastry square. Cut vents. Bake at 375° for 25 to 30 minutes until pastry is golden.

INGREDIENTS:

QUICK RUSSIAN PASTRY:
2½ cups sifted flour
1½ teaspoons baking powder
1 teaspoon salt
½ cup vegetable shortening
2 tablespoons butter
1 egg lightly beaten
ice water, as needed

CABBAGE FILLING:
2 onions, chopped
1 tablespoon butter
5 cups finely chopped cabbage
salt, to taste
2 hard cooked eggs, chopped

Eggplant and Tomato Casserole

MARY BRETT

INSTRUCTIONS: Place bread crumbs in a greased casserole dish. Sprinkle with melted butter.

Sauté onion in oil until clear. Combine onion with tomatoes, brown sugar, basil, and salt. Pour mixture into prepared casserole dish. Bake uncovered at 325° for 2 hours.

Cover eggplant with water in medium saucepan. Simmer until tender. Stir eggplant and optional corn into casserole. Bake an additional 45 minutes. This dish can be prepared ahead and reheated.

INGREDIENTS FOR 6 SERVINGS:

1 cup fresh bread crumbs

¼ cup melted butter

1 medium onion, chopped

1 tablespoon oil

1 (26 ounce) carton tomatoes, chopped

4 tablespoons brown sugar

½ teaspoon dried basil

¼ teaspoon salt

1 medium eggplant, pared and diced

1 cup corn kernels (optional)

Stuffed Spinach

SUZANNE LEAVER

I was away from home for the first time, attending massage school in Colorado. A group of students got together for a potluck Thanksgiving dinner. Not knowing very much about holiday cooking, I called home to get this recipe from my Mom. It's been a favorite at my holiday table ever since!

INSTRUCTIONS: Cook spinach and drain. Combine with remaining ingredients. Place in greased casserole. Top with remaining stuffing. Bake at 350° for 30 minutes.

INGREDIENTS FOR 4 TO 6 SERVINGS:

2 (10 ounce) packages frozen spinach

1 tablespoon chopped onion

1 (10 ounce) can cream of mushroom soup

1 egg, lightly beaten

½ cup butter, melted

¾ cup grated Cheddar cheese

1 cup herb bread stuffing.

TOPPING:

¾ cup herb bread stuffing

Great Aunt Agnes' Mushroom Casserole

MARY T. MACDONALD

Aunt Agnes made this fabulous mushroom casserole on every festive occasion. Throughout the years (she's now 94), children, grandchildren, nieces, and friends have attempted this recipe, but say it is not as special as Aunt Agnes'. Personally, I think mine is the same! The sauce and dumplings are compatible with many food combinations; for example try broccoli, mushrooms and chicken, or asparagus, tomatoes and veal, etc.

INSTRUCTIONS: FOR SAUCE: Chop stems and sauté in the butter. Add flour and blend until smooth. Add milk gradually, then salt. Stir until thickened. Add 3 ounces grated Gruyère cheese.

FOR DUMPLINGS: Melt butter in a saucepan. Add boiling water, flour, and salt. Stir until a ball of dough is formed. Remove from heat. Add eggs, one at a time, beating thoroughly after each addition. Continue beating mixture until smooth and shiny. Drop batter by teaspoonful into a large pot of boiling salted water. Cook for 2 to 3 minutes. Remove dumplings and drain on paper towels.

TO ASSEMBLE: Wipe mushrooms and dip in lemon juice with a little salt added. Place in baking dish. Add sauce to mushrooms in baking dish. Top with drained dumplings. Sprinkle with ¼ cup grated Gruyère cheese. Bake at 375° for 20 to 25 minutes.

INGREDIENTS:
1 pound fresh mushrooms, stems removed and set aside
lemon juice mixed with a dash of salt

SAUCE:
chopped mushroom stems
¼ cup butter
¼ cup flour
2 cups milk
½ teaspoon salt
3 ounces Gruyère cheese, grated

DUMPLINGS:
½ cup butter
1 cup boiling water
1 cup flour
½ teaspoon salt
4 eggs
large pot boiling salted water

TOPPING:
¼ cup Gruyère cheese, grated

Do not dip mushrooms in lemon/salt mixture until ready to assemble the dish.

Mushroom Moussaka

PATRICIA FERRIN

his is a meatless and eggless version of the famous Greek eggplant casserole, with two deceptively rich-tasting sauces. One is tomato-based, loaded with mushrooms; the other is a traditional béchamel.

INSTRUCTIONS FOR EGGPLANT PREPARATION:
Slice eggplants into ¼-inch thick rounds. Lightly salt slices on both sides. Layer them in a colander placed over a bowl. Let them stand for 30 minutes so that they sweat out their bitter juices.

Retrieve the eggplant slices from their spa, and pat them dry. Bake them on a lightly oiled baking sheet at 375° for 20 to 25 minutes until tender. Set aside.

FOR MUSHROOM-TOMATO SAUCE: Heat oil in a large, deep skillet. Add onions and salt. Sauté until translucent. Add mushrooms and garlic. Stir and cover. Cook over medium heat an additional 8 to 10 minutes.

Add tomatoes, tomato paste, cinnamon, oregano, basil, and pepper. Bring to a boil. Reduce heat. Simmer, uncovered, for 12 to 15 minutes. Remove from heat. Stir in parsley, bread crumbs, and Parmesan. Set aside.

FOR BÉCHAMEL SAUCE: In a medium saucepan, melt butter over low heat. Whisk in 4 tablespoons of flour. Whisk constantly to cook for several minutes.

Slowly whisk in hot milk. Stir and cook until sauce is smooth and slightly thickened. Sift in the remaining 2

INGREDIENTS FOR 6 SERVINGS:
3 medium eggplants
pinch of salt

MUSHROOM-TOMATO SAUCE:
2 tablespoons olive oil
2 cups chopped onion
1¼ teaspoons salt
1½ pounds mushrooms, coarsely chopped
5 cloves garlic, minced
1 (14½ ounce) can tomatoes with liquid, broken into small pieces
1 (6 ounce) can tomato paste
1 teaspoon cinnamon
1 teaspoon oregano
1 teaspoon basil
black pepper, to taste
1 cup fresh parsley, minced
½ cup fine bread crumbs
½ cup grated Parmesan cheese

BÉCHAMEL SAUCE:
3 tablespoons butter or margarine
6 tablespoons flour
2½ cups hot milk
½ cup grated Parmesan cheese
¼ teaspoon nutmeg

Continued on next page

tablespoons of flour. Whisk well to prevent lumps. Cook for an additional 5 to 8 minutes. Stir in Parmesan and nutmeg.

TO ASSEMBLE: Preheat oven to 375°. Oil a 9x13x2-inch baking pan. Place two layers of eggplant slices on the bottom. Top with all of the tomato-mushroom sauce. Add remaining eggplant slices. Spread evenly with béchamel sauce. Dust with bread crumbs and Parmesan cheese. Bake, uncovered, for 35 to 40 minutes, until bubbly and lightly browned.

TOPPING:
fine bread crumbs
grated Parmesan cheese

Dinner Party Potatoes

ELEANOR MALONEY GAYNOR

INSTRUCTIONS: Wash, peel, and boil potatoes. Meanwhile, thoroughly blend cream cheese and sour cream together in a large bowl. Add hot potatoes. Beat until light, slowly incorporate milk. Add salt and pepper to taste.

Place in greased casserole dish. Brush with melted butter. Sprinkle with paprika. Bake at 350° for 25 minutes.

INGREDIENTS FOR 8 TO 10 SERVINGS:
10 medium potatoes
8 ounces cream cheese, softened
½ cup sour cream
¼ cup milk
salt and pepper, to taste
2 tablespoons butter, melted
paprika

Homestyle Roast Potatoes

RUTH McCREA

his is a very simple dish. But like so many simple things, it's easy to overlook. Yet, it's everyone's favorite!

INSTRUCTIONS: Peel potatoes. Cut into manageable pieces. If preparing in advance, keep potatoes covered with cold water.

Dry potatoes. Brush entire surface of each potato piece with butter. Use more butter if needed. Place in a Pyrex baking dish. Sprinkle with salt.

Bake at 375° for approximately 1 hour. Timing is flexible. Watch carefully. Turn potatoes occasionally so that the entire surface develops a nice color. Potatoes are done when they are "golden", more or less, all over.

Note: The potatoes are excellent to serve with cold meats, such as smoked turkey or baked ham.

INGREDIENTS FOR 6 SERVINGS:
6 medium potatoes
4 tablespoons butter, melted
salt, to taste

Apple and Onion Casserole

MRS. J.D. HEDGES, 1908 L.V.I.S. COOKBOOK

For people who like apples and onions a good dish is produced by slicing them in alternate layers into a baking dish, with a little butter, pepper, and salt added to each layer, and only sufficient water to prevent burning; cover them and bake till done; the flavor of the onions is much more delicate, and the odor while cooking is almost entirely overcome.

Sweet Potatoes with Cognac

BOB GIBSON

*I*nstructions: Boil potatoes. Mash enough for four cups. Whip in remaining ingredients. Place in ovenproof casserole dish. Dot with butter. Bake at 375° for 30 minutes.

INGREDIENTS FOR 4 SERVINGS:

4 sweet potatoes

4 tablespoons butter

⅓ cup heavy cream or half-and-half

⅓ to ½ cup cognac

¼ teaspoon cinnamon

¼ teaspoon mace

pinch of nutmeg

salt to taste

Onion Pie

JANET DAVIS

*I*nstructions: Sauté onions in butter until lightly browned. The onions must be browned to impart a rich flavor. Cover the bottom of a 9-inch quiche pan with the onions. Thoroughly combine remaining ingredients. Pour over onions. Bake at 350° for 35 to 45 minutes until mixture is set.

INGREDIENTS FOR 6 TO 8 SERVINGS:

3 or 4 large onions, thinly sliced

4 tablespoons butter or margarine

¾ cup milk

3 large eggs

¾ cup sharp Cheddar cheese, shredded

¾ cup Swiss or Monterey Jack cheese, shredded

¾ teaspoon nutmeg

½ teaspoon salt

½ teaspoon white pepper

Fort Pond Creamed Onions

KIRK WILLARD THOMPSON

INSTRUCTIONS: Peel onions and score each end with an X. Gently simmer onions in broth until just tender, about 35 minutes. Remove onions from broth. Layer them in a shallow baking dish.

Make a roux. Melt butter in medium saucepan. Whisk in flour until mixture is free of lumps. Cook 2 to 3 minutes. Set aside.

Measure 3 cups of broth in which onions were simmered. Heat to a brisk boil. Whisk in cheeses, stirring constantly until melted. Whisk in lumps of roux, until a very thick sauce is formed. At this point, sauce may be set aside until 20 minutes before serving.

Before serving, drain any excess liquid that may have accumulated in the bottom of the baking dish. Return sauce to a boil. Pour sauce over onions. Dust with Parmesan cheese and paprika. Broil until sauce is bubbly and lightly browned.

INGREDIENTS FOR 6 TO 8 SERVINGS:

2 ¼ pounds white boiling onions

2 (13¾ ounce) cans low salt chicken broth

1 ½ sticks butter

¾ cup flour

¾ cup Gruyère and Swiss cheese combined, cut into ¼-inch cubes

⅓ cup heavy cream

Parmesan cheese

paprika

Swiss Chard with Garlic

HARRY ACTON STRIEBEL

Swiss chard - green or Ruby red leaf - is the most rewarding vegetable I grow. It is planted as early as lettuce or spinach, but it does not wilt in hot weather. I continually pick the outer leaves from early summer until frost.

INSTRUCTIONS: Wash Swiss chard two times to remove sand. Let drain, but do not dry. Separate leaves from stems. Chop.

Cover the bottom of a large, heavy pot with ⅛-inch of oil. Heat oil and gently sauté garlic until translucent.

Add Swiss chard. Some people remove the stems and use only the leafy part. I cook the chopped stems first until tender, approximately 8 minutes. Add chopped moist leaves in batches. As chard cooks down, it shrinks tremendously. Season to taste with salt and pepper. Cover and cook on low until tender. Let sit 5 to 10 minutes before serving. This dish freezes well.

INGREDIENTS:
4 bunches of Swiss chard (approximately 100 leaves)
2 or 3 cloves of garlic, coarsely chopped
olive oil
salt and pepper to taste

Tomatoes Country Style

WENDY VAN DEUSEN, CHEF, THE 1770 HOUSE

INSTRUCTIONS: Using a mixer or a food processor, beat together the two cheeses, the garlic, parsley, and basil.

Cut tomatoes into 12 even slices, about ½-inch thick. Spread 6 slices of tomato with about 2 tablespoons of cheese mixture. Top with remaining slices to make 6 sandwiches.

Dip each in flour, then in the egg mixture, and finally in the bread crumbs. Fry on both sides over medium heat in mixture of butter and olive oil until golden. Garnish with fresh basil or parsley.

INGREDIENTS FOR 6 SERVINGS:

4 ounces cream cheese, softened

4 ounces chèvre (goat cheese)

1 clove garlic, minced

¼ cup minced parsley

1 teaspoon chopped fresh basil, or ½ teaspoon dried basil

4 beefsteak tomatoes

½ cup all-purpose flour

1 egg, beaten with 1 tablespoon of milk

⅔ cup dry bread crumbs

3 tablespoons butter

3 tablespoons olive oil

GARNISH:

fresh basil or parsley

Zucca con Fagioli

BEPPE DESIDERO. QUISISANA. NEW YORK CITY

As a child, squash or "zucca" was not one of my favorite dishes that my mother would prepare for us. One day, I suggested to her to make it with beans, which I loved. To my surprise, my mother came up with this dish which everyone loves. God bless my mother for her great sense of flavor and taste.

INSTRUCTIONS: Steam sliced squash for 2 minutes. Let dry on paper towels.

Set aside 5 ounces of the beans. Purée 25 ounces of the beans with the onions. Stir in rosemary and oil.

Place a thin layer of bean purée in a greased ovenproof dish. Add a layer of squash. Sprinkle with Parmesan. Repeat procedure. Top with remaining Parmesan and reserved beans. Bake at 375° for 12 minutes.

INGREDIENTS FOR 4 SERVINGS:

2 pounds butternut squash, peeled and sliced very thinly

1 (30 ounce) can cannellini beans

1 Bermuda onion, peeled and finely chopped

1 teaspoon fresh rosemary, finely chopped

1 tablespoon olive oil

2 ounces grated Parmesan cheese

VEGETABLE CROQUETTES

BARBARA MACKLOWE

When my husband became a vegetarian, I had to find new and interesting dishes that looked pretty and had universal appeal to serve for dinner. This one is a hit! Use as a vegetarian main course with a grain and a salad, or use as a side dish. Buy the freshest vegetables for better flavor.

INSTRUCTIONS: In a food processor, chop carrots, broccoli, and cauliflower. Chop finely for a smooth texture and more coarsely for a crunchier texture. Stir in peas. Set aside.

Beat egg whites until soft peaks form. Fold into matzoh meal or bread crumbs. Gently stir in vegetable mixture. Season to taste.

Form mixture into 4 patties. Cover with waxed paper and refrigerate at least one hour, preferably overnight. Heat non-stick skillet. Sauté in butter until browned on each side. Serve with mushroom or tomato sauce. Also great with salsa.

INGREDIENTS FOR 4 SERVINGS:

1 cup carrots
1 cup broccoli
1 cup cauliflower
1 cup frozen petite peas, defrosted
3 egg whites
½ cup matzoh meal or unflavored bread crumbs
salt and pepper, to taste
1 to 2 tablespoons butter

Summer Vegetable Casserole

HILLARY ROSNER

Instructions: Peel and cube eggplant. Slice cauliflower florets into thick, even slices. Steam eggplant and cauliflower for 15 minutes. Add corn during the last 3 minutes of steaming.

Gently combine steamed vegetables with scallions and red pepper. Season to taste. Place in buttered casserole dish.

Beat together eggs, milk, and mace. Pour over vegetables. Bake at 350° for 40 minutes. Top casserole with cheese during the last 5 minutes of baking time.

Ingredients for 4 servings:

1 medium firm eggplant
1 cup cauliflower florets
1 cup fresh corn kernels
5 scallions, chopped
½ cup red pepper, diced
salt and freshly ground pepper, to taste
4 eggs
2½ cups skim or whole milk
pinch of mace
3 tablespoons grated Parmesan cheese

Zucchini Fritters

JUDY LAUGHLIN

Instructions: Sprinkle grated zucchini lightly with salt. Let sit for half an hour. Squeeze dry with paper towels. Combine zucchini with onion and celery. In a separate bowl, beat together eggs and flour. Stir in vegetable mixture.

In a heavy skillet, heat a small amount of vegetable oil. To form fritters, drop the batter by tablespoons into the hot oil. Fry until golden on each side. Drain well on paper towels.

Ingredients:

4 large zucchini, coarsely grated
salt
1 large onion, finely chopped
2 stalks celery, finely chopped
2 eggs, lightly beaten
¼ cup flour
vegetable oil for frying

Zucchini Tomato Gratin

INSTRUCTIONS: In large skillet, sauté onion in 2 tablespoons of butter and oil until soft, about 5 minutes. Add garlic; sauté 2 minutes longer. Stir in tomatoes, basil, nutmeg, salt, and pepper. Cook 8 minutes over medium high heat, stirring occasionally, until moisture evaporates.

In separate skillet, sauté zucchini in 2 tablespoons of butter until tender. Drain well on paper towels.

Whisk eggs in large bowl. Whisk in ricotta, cream, and Parmesan.

TO ASSEMBLE: Arrange half of zucchini in a 10-inch deep dish. Spread tomato mixture evenly over this. Add remaining zucchini. Top with egg-cheese mixture. Bake at 450° for 10 minutes. Reduce heat and continue baking at 375° for about 25 minutes longer. Let stand 5 minutes before serving.

INGREDIENTS FOR 6 SERVINGS:

4 tablespoons butter
1 tablespoon olive oil
1½ cups chopped onion
1 clove of garlic, minced
1 (48 ounce) can whole tomatoes, drained and sliced
¼ teaspoon dried basil
pinch freshly grated nutmeg
salt and pepper to taste
¾ pound zucchini, thinly sliced
2 eggs
1 cup ricotta cheese, passed through a sieve
1 cup heavy cream
¾ cup grated Parmesan cheese

Baseball Bat Casserole

SUE BULLOCK

There's a period in every summer when gardeners discover that the wimpy zucchini that was only 2 inches long the previous evening has turned into a murder weapon overnight. This is a delicious solution to that problem.

INSTRUCTIONS: Halve the zucchini lengthwise. Remove the seeds and cut into ½-inch slices. Steam until soft; reserve the liquid.

Sauté onion in butter until soft and golden. Stir in flour, and cook briefly over low flame. Gradually add milk, reserved cooking liquid, and wine. Stir constantly until a creamy sauce is formed.

Place steamed zucchini in a buttered casserole. Cover with the sauce. Top with Parmesan cheese. Bake uncovered at 350° for 40 minutes. This dish may be made ahead and reheated.

INGREDIENTS:
1 oversize zucchini
½ large onion, chopped
2 tablespoons butter
2 tablespoons flour
½ cup milk
¼ cup reserved cooking liquid
¼ cup white wine
4 tablespoons Parmesan cheese

Child eating cookie at L.V.I.S. Summer Fair. Child unknown.

Desserts

Beverages

Amazing Apple Cake

PAT MERCER

*T*his is a very forgiving cake. It improves with age, so bake it a day or two early. For a special touch, garnish with fresh seasonal flowers.

INSTRUCTIONS: Process the flour, baking powder, baking soda, cinnamon, cloves, ginger, and salt with the metal blade of a food processor until well combined. Transfer to a large bowl. Process nuts until coarsely chopped; add to flour mixture.

Add apples to processor. Coarsely chop. Set aside. Process butter and sugar until creamy. Add eggs; process 30 seconds. Add vanilla and buttermilk; process 30 seconds. Add this wet mixture to the flour mixture, stirring gently until blended. Incorporate chopped apples and raisins.

Pour batter into a greased and floured 9-inch tube pan or 12-cup Bundt pan. Bake at 350° for 1 hour, or until inserted toothpick comes out clean. Let cool in pan for 1 hour. Drizzle with glaze.

FOR GLAZE: In food processor, mix all ingredients together until the orange peel is finely grated. Add more orange juice, if desired, to adjust consistency.

INGREDIENTS:
2¼ cups all-purpose flour
2½ teaspoons baking powder
½ teaspoon baking soda
1 teaspoon cinnamon
½ teaspoon ground cloves
½ teaspoon ground ginger
pinch of salt
½ cup nuts (pecans, walnuts, or almonds)
4 large apples, peeled and cored
¾ cup unsalted butter, softened
¾ cup brown sugar, packed
3 large eggs
1 teaspoon vanilla
½ cup buttermilk
½ cup golden raisins

GLAZE:
12 ounces cream cheese, softened
½ cup powdered sugar
1 teaspoon vanilla
1 to 2 tablespoons orange juice
strip of orange peel, 3x½-inch

Banana Cake

JANET DAVIS

Kids love to have this cake left on the counter with a knife on the plate. It disappears fast.

INSTRUCTIONS: Cream together butter and sugar. Beat in eggs. Stir in milk and sour cream or yogurt. Combine flour, baking powder, and salt. Gradually add flour mixture. Gently mix in vanilla, mashed bananas, and optional chocolate chips. Do not overmix.

Divide batter between 2 greased and lightly floured 5x7-inch loaf pans. Bake at 325° for 40 to 45 minutes. Test for doneness with a toothpick.

INGREDIENTS FOR 2 LOAVES:

½ cup butter, softened

1 ½ cups sugar

2 large eggs

½ cup milk

½ cup sour cream or yogurt

3 cups flour

2 teaspoons baking powder

¼ teaspoon salt

3 to 4 teaspoons vanilla (or less, to taste)

3 very ripe bananas, mashed

½ cup mini chocolate chips (optional)

Cranberry Upside Down Cake

BETTY WHITE

INSTRUCTIONS: Combine cranberries, ½ cup sugar, and walnuts. Place in the bottom of a greased 10-inch pie pan. Combine 1 cup sugar, butter, shortening, eggs, and flour. Pour over cranberry mixture. Bake at 325° for 45 to 60 minutes.

While still warm, loosen sides of cake from pan with a leveling spatula. Place an inverted plate on top of pan. Flip to remove cake. Lightly brush with apricot preserves thinned with warm water.

INGREDIENTS:

2 cups fresh cranberries

1 ½ cups sugar

½ cup chopped walnuts

½ cup butter, melted

2 tablespoons shortening, melted

2 eggs

1 cup all-purpose flour

2 to 3 tablespoons apricot preserves

1 tablespoon water

CRANBERRY SAUCE SWIRL CAKE

DORI K. LYONS

his cake has welcomed new neighbors and new babies. It's been a hit at many Christmas brunches. It's good for everything and nothing!

INSTRUCTIONS: With an electric mixer, cream margarine. Gradually beat in sugar. Add eggs, one at a time, on medium speed.

In a small bowl, combine flour, baking powder, baking soda, and salt. On low speed, alternately add flour mixture and sour cream. Add almond extract.

Place half the batter in a greased and floured 12-cup Bundt pan. Spoon on half of the cranberry sauce and swirl with a fork. Repeat process. Sprinkle with chopped nuts.

Bake at 350° for 55 to 60 minutes. Cool slightly; remove from pan and spread icing on warm cake.

FOR ICING: Blend all ingredients thoroughly.

INGREDIENTS:

¼ cup margarine

1 cup sugar

2 eggs

2 cups all-purpose flour

1 teaspoon baking powder

1 teaspoon baking soda

½ teaspoon salt

1 cup sour cream

1½ teaspoons almond extract

1 (16 ounce) can whole cranberry sauce

½ cup chopped walnuts

ICING:

¾ cup confectioners' sugar

1 tablespoon warm water

½ teaspoon almond extract

Golden Fruit Cake

BETTY CAFISO

INSTRUCTIONS: Combine flour and salt. Mix in raisins and pecans. Set aside. Cream butter and sugar until light. Beat in egg yolks. Add the baking soda dissolved in water, ¼ cup Grand Marnier, and the orange extract. Stir in flour mixture. The batter will be heavy and hard to mix.

In a separate bowl, beat egg whites until foamy. Add cream of tartar; beat until whites are stiff. Fold into batter. Spoon batter into a 10-inch tube pan that has been buttered, lined with waxed paper, and buttered again. Smooth top of batter. Bake at 300° for 2 hours.

Cool cake in pan for 20 minutes before removing. Drizzle with remaining Grand Marnier. When cake is cool, wrap tightly and store in refrigerator.

INGREDIENTS:

3 cups flour

1 teaspoon salt

1 pound golden raisins

4 cups chopped pecans

1 pound butter

2 cups sugar

6 eggs, separated

1 teaspoon baking soda dissolved in 1 tablespoon warm water

½ cup plus 1 tablespoon Grand Marnier, Cointreau, or Triple Sec

3 teaspoons of orange extract

pinch of cream of tartar

PUMPKIN CAKE

BONNIE PIZZORNO

his cake freezes well. It's nice to serve it with sweetened whipped cream.

INSTRUCTIONS: Combine flour, baking powder, baking soda, salt, and cinnamon. Set aside.

In a large bowl, mix together eggs and sugar. Stir in pumpkin, then oil. Gradually stir in flour mixture. Fold in raisins and nuts. Bake at 325° for 60 to 70 minutes in a greased 10-inch tube pan.

INGREDIENTS:

3 cups flour
2 teaspoons baking powder
2 teaspoons baking soda
1 teaspoon salt
2 teaspoons cinnamon
4 eggs, beaten
2 cups sugar
1½ cups canned pumpkin
1½ cups vegetable oil
1 cup dark and/or white raisins
½ cup chopped walnuts

Strawberry Shortcake

here are none better than the Wainscott strawberries, and you can pick your own on the day that you make this.

INSTRUCTIONS: Wash and hull strawberries. Crush and sugar to taste. Chill until ready to serve.

Combine flour, sugar, and baking powder. Cut in ¼ cup butter until coarse crumbs are formed. Using a fork, stir in milk to form dough. Roll dough into a 9-inch circle, ½-inch thick. Place in a 9-inch layer cake pan. Dot dough with remaining tablespoon of butter. Bake at 450° for 15 minutes.

Just before serving, cut shortcake into 6 or 8 wedges. Split and fill with prepared strawberries. Top with more strawberries, and whipped cream, if desired.

INGREDIENTS FOR 6 TO 8 SERVINGS:
1 quart strawberries
2 cups flour
1 tablespoon sugar
4 teaspoons baking powder
¼ cup plus 1 tablespoon butter or margarine
⅔ cup milk
1 cup heavy cream, whipped (optional)

Apple Pound Cake

WENDY KOWALSKI

his is a very easy cake to make and serve. Granny Smith or Macintosh apples are the best choice.

INSTRUCTIONS: Mix cinnamon with 3 tablespoons sugar. Pour over prepared apples. Set aside.

In a large mixing bowl, combine flour, sugar, and baking powder. Mix together remaining ingredients. Stir in and mix until smooth.

Grease and flour a 9-inch tube pan. Layer batter and apples, ending up with batter on top.

Bake at 375° for 1 to 1-¼ hours. Cool completely, right side up, in pan set on a wire rack.

INGREDIENTS:

4 to 5 large apples, peeled and sliced

2 tablespoons cinnamon

3 tablespoons sugar

3 cups flour

1½ cups sugar

1 tablespoon baking powder

4 eggs

2½ teaspoons vanilla

1 cup oil

¼ cup orange juice or unsweetened pineapple juice

Cream Cheese Pound Cake

This cake is easy to make. It stays moist and has wonderful flavor!

INSTRUCTIONS: Cream together butter and cream cheese. Gradually add sugar, beating thoroughly. Add almond extract.

On low speed, alternately add in flour and eggs, beating thoroughly after each addition.

Pour batter into a greased and floured 10-inch tube pan. Place on the middle rack of a COLD oven. Bake at 300° for about 1½ hours. Up to 15 minutes more baking time may be required. Cake is done when a toothpick inserted in center comes out clean. Cool in pan set on wire rack for 30 minutes before turning out.

INGREDIENTS:
1 ½ cups sweet butter, softened
8 ounces cream cheese, softened
3 cups sugar
1 ½ teaspoons almond extract
3 cups cake flour
6 large eggs

Great-Great-Grandmother Joan Huntting's Plain Cake

MARY HUNTTING RATTRAY, 1939 L.V.I.S. COOKBOOK

One cup sugar, 2 tablespoons butter, 2 eggs, ¾ cup milk, 2 cups sifted flour, 2 teaspoons baking powder, 1 teaspoon vanilla. I like a modern filling: 1 cup sifted confectioners' sugar, 1 egg or 2 egg yolks, ¼ cup milk, ½ teaspoon vanilla, 2 to 4 squares Baker's Unsweetened Chocolate, melted, 1 tablespoon softened butter. Combine ingredients in order given, beating with egg beater until blended. Place bowl in pan of ice water and continue beating until of right consistency to spread, about 3 minutes. If 4 squares of chocolate are used, and frosting is beaten 5 minutes, no ice is needed.

Italian Country Easter Cake

GAIL LEVIN

his is an old family recipe that was given to me by an elderly Italian woman. It is especially appropriate for Easter, but good all year long!

INSTRUCTIONS: Mix together all the ingredients in order as listed. Pour batter into a greased 9-inch tube pan. Bake at 350° for 1 hour until golden brown.

INGREDIENTS:

1 cup sugar
1 cup vegetable oil
3 eggs
1 cup non-fat yogurt
3 cups flour
1 tablespoon baking powder
pinch nutmeg
grated peel of 1 lemon

Sponge Cake

ROSALIE BAKER, 1862 EAST HAMPTON COOK BOOK

Obtain the exact weight of any number of eggs in pulverized sugar and half of the weight of the eggs in good flour. Break the eggs very carefully putting the yolks in the sugar and the whites on a platter or in a tin pan if you use an egg beater, but if a knife is used a platter is best. After the yolks and sugar are very thoroughly beaten together add the whites beaten to a stiff froth. Then add the grated peel of a fresh lemon and the juice. Then, immediately before baking add the flour and bake in a quick oven.

I have written the directions very explicitly because a great many persons do not make a good sponge cake and mine is always good made in the manner I have described.

Good and Fattening Cheesecake

*I*f you're fed up with low-calorie this and non-fat that, then this is the dessert for you! The only healthy ingredient in it is the lemon juice, and in a few years, the scientists will probably decide that even that will nail you as fast as anything else. Meanwhile, this is a delicious way to ignore all their gratuitous advice.

INSTRUCTIONS FOR CRUST: Combine crumbs and sugar. Stir in melted butter, mixing thoroughly. Pour mixture into a lightly greased springform pan. Press to cover bottom and sides of pan.

FOR FILLING: Blend together all ingredients except the cream cheese. Add cream cheese and blend again. Pour mixture into prepared pan. Bake at 325° for 30 to 40 minutes. Cool, then chill thoroughly, before releasing cake from pan.

VARIATION: Before baking, fold in any of the following: fresh raspberries, drained sweet Bing cherries, or orange peel slivers.

INGREDIENTS:

CRUST:

3 cups graham cracker crumbs

¾ cup sugar

⅓ pound butter, melted

FILLING:

2¼ cups sour cream

¾ cup sugar

3 eggs

3 teaspoons vanilla

1½ teaspoons lemon juice

16 ounces cream cheese, softened

Mocha Cheesecake

MRS. BARRY BISTRIAN

INSTRUCTIONS FOR CRUST: Grind wafer crumbs in food processor until fine. Pulse in butter and sugar; process for 10 seconds. Press into bottom of springform pan. Bake at 375° for 6 minutes.

FOR CAKE: Blend together sugar and eggs in bowl of food processor. Pulse in 1 pound of cream cheese until smooth. Transfer mixture to a large bowl.

Add remaining cream cheese to food processor bowl. Blend with chocolate, cocoa powder, coffee dissolved in rum, vanilla, and sour cream until smooth. Pulse machine as melted butter is added gradually. Whisk the two cheese mixtures together.

Bake at 350° for 1 hour. Although cake may appear runny, it will become firm when chilled. Chill for at least 5 hours.

INGREDIENTS:

CRUST:

1½ cups chocolate wafer crumbs
5 tablespoons softened butter
¼ cup sugar

CAKE:

1 cup sugar
3 eggs
1½ pounds cream cheese, cut in cubes
6 ounces semi-sweet chocolate bits, melted
2 tablespoons cocoa powder
1 tablespoon instant coffee powder
2 tablespoons rum
1 teaspoon vanilla
3 cups sour cream
¼ cup melted butter

DIRT CAKE

RUTH MUELLER

This cake looks adorable.

INSTRUCTIONS: Process the Oreo cookies with the metal blade of a food processor until fine crumbs are formed. Set aside. Cream together margarine, cream cheese, and sugar. In a separate bowl, beat together pudding and milk until thickened; fold in Cool Whip. Combine cream cheese and pudding mixtures. Refrigerate 30 minutes. Line the bottom of the flower pot with foil. Alternately layer the cream cheese-pudding mixture with the crushed Oreos, ending with the Oreos on the top. Chill until firm. To decorate, insert a small vase filled with flowers in the center of the "cake."

INGREDIENTS:

1 (1¼ pound) package Oreo cookies

¼ cup margarine, softened

8 ounces cream cheese, softened

1 cup confectioners' sugar

2 (3.4 ounce) packages French vanilla instant pudding mix

3½ cups milk

12 ounces Cool Whip

SUPPLIES:

1 (8-inch) plastic flower pot

foil

1 small plastic shovel

flowers in a small vase

Double Diabolo

MARTHA STEWART

This is one of the richest, most irresistible chocolate confections you will ever make. I like to bake it in a 12-inch cake pan. Leftovers stay fresh for weeks in the refrigerator. Bake the cake at least 1 day before serving. It may be made days ahead, wrapped and refrigerated until ready to use, and served the day of the party.

INSTRUCTIONS: Soak raisins overnight in the whiskey. Preheat oven to 350°. Butter a 12-inch cake pan, line bottom with waxed paper, and butter and flour the paper.

In the top of a double boiler, melt the chocolate with the water. Stir in the butter bit by bit until mixture is smooth. Beat the egg yolks with the sugar until thick and creamy. Stir into the chocolate. Add the flour and almonds, then the raisins and whiskey. Mix together gently.

Beat the egg whites with salt until stiff but not dry. Fold by thirds into the chocolate mixture, taking care to deflate the mixture as little as possible. Pour the batter into the prepared pan, smooth the top, and bake for approximately 25 minutes. The cake should be moist in the center, but just beginning to shrink from the sides of the pan. Let the cake rest in the pan for 10 minutes before turning out onto a rack to cool.

To make the icing, melt the chocolate in the cream, whisking until smooth. If too thin, cool slightly over ice. Pour over cake, smoothing with a spatula.

INGREDIENTS:
½ cup raisins
½ cup Scotch whiskey
14 ounces semi-sweet chocolate
¼ cup water
½ pound (2 sticks) unsalted butter
6 eggs, separated
1⅓ cups sugar
9 tablespoons cake flour
1⅓ cups finely ground blanched almonds
pinch salt

ICING:
8 ounces semi-sweet chocolate
1 cup heavy cream

Grandma Kate's Chocolate Cake

KAREN COHEN

This was my Grandma Kate's favorite chocolate cake. When she was a young woman, she got this recipe from a lady named J.I. Goldstone, whose family was one of the Warner Brothers Pictures' Founders. She was famous for her baking. My grandma was born in Pennsylvania about 100 years ago.

INSTRUCTIONS FOR CAKE: Place chocolate, milk, and butter in top of a double boiler. Cook over low heat until thick. Transfer mixture to a large bowl. Let cool. Add sugar. Mix well.

In a separate bowl, sift together flour and baking powder. Alternately add dry ingredients and egg yolks to chocolate mixture. Add vanilla and beat well.

Beat egg whites until stiff peaks form. Fold into batter. Pour into 2 buttered 8-inch round pans. Bake at 300° for 45 minutes, then at 350° for 15 minutes. Do not overbake. Cool on wire racks.

FOR ICING: Melt chocolate in top of double boiler over low heat. Add sugar, salt, and butter. Let cool. Beat in eggs, milk, and vanilla.

Transfer icing to a stainless steel bowl. Place in a larger bowl filled with ice water. Using an electric mixer, beat on high speed until icing is stiff and light brown in color. After icing cake, refrigerate it for 1 hour to set. Stand at room temperature before serving.

INGREDIENTS:

CAKE:

8 squares of unsweetened chocolate

2 cups milk

2 tablespoons butter

4 cups sugar

2 cups flour

2 teaspoons baking powder

8 eggs, separated

2 tablespoons vanilla

ICING:

4 squares unsweetened chocolate

2 cups confectioners' sugar

pinch of salt

6 tablespoons butter, softened

2 eggs

4 tablespoons milk

1 teaspoon vanilla

Great Chocolate Cake

MRS. MACRAE SYKES

INSTRUCTIONS FOR CAKE: Cream together butter and sugar. Stir in eggs. Place can of syrup under hot water before opening. Alternately add chocolate syrup and flour. Add vanilla and mix well.

Pour batter into a 9x13x2-inch Pyrex dish that has been buttered, lined with waxed paper, and buttered again. Bake at 350° for 30 to 35 minutes. Cake is done when firm to the touch.

FOR ICING: Melt butter, water, and chocolate in top of a double boiler. Gradually add sugar. Stir in vanilla, mixing thoroughly. Frost cake. This cake freezes well.

INGREDIENTS:
½ cup butter
1 cup sugar
4 eggs, beaten
1 (16 ounce) can chocolate syrup
1 cup flour
1 tablespoon vanilla

ICING:
3 tablespoons butter
5 tablespoons water
3 squares unsweetened chocolate
2 cups confectioners' sugar, sifted
1 teaspoon vanilla

Mouthwatering Chocolate Cake

PAM CATALETTO

INSTRUCTIONS FOR CAKE: Melt chocolate and butter in top of double boiler over low heat. Add boiling water. Mix well. Transfer to large bowl. Let cool.

Add remaining ingredients in order as listed, stirring well after each addition.

Pour batter into greased and floured 9x9-inch pan. Bake at 350° for 20 to 30 minutes. A toothpick inserted will come out clean when cake is done.

FOR ICING: Melt chocolate and butter in top of double boiler over low heat. Gradually stir in sugar. Add milk, one tablespoon at a time, until desired consistency is achieved.

INGREDIENTS:

2 squares unsweetened chocolate

½ cup butter or margarine

1 cup boiling water

1 cup sugar

1 egg

1⅓ cups flour

1 teaspoon baking soda, dissolved in a small amount of the boiling water

1 teaspoon baking powder

1 teaspoon vanilla

ICING:

1 square unsweetened chocolate

4 tablespoons butter

3½ cups confectioners' sugar, sifted

3 to 4 tablespoons milk

Ice Box Cake Supreme

JANET SCHWITTER

This recipe is from my mother-in-law who was originally from Switzerland.

INSTRUCTIONS: Line the bottom and sides of a 10-inch springform pan with ladyfingers. In a large bowl, cream together butter and sugar. Beat in egg yolks. Stir in almonds, cookies, rum, and vanilla. Beat egg whites with salt until stiff. Fold egg whites and 1 pint of whipped cream into mixture.

Pour half of the mixture over ladyfingers in pan. Add another layer of ladyfingers. Top with remaining mixture. Cover and refrigerate overnight.

Before serving, decorate with 1 cup of whipped cream. Garnish with cherries.

INGREDIENTS:
2 packages ladyfingers
2 cup sweet butter, softened
½ cup granulated sugar
8 eggs, separated
dash of salt
1 cup finely chopped almonds
12 ounces almond cookies, crumbled
1 ounce rum
1 teaspoon vanilla
1 pint heavy cream, whipped

GARNISH:
1 cup heavy cream, whipped
candied dried cherries

Orange Ice Box Cake

RUTH MC CREA

 favorite dessert of ours in the '30s. It's originally from the Boston Cookbook, but we have made changes.

INSTRUCTIONS: Mix together the first 8 ingredients in order as listed. Cook in the top of a double boiler, stirring constantly, for 15 minutes. Cool. Fold in whipped cream.

Line a 9x5-inch loaf pan with waxed paper. Cover bottom with ladyfingers which have been split in half. Layer with half the filling. Repeat process, and add a final layer of split ladyfingers on the top.

Cover and chill for 24 hours. After this time, it can be frozen for several months if wrapped in foil in its pan. Thaw before serving. Invert on a plate, and remove waxed paper.

INGREDIENTS FOR 6 TO 8 SERVINGS:
1 cup sugar
5 tablespoons flour
grated rind of 2 oranges
grated rind of 1 lemon
½ cup orange juice
1 tablespoon lemon juice
2 eggs, slightly beaten
2 teaspoons butter
½ cup heavy cream, beaten stiff
1 ½ packages ladyfingers

Never Fail Seven-minute Frosting

HESTER F. CHENEY

I discovered this recipe in an old cookbook, and used it on a devil's food layer cake. It was so popular with family and friends, that I have made dozens of the layer cakes so frosted.

INSTRUCTIONS: Place egg whites, cold water, sugar, and cream of tartar in top of double boiler. Beat with an electric hand mixer until thoroughly blended. Put double boiler top over rapidly boiling water. Beat mixture constantly for about 7 minutes. Remove from heat, add vanilla, and beat until right consistency to spread is achieved.

INGREDIENTS:
2 unbeaten egg whites
5 tablespoons cold water
1 ½ cups sugar
¼ teaspoon cream of tartar
1 teaspoon vanilla

Silky Chocolate Frosting

CHARLOTTE GORDON EDISON

INSTRUCTIONS: Boil 1 cup of water in a medium saucepan. Add sugar, and boil until dissolved. Add chocolate, stirring continuously until chocolate is melted.

In a cup, dissolve cornstarch in cold water. To thicken chocolate mixture and to avoid lumping, slowly begin to stir a small amount of the hot chocolate mixture into the dissolved cornstarch. Then, add some of the blended cornstarch-chocolate mixture back into the simmering chocolate mixture. Repeat this process, back and forth, several times while stirring until all of the dissolved cornstarch is incorporated into the hot chocolate mixture. Continue to stir for 10 to 15 minutes over medium flame until thickened.

Reduce heat. Add butter and vanilla. Blend thoroughly. When frosting cools slightly, it is perfect for topping your favorite layer cake or 8 to 10 cupcakes.

INGREDIENTS:

1 cup water
1 cup granulated sugar
2 squares unsweetened chocolate
3 tablespoons cornstarch
1½ teaspoons cold water
1 tablespoon butter
1 teaspoon vanilla

Apricot Squares

ANDREA COOPER

n easy to make dessert given to me by Sybil Passarella. Prune preserves work equally well.

INSTRUCTIONS: Cream together butter and sugar. Beat in egg yolks. Combine flour and baking powder; stir into creamed mixture. Press mixture into a 9x13-inch greased pan.

Using a leveling spatula, spread preserves over dough. Sprinkle nuts evenly on top.

Bake at 325° for 50 minutes. Cool and cut into squares.

INGREDIENTS FOR 2 TO 3 DOZEN:
1 cup butter
1 cup sugar
2 egg yolks
2 cups flour
1 teaspoon baking powder
1 (15 to 18 ounce) jar apricot preserves
½ cup finely chopped walnuts

Thumbprint Christmas Cookies

PATRICIA AND KEN FERRIN

INSTRUCTIONS: Mix shortening, sugar, egg yolk, and vanilla thoroughly. Blend together flour and salt. Add to creamed mixture.

Using 1 teaspoon of dough per cookie, form balls. Dip each ball into lightly beaten egg white. Roll in nuts.

Place balls about one inch apart on ungreased baking sheet. Press thumb gently in center of each.

Bake at 350° for 10 to 12 minutes, or until set. When cool, fill thumbprint impressions with jelly.

INGREDIENTS FOR 2 DOZEN:
½ cup shortening
¼ cup brown sugar, packed
1 egg, separated
½ teaspoon vanilla
1 cup all-purpose flour
¼ teaspoon salt
¾ cup nuts, finely chopped
jelly, red or mint

Chewy Ginger Cookies

RUTH MC CREA LIZARS

INSTRUCTIONS: Cream together sugar, shortening, butter, eggs, and molasses until fluffy.
Sift together dry ingredients. Add to creamed mixture. Roll small, walnut-sized balls of dough in ¼ cup sugar. Bake at 350° for 10 minutes or until surface is cracked and brown.

INGREDIENTS FOR 3 1/2 TO 4 DOZEN:
2 cups sugar
¾ cup shortening
¾ cup butter
2 eggs
½ cup molasses
4½ to 5 cups unbleached flour
3½ teaspoons baking soda
½ teaspoon salt
2 teaspoons cinnamon
1½ teaspoons ginger
1½ teaspoons ground cloves
½ teaspoon freshly grated nutmeg

TOPPING:
¼ cup sugar

Bird's Nest Cookies

MRS. EDWARD H. JEWETT, JR.

INSTRUCTIONS: Melt morsels in top of double boiler. Remove from heat and add nuts and noodles. Stir to mix well. Drop by teaspoonfuls onto waxed paper. Let cool.

INGREDIENTS:
1 (12 ounce) package butterscotch morsels
1 (11.5 ounce) can salted peanuts
1 (5 ounce) can Chinese noodles

Chocolate Chip Cookie Sticks

DEBORAH WALTER

INSTRUCTIONS: Mix sugars, oil, vanilla, and egg in large bowl until smooth. Combine flour, baking soda, and salt. Gradually stir in dry ingredients.

Divide dough in half. Shape each half into two 15x3-inch rectangular strips. Place strips 3 inches apart on lightly greased cookie sheets. Sprinkle strips with chocolate chips and walnuts, pressing lightly.

Bake at 375° for about 7 to 9 minutes, until golden brown. Cool 2 minutes. Cut each strip crosswise into 1-inch segments; remove from cookie sheet. Store loosely covered.

INGREDIENTS FOR 5 DOZEN:
½ cup granulated sugar
½ cup brown sugar, packed
½ cup vegetable oil
1 teaspoon vanilla
1 egg
1 ½ cups all-purpose flour
½ teaspoon baking soda
½ teaspoon salt
1 cup semi-sweet mini chocolate chips
½ cup chopped walnuts

Crispy Cookies

ELEANOR MALONEY GAYNOR

INSTRUCTIONS: Cream butter and sugar thoroughly. Add flour, a little at a time. Stir in potato chips and vanilla. Mix thoroughly.

Drop by rounded teaspoonfuls onto ungreased cookie sheet. Sprinkle with chopped walnuts.

Bake at 350° for 12 to 14 minutes, until bottom of cookies are light brown. Cool 10 minutes before removing from cookie sheet. Dust liberally with confectioners' sugar.

INGREDIENTS FOR 3 DOZEN:
1 cup lightly salted butter
½ cup granulated sugar
1 ½ cups all-purpose flour
½ cup crushed potato chips
1 tablespoon vanilla extract
¼ cup finely chopped walnuts
confectioners' sugar

Cranberry Bog Bars

PAM CATALETTO

INSTRUCTIONS: Cream together margarine and sugar. Stir in flour and oats. Spread evenly in ungreased 9x13-inch pan. Batter will be thick. Spread cranberry sauce on top of mixture.

Mix together all topping ingredients and sprinkle on top. Bake at 350° for about 30 to 40 minutes, until brown.

INGREDIENTS:
1 cup margarine
1 cup brown sugar
1 cup flour
2½ cups old-fashioned oats
1 (16 ounce) can whole berry cranberry sauce

TOPPING:
¼ cup margarine
½ cup brown sugar
1 cup old-fashioned oats
½ cup chopped pecans

French Butter Cookies

ELIZABETH J. MAGILL

A lovely delicate cookie!

INSTRUCTIONS: Cream together butter and sugar. Beat in egg yolk. Gradually add flour.

Divide dough in half and roll into cylinder shapes, 1½x6-inches long. Wrap and place in freezer until firm. Slice dough into ¼-inch rounds. Brush tops with egg white and sprinkle with sliced almonds.

Place cookies on two greased baking sheets. Bake at 375° for about 12 minutes.

INGREDIENTS FOR 4 DOZEN:
½ cup sweet butter
¼ cup plus 2 tablespoons super fine sugar
1 egg yolk
1 cup flour
1 egg white, lightly beaten
¼ cup sliced almonds

Dog Biscuits

CRISTA G. MARTIN

s many families in East Hampton have dogs, I offer this recipe which I developed for my own dogs, Barkley, a Yorkshire terrier, and Capi, a miniature white poodle, whose real name is Capital, because I found her near our nation's capital. These biscuits freeze very well.

INSTRUCTIONS: Blend flours, cornmeal, dry milk, and salt together. Set aside. Heat stock to warm. Dissolve yeast in ¼ cup warm water. Add yeast, stock, and bacon fat to dry ingredients.

Roll dough ¼-inch thick and cut with dog biscuit or other cutter.

Bake at 300° for 45 minutes. Turn off oven and leave overnight.

INGREDIENTS:
3½ cups flour
2 cups whole wheat flour
2 cups cracked rye flour
1 cup cornmeal
½ cup nonfat dry milk
4 teaspoons salt
1 pint chicken or beef stock
1 package dry yeast
¼ cup warm water
reserved fat from 1 pound bacon

Easy Snack Cookies

ANN KIRK WILLARD

INSTRUCTIONS: Grease a 10½x 15½-inch jelly roll pan. Line bottom with graham crackers. Melt butter and sugar together and pour over crackers. Top with walnuts. Bake at 350° for 10 minutes. Cut into squares.

INGREDIENTS:
1 box graham crackers
¾ cup butter
1 cup brown sugar
1 cup chopped walnuts

Grandpa's Macaroons

BILL RUDER

Wonderful for Passover traditional desserts, and great year-round. Your grandchildren will adore them!

INSTRUCTIONS: Mix all ingredients together. Shape dough into 1½-inch balls. Line cookie sheet with parchment paper, or butter cookie sheet amply. Bake at 350° for about 15 minutes, or until browned.

INGREDIENTS FOR 2 1/2 DOZEN:
2 (7 ounce) bags coconut flakes
2 egg whites, beaten stiff
1 (14 ounce) can sweetened condensed milk
1 teaspoon vanilla extract
1 tablespoon soft butter

Hung Yen Bing Cookies

MRS. GREYDON A. RHODES, 1948 L.V.I.S. COOKBOOK

One cup shortening, ⅓ cup sugar, ¼ teaspoon salt, ⅔ cup ground almonds (blanched) or ⅔ cup fine soy grits, 1 tablespoon milk; almond flavoring, 1⅔ cups sifted flour, 24 (1½ ounces) blanched almonds. Cream shortening and sugar until light and fluffy. Add salt, stir in ground almonds or soy grits. Sift in flour and knead lightly into smooth ball. Chill for 10 minutes. Form into 1¼-inch balls and place on ungreased baking sheet. Press down with palm of hand to make a cake ½ inch thick. Place a blanched almond in center of each cookie. Bake in moderate oven 350° for 12 minutes.

Old East Hampton Cookies

MRS. NORMAN W. BARNS, 1939 L.V.I.S. COOKBOOK

Two cups brown sugar, 1 cup butter, 1 cup very thick sour cream. Stir 1 teaspoon soda in the cream and beat well. Large pinch of salt, 2 teaspoons nutmeg, 2 eggs. Roll soft and bake in hot oven. Raisins may be put on top if desired.

This recipe is one used in the early days in the village and has been handed down for several generations in Norman Barns' family. It came from his grandfather Madison Huntting's family.

Back to Basics Brownies

MRS. DONALD KIRK

INSTRUCTIONS: Cream together butter and sugar in a bowl. Add eggs and mix well. Add flour and baking powder, then the vanilla and melted chocolate.

Pour mixture into a greased 8x8-inch pan. If desired, sprinkle with chocolate chips. Bake at 350° for 25 minutes. The brownies may look a bit runny, but this makes fudgy insides. Cook in pan for ½ hour. Cut into squares and remove with spatula. Store in a cookie tin when completely cooled.

INGREDIENTS:

½ cup butter, softened

1 cup sugar

2 eggs

¾ cup flour

1 teaspoon baking powder

½ teaspoon vanilla

2 (1 ounce) squares semi-sweet chocolate, melted

6 ounces chocolate chips (optional)

One Pot Brownies

ANNETTE LUBIN

This recipe has become a favorite with family and friends, because it is "no fail."

INSTRUCTIONS: Melt butter and cocoa in top of double boiler. Remove from heat. Add sugar, salt, and eggs, one at a time, stirring batter after each addition.

Sift together flour and baking powder and add to mixture, stirring thoroughly. Add vanilla and walnuts. Spread evenly in buttered 8-inch square pan.

Bake at 375° for about 25 to 30 minutes, or until toothpick inserted in center comes out clean.

INGREDIENTS:

½ cup butter or margarine
½ cup cocoa
1 cup sugar
pinch of salt
2 eggs
½ cup flour
½ teaspoon baking powder
1 teaspoon vanilla
¾ cup chopped walnuts

Pecan Dainties

THERESE FURST

INSTRUCTIONS: Beat egg white until stiff. Add brown sugar gradually, beating constantly.

Fold in nuts and extract. Drop by teaspoonfuls onto a greased cookie sheet.

Bake at 250° for 30 minutes. Remove from cookie sheet immediately and cool.

INGREDIENTS FOR 3 DOZEN:

1 egg white
1 cup light brown sugar
1½ cups pecan halves
¼ teaspoon almond extract

Shirley Cooper's Highland Shortbread

ETHEL ROSNER

My mother was renowned for her shortbread, a recipe she learned at her home in Inverness. Those who once received a gift of these wonderful Scottish cookies spoke of them for years. They are simple to make and bring many compliments.

INSTRUCTIONS: Cream together butter and sugar with wooden spoon until smooth. Add flour slowly and blend evenly.

When almost entirely blended, turn out on lightly floured surface. Knead gently until dough is smooth and soft.

Shape dough into a ½-inch thick square. Cut dough into finger shapes and pierce with fork.

Bake at 325° for 8 to 10 minutes, until golden in color. Place on rack to cool and dry, until firm to touch.

INGREDIENTS:

2 cups sweet butter, room temperature
1 cup extra-fine granulated sugar
4 cups all-purpose flour

Soft Molasses Cookies

FLORENCE FITHIAN STONE WESSBERG

This recipe was handed down from my maternal grandmother, Sybil Rae (Fithian) Anderson. She always had plenty of these cookies for her 12 children. Have a tall glass of cold milk waiting when the first batch is done!

INSTRUCTIONS: Cream together shortening and sugar. Add eggs.

In a separate bowl, combine boiling water, molasses, and dissolved baking soda. Set aside.

In a third bowl, sift together dry ingredients. Add dry ingredients alternately with liquids to base mixture. Mix well.

Drop by rounded teaspoonfuls onto ungreased cookie sheets. Bake at 375° for 12 to 15 minutes.

INGREDIENTS:
1 cup shortening
1 cup sugar
2 eggs, beaten
1 cup boiling water
1 cup unsulfured dark molasses
2 teaspoons baking soda, dissolved in a little water
4 cups flour
2 teaspoons baking powder
1 teaspoon ginger
1 teaspoon cinnamon
1 teaspoon ground cloves

Swedish Spritzbaaken Cookies

MRS. DWIGHT EISENHOWER, THE WHITE HOUSE, WASHINGTON, D.C., 1955 L.V.I.S. COOKBOOK

One pound butter, 1 cup sugar, 2 whole eggs, 2 extra yolks, 4½ cups sifted flour, vanilla. Cream sugar and butter. Add beaten eggs, then flour gradually, then vanilla to taste. Use cookie press and form your own design. Bake in a moderate oven (350° or 375°) twenty minutes or until done. Should be light in color. These bake very quickly and need to be watched constantly.

Makes 100 cookies.

Viennese Fruit Squares

DEBBIE CLEMENCE

*I*NSTRUCTIONS: Using a pastry blender, cut butter into flour and sugar until mixture resembles small peas. Add extract. Reserve ⅓ of mixture for topping.

Knead remaining dough 5 times. Press well into ungreased 10½x15½-inch jelly roll pan. In a small bowl, beat jam well with a fork. With a leveling spatula, spread jam over dough, leaving ¼-inch border clean from pan edge.

Work reserved dough with fingers until crumbs are formed. Be careful not to overwork dough. Sprinkle onto jam.

Bake at 350° for 20 minutes. Cool 5 minutes. Cut into small squares, 5 rows by 8 rows to yield 40 squares. These freeze well.

INGREDIENTS FOR 40 SQUARES:
3 cups flour
1 cup sugar
1 cup sweet butter
1 teaspoon almond extract
1 (12 ounce) jar apricot or raspberry jam or preserves

Banana Pie

MRS. GILBERT P. SMITH, 1955 L.V.I.S. COOKBOOK

*B*ake your favorite crust. Mash two very ripe bananas, add 1 cup sugar, ⅓ teaspoon salt, 2 unbeaten egg whites, ⅓ teaspoon almond extract. Beat until stiff like meringue. Pour into shell and bake at 300° for 20 minutes. Before serving spread with whipped cream and chopped nuts.

 Beach Plum Pie

MRS. EVERETT J. EDWARDS, 1939 L.V.I.S. COOKBOOK

Prepare standard pie crust, for top and bottom. Slip pits from enough fresh beach plums to fill pie-plate; to 1 cup pitted plums, packed solid, add ¾ cup sugar mixed with 1 teaspoon flour. Mix well. Bake in rather slow oven 350° to 400°. Canned beach plums may be used. Drain off juice, adding 2 teaspoons flour to 3 cups drained beach plums; then put back juice needed.

 Blueberry Cream Cheese Tart

ANN KIRK WILLARD

INSTRUCTIONS: Combine cream cheese, sugar, and vanilla. Set aside. Whip heavy cream until stiff and fold into cream cheese mixture thoroughly. Spread into tart shell. In small saucepan, melt jelly with rum. Cool. Add dry blueberries and mix carefully. Spoon over pie filling. This recipe may be made with fresh raspberries or strawberries as well. Stand strawberries upright on pie filling and spoon jelly mixture over them.

INGREDIENTS FOR 6 TO 8 SERVINGS:
3 ounces cream cheese, room temperature
½ cup sugar
1 teaspoon vanilla
1 cup heavy cream
½ cup currant jelly
1 tablespoon rum
1 pint fresh blueberries
1 (9-inch) pre-baked tart shell

Lemon Fluff Pie

ANN CREAMER

his tart, lemony-flavored pie is delicious in spring and summer. The crust can also be made with graham crackers.

INSTRUCTIONS FOR CRUST: Combine butter and vanilla wafers. Line a 10-inch springform pan with mixture.

FOR FILLING: Grate rinds from lemons. Place in top of double boiler along with juice squeezed from lemons. Add 1 cup sugar. Stir until dissolved. Slowly add egg yolks. Cook and stir until mixture coats a spoon.

Soak gelatin in cold water for 5 minutes. Add to egg mixture and stir until dissolved. Remove from heat and cool.

Beat egg whites until stiff. Gradually beat in ¾ cup sugar. Fold into base mixture and pour into pan.

Refrigerate for several hours. To serve, decorate with whipped cream, if desired.

INGREDIENTS:

CRUST:
¾ pound vanilla wafers, finely crushed
1 cup butter or margarine

FILLING:
4 lemons
1 cup sugar
7 egg yolks, beaten
1 tablespoon gelatin
½ cup cold water
7 egg whites
¾ cup sugar

TOPPING (OPTIONAL):
freshly whipped cream

Lemon Sponge Pie

WINGS WHITE

This pie has been the centerpiece of birthday celebrations at our house for forty years. It is my grandmother's recipe.

INSTRUCTIONS: In a large bowl, mix together sugar and flour. Cream in butter. Grate in the rind of lemon; squeeze in its juice. Stir in egg yolks. Blend in milk.

In separate bowl, beat egg whites to soft peaks. Fold into mixture. Spread into pie shell.

Bake at 425° for 10 minutes, then reduce temperature to 375° and cook 30 to 40 minutes longer. Pie is done when knife inserted halfway between side and middle comes out clean.

INGREDIENTS:

1 cup sugar
1 tablespoon flour
1 ½ teaspoons butter
1 lemon
3 eggs, separated
1 cup milk
1 unbaked pie shell

Old-Fashioned Peach Pie

BARBARA DUBITSKY

Instructions for pastry shell: Mix flour and salt in large bowl. Cut in shortening with pastry blender or two knives. Mix lightly until dough resembles coarse meal or tiny peas. Sprinkle water over dough, one tablespoon at a time, mixing lightly and using only enough water so that pastry forms a ball.

Roll dough on lightly floured surface 2 inches larger than pie pan. Fit loosely, but firmly, into pan. Crimp or flute edges.

FOR FILLING: Arrange peach halves, cut side up, close together over pastry. Mix sugar and flour together, then sprinkle over peaches. Mix egg yolk, cream, and almond extract and drizzle over fruit.

Bake at 450° for about 25 minutes on lower rack in oven. Serve plain or with ice cream, if desired.

INGREDIENTS:

PASTRY SHELL:
1 ½ cups flour
¼ teaspoon salt
½ cup shortening or sweet butter
4 to 5 tablespoons cold water

FILLING:
6 to 8 peaches, peeled and halved
½ cup sugar
2 tablespoons flour
1 egg yolk
3 tablespoons heavy cream
1 teaspoon almond extract

℘lum ℑart

MONIQUE EASTMAN

liced apples may be substituted for the plums, but brush apples with melted apricot jam before serving.

INSTRUCTIONS FOR TART SHELL:
In a large bowl, combine flour, sugar, and salt. Cut in butter until mixture resembles coarse meal. Add water. Mix until dough forms a ball. Wrap in foil. Chill or refrigerate over night.

Roll dough as thin as possible on a lightly floured surface. Line a 12-inch tart pan (with detachable bottom) with dough.

FOR FILLING: Slice plums in half. Arrange, cut side down, symmetrically and close together over dough. Sprinkle lightly with lemon juice, sugar, and cinnamon. Bake at 400° for 45 minutes to 1 hour, until tart shell is crisp and plums are slightly browned. Cool before slicing.

INGREDIENTS:

TART SHELL:
2 cups all-purpose flour
1 teaspoon sugar
¼ teaspoon salt
¾ cup sweet butter, cut into ¼-inch cubes
⅓ cup ice water

FILLING:
35 to 40 Italian plums
lemon juice
sugar
cinnamon

RHUBARB PIE

MRS. BERNICE LEAK

 e all have a favorite recipe from our childhood which echoes in our memory. This is mine - my mother's rhubarb pie. It combines both a sweet and tart taste with an unexpected accent of orange peel.

INSTRUCTIONS FOR PASTRY: Combine flour and sugar in a bowl. Cut in shortening until mixture resembles coarse meal. Gradually mix in ice water, stirring with a fork until a ball is formed. For best results, chill dough before rolling. Roll dough out for bottom crust and lattice topping for a 9-inch pie pan.

FOR FILLING: Line bottom crust with rhubarb. Blend together sugar, flour, orange peel, and butter. Beat in eggs until smooth. Pour over rhubarb. Top with lattice crust.

Bake at 450° for 10 minutes. Reduce heat. Cook at 350° for 30 minutes until rhubarb is tender.

INGREDIENTS:

PASTRY:
2 cups all-purpose flour
1 tablespoon sugar
1 cup shortening
⅔ cup ice water

FILLING:
3 cups fresh rhubarb, cut into ½-inch pieces
1 cup sugar
2 tablespoons all-purpose flour
1 tablespoon grated orange peel
1 tablespoon butter
2 eggs, lightly beaten

Green Tomato Mincemeat Pie Filling

ANN KIRK WILLARD

INSTRUCTIONS: Put all ingredients into a large kettle. Cook over low heat until thick. Stir frequently.
Seal in hot sterilized jars. This recipe makes a delicious pie filling.

INGREDIENTS FOR 4 QUARTS:

4 quarts chopped green tomatoes
1 quart tart unpeeled apples, chopped
½ pound beef suet, chopped
2 pounds dark brown sugar
2 (15 ounce) boxes raisins
½ pound dried currants
¾ cup vinegar
1 tablespoon salt
2 teaspoons allspice
2 teaspoons ground cloves
1 teaspoon nutmeg
4 ounces candied orange peel
4 ounces candied lemon peel
4 ounces citron

Sweet Potato Pie

SANDRA DOOLEY-GILLIAM

This old Southern recipe has been handed down from generation to generation as a holiday dessert after the Fall harvest. Always look for farm-fresh potatoes; the redder the better!

INSTRUCTIONS FOR PIE CRUST: In small bowl, combine flour and salt. Cut in shortening with pastry blender until mixture resembles small peas. Sprinkle water over dough and stir with fork to form a ball.

Roll dough on lightly floured surface to ⅛-inch thickness. Let rest a few minutes before shaping. Fold in half and place in a 9-inch pie plate.

FOR FILLING: Cover potatoes with water. Boil until tender, about 20 to 30 minutes. Drain, reserving ½ cup of the cooking water. Add reserved cooking water, margarine, and sugar to potatoes. Mash. Add milk, egg, and cinnamon. Cream potato mixture with an electric mixer until thoroughly blended.

Pour mixture into pie shell. Bake at 350° for 1 hour and 10 minutes.

INGREDIENTS:

PIE CRUST:
1 cup unsifted all-purpose flour
1 teaspoon salt
6 tablespoons shortening
2 tablespoons ice water

FILLING:
3 large sweet potatoes, peeled and cut into chunks
½ cup water, reserved from boiled potatoes
½ cup margarine
1 ½ cups sugar
½ cup milk
1 egg
1 teaspoon cinnamon

Peanut Butter Pie

MRS. KENNELL SCHENCK

This pie is rich and full of cholesterol, but delicious, quick, and easy!

INSTRUCTIONS: In a large bowl, beat sugar, peanut butter, and cream cheese until smooth. Fold in the whipped heavy cream.

Fill pie shell with mixture, cover with waxed paper, and refrigerate. Bring to room temperature before serving.

INGREDIENTS:
1 cup confectioners' sugar
1 cup crunchy peanut butter
1 cup cream cheese, at room temperature
1 cup heavy cream, whipped very stiff
1 (9-inch) graham cracker pie shell

Plantation Pie

MRS. FRANK DAYTON, 1965 L.V.I.S. COOKBOOK

One crust, 4 eggs, 1 cup sugar, 4 tablespoons flour, 1½ cups dark corn syrup, 1 teaspoon vanilla, 1 cup salted roasted peanuts.

Beat eggs, mix together flour and sugar. Add syrup, vanilla and peanuts. Pour in shell and bake until almost set, at 350° (but center still soft) about 45 minutes. Cool at least an hour. Serve slightly warm or cold.

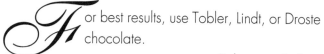

Bittersweet Chocolate Tart

ANN AND DICK ROBERTS

For best results, use Tobler, Lindt, or Droste chocolate.

INSTRUCTIONS: Bake tart shell at 375° until light brown, about 30 minutes.

Melt chocolate slowly in top of double boiler. In a separate bowl, beat egg yolks and granulated sugar together until mixture is pale yellow. Gradually add melted chocolate to mixture, beating briskly with whisk.

Pour mixture into baked shell. Bake at 375° for 10 minutes. Cool and sprinkle with powdered sugar.

INGREDIENTS:

1 (9- or 10-inch) sweet tart shell (with a depth of 1 inch)

6 ounces bittersweet chocolate

3 egg yolks

2½ tablespoons granulated sugar

1 tablespoon powdered sugar

French Silk Chocolate Pie

BETTY STRONG

INSTRUCTIONS: In a large bowl, cream together butter and sugar. Add chocolate and vanilla, blending well. Add eggs, one at a time, beating for 5 minutes on medium speed after each addition.

Pour into prepared pie crust. Refrigerate. Cover with freshly whipped cream at time of serving.

INGREDIENTS:

½ cup butter

¾ cup sugar

1 square unsweetened chocolate, melted and cooled

1 teaspoon vanilla

2 eggs

1 (8-inch) baked pie crust

TOPPING:

freshly whipped cream

Reminiscent S'mores Tart

CHAD VANDERSLICE, PASTRY CHEF, EAST HAMPTON POINT RESTAURANT

*A*ah yes, just one bite into a S'mores Tart rockets you back in time to a certain place, probably around a campfire. I was at a barbecue recently where we had S'mores for dessert. It made me think, "This is so good, people would probably enjoy this for dessert at the restaurant."

INSTRUCTIONS FOR CRUST: Cream butter and sugars together with a mixer. Beat in whole eggs and yolks, scraping down sides of bowl. Add remaining dry ingredients; mix completely. Refrigerate for 30 minutes.

Roll dough on floured surface to 1/8-inch thick. Place in 3½-inch tartlet molds. Prick dough. Bake at 325° for 20 minutes. Let cool for about 30 minutes. Remove from tartlet molds and set aside.

FOR GANACHE: Place chocolate in bowl. Set aside. Place remaining ingredients in a medium saucepan; bring to a boil. Strain over chocolate. Whisk slowly for 15 minutes, or until a thick, fudgy consistency is attained. Pour into prepared tartlet shells. Refrigerate 1 hour.

FOR MARSHMALLOWS: Dilute gelatin in 1 tablespoon water. Set aside. In top of a double boiler, stir egg whites, sugar, and vanilla bean until mixture reaches 125°, or until hot to the touch. Remove from heat, and remove vanilla bean.

Whip egg white mixture at high speed, until it begins to thicken. Add diluted gelatin. Whip until cool and thick. Spoon onto top of tartlets and smooth. Marshmallow Fluff may be substituted.

Bake at 350° for 5 minutes, or until golden brown. Enjoy with vanilla ice cream. Tartlets may be made 1 day in advance. Marshmallows, however, should be added just prior to baking.

INGREDIENTS:

GRAHAM CRACKER CRUST:
1 cup unsalted butter
¾ cup sugar
½ cup brown sugar
2 whole eggs
2 egg yolks
2 cups all-purpose flour
1¼ cups graham cracker crumbs
pinch of baking powder
½ teaspoon cinnamon
¼ teaspoon ground cloves
⅛ teaspoon nutmeg

HONEY CHOCOLATE GANACHE:
2 pounds semi-sweet chocolate, chopped
6 tablespoons butter
1½ cups heavy cream
2 whole cloves
1 cinnamon stick
⅓ cup honey

HOMEMADE VANILLA MARSHMALLOW:
1 teaspoon gelatin
1 tablespoon water
½ cup egg whites
1 cup sugar
1 vanilla bean

Apple Candy Pie

MRS. JOHN NAGEL

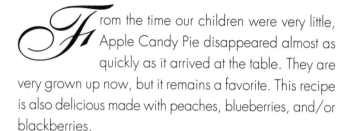

From the time our children were very little, Apple Candy Pie disappeared almost as quickly as it arrived at the table. They are very grown up now, but it remains a favorite. This recipe is also delicious made with peaches, blueberries, and/or blackberries.

INSTRUCTIONS: Arrange apples in a 7x11-inch baking pan; add water.

Blend the remaining ingredients with a fork. Pat the mixture over the apples. Bake at 350° for 30 minutes, until the apples are tender and the crust is browned. Serve warm.

INGREDIENTS:
- 4 cups tart apples, peeled and sliced
- ½ cup water, or less for juicy apples
- ¾ cup flour
- ½ cup granulated sugar
- ½ cup brown sugar
- 1 teaspoon cinnamon
- ½ cup butter

Caramel Baked Bosc Pears

CAROL MC CALLION

INSTRUCTIONS: Halve and core pears; brush with lemon juice. Place pears cut side up in a baking dish.

Combine brown sugar, butter, and water in a saucepan. Bring to a boil and cook for 2 to 3 minutes. Pour caramel over pears. Cover with foil; bake at 350° for 30 minutes. Uncover, and bake 10 minutes longer, basting occasionally with caramel. Serve with whipped cream or ice cream.

INGREDIENTS FOR 4 SERVINGS:
- 4 ripe Bosc pears
- lemon juice
- ¾ cup brown sugar
- 2 tablespoons butter
- ½ cup water

Danish Currants

JOANNA S. ROSE

INSTRUCTIONS: Wash currants and remove any stray stems. Wash and pick over raspberries. In a large saucepan, cook both fruits in water for 10 minutes. Work the cooked fruits through a sieve or food mill thoroughly. Return puréed fruits to saucepan. Add tapioca, sugar, and salt. Cook over low heat, stirring constantly, until mixture thickens. This takes about 10 minutes. If desired, serve with freshly whipped cream.

INGREDIENTS FOR 8 SERVINGS:
1 quart red currants
1 pint raspberries
2 cups water
½ cup quick-cooking tapioca
¾ cup sugar
dash salt
whipped cream (optional)

Fruit Crisp

VIVIENNE EVANS

After baking different fruit pies over the years, I have come to the conclusion that this is the easier dessert and my most favorite. For quick baking, use canned fruit. My favorite is fresh Granny Smith apples, which require an additional ¾ cup sugar and 20 to 30 minutes more baking time.

INSTRUCTIONS: Mix the fruit, sugar, butter, and nutmeg in a baking dish. Set aside.

For topping, combine flour, oats, sugar, and cinnamon. Cut in butter. Sprinkle topping over fruit mixture. Bake at 350° for 30 to 40 minutes. This is especially delicious served with vanilla ice cream.

INGREDIENTS:
2 cans apples, blueberries, or peaches
½ cup sugar
3 tablespoons butter
1 teaspoon nutmeg

TOPPING:
2½ cups flour
½ cup quick oats
1 cup sugar
1 teaspoon cinnamon
1 cup butter or margarine

FRUIT PIZZA

KIRK WILLARD THOMPSON

INSTRUCTIONS FOR CRUST:
Combine flour and sugar; cut in butter to form dough. With floured fingers, pat dough evenly on a large, round pizza pan. Bake at 325° for 20 minutes. Let cool.

FOR FILLING: Cream together the cream cheese and sugar. Stir in vanilla. Spread evenly on cooled crust.

FOR TOPPING: Slice and arrange fruit in desired pattern.

FOR GLAZE: Heat juice, sugar, and cornstarch in a small saucepan. Stir constantly until slightly thickened. Generously brush glaze over fruit topping.

INGREDIENTS:

CRUST:
1 ½ cups flour
½ cup confectioners' sugar
¾ cup butter

FILLING:
8 ounces cream cheese
½ cup confectioners' sugar
2 teaspoons vanilla

TOPPING (USE ANY OR ALL):
apricots
blueberries
grapes
kiwis
mandarin oranges
pineapple slices
strawberries

GLAZE:
1 cup orange or pineapple juice
½ cup sugar
1 to 1 ½ tablespoons cornstarch

Peaches Jean

MRS. LAWRENCE CLARKE

This recipe may also be made with pears. INSTRUCTIONS: Place peach halves, cavity side up, in a shallow, oven-proof casserole dish. Combine the remaining ingredients to create a filling. Fill each cavity with a spoonful of the mixture. Bake at 350° for 10 to 15 minutes. Serve hot. If you like, add a dollop of whipped cream on each peach half.

INGREDIENTS FOR 8 SERVINGS:
16 canned peach halves, drained
16 small almond macaroons, dried and crumbled
1 cup apricot preserves
½ cup Grand Marnier
½ cup slivered almonds

Orange Delight

PIDDY CLAY

INSTRUCTIONS: Carefully cut away the orange peels and pith. Slice oranges into thin rounds. Arrange in a pretty bowl. Generously splash with orange liqueur. Refrigerate. Combine marmalade, sugar, and water in a small sauce-pan. Bring to a boil. Cook for 10 to 15 minutes. Let cool. Pour over prepared oranges. Refrigerate until ready to serve. Garnish with sprigs of fresh mint.

INGREDIENTS:
6 large navel oranges
orange liqueur, such as Grand Marnier or Triple Sec
¾ cup orange marmalade
½ cup granulated sugar
¼ cup water
sprigs of fresh mint

Oranges Piquant

MARY KILROE

This is a light, no-fuss dessert made with ingredients off the pantry shelf.

INSTRUCTIONS: Arrange orange segments in 4 dessert compotes. Chop any large orange and ginger pieces in the marmalades. Combine marmalades and heat just to the melting point. Spoon 1 tablespoon of the marmalade mixture over oranges in each compote. Chill. Just before serving the first course of dinner, put the compotes in the freezer. At dessert time, they will be icy cold, but not frozen. To serve, top with a generous spoonful of sour cream.

INGREDIENTS FOR 4 SERVINGS:
2 (10 ounce) cans mandarin oranges, drained
3 tablespoons orange marmalade
1 tablespoon ginger marmalade
sour cream

Café du Fluffette

RUTH McCREA

This dessert can be made well in advance.

INSTRUCTIONS: Dip scissors into a glass of cold water and cut the marshmallows into quarters. Place them in the top of a double boiler. Add the coffee; cook, stirring until marshmallows melt. Cool. When slightly thickened, stir in the Kahlúa and vanilla. Fold in whipped cream. Spoon into dessert glasses. Chill. When ready to serve, garnish with whipped cream and chocolate shavings.

INGREDIENTS FOR 5 TO 6 SERVINGS:
16 marshmallows
¼ cup hot, black coffee
¼ cup Kahlúa
½ teaspoon vanilla
1 cup heavy cream, stiffly beaten

GARNISH:
whipped cream
chocolate shavings

Lemon Sherbet

ANN KIRK WILLARD

Limes may be substituted for the lemons. INSTRUCTIONS: Mix together lemon juice, rind, and sugar until the sugar is thoroughly dissolved. Gradually stir in milk. If desired, add food coloring. Freeze mixture in a bowl, stirring several times as it freezes to achieve desired consistency.

INGREDIENTS FOR 6 SERVINGS:
juice of 2 lemons, about ⅓ cup
grated rind of 1 lemon
¾ cup sugar
2 cups milk
yellow food coloring (optional)

Bread Pudding

MISS SARAH D. GARDINER, 1939 L.V.I.S. COOKBOOK

This recipe for bread pudding was contained in a letter written by Mrs. J.L. Gardiner of Gardiner's Island, December 11, 1852, to her granddaughter, Miss Sarah G. Thompson. "You inquire about the bread crumb pudding. I have no particular rule about it. Make your custard — 4 eggs to a quart of milk. Make it sweet. A coffee cup heaping full of bread crumbs not too fine. Two-thirds of a cup of seeded raisins, half a tea cup of melted butter. Spice to your taste. Put in the crumbs just as it is going in oven. If they stand any time in the custard they will sink to the bottom of the dish. Bake about as long as custard or until it rises in the dish. When done cover it thick with powdered sugar. If you find that it is not quite right, you can improve it next time. Have your dish large enough so as not to have the butter run over. That enriches the bread crumbs."

Classic Rice Pudding

BABE BISTRIAN

INSTRUCTIONS: Rinse a large sauce-pan with cold water; do not dry. Pour in milk and bring to a boil over medium heat. Stir in rice and return to a boil. Reduce heat. Simmer, uncovered, stirring occasionally until rice is tender (about 55 minutes).

Meanwhile, in a small bowl, combine cream, sugar, egg yolks, vanilla, and salt. When rice is tender, stir in cream mixture until completely combined. Bring to a boil. Remove from heat.

Pour pudding into a 2-quart oblong or oval serving dish. Sprinkle top with cinnamon. Chill at least 4 hours before serving.

INGREDIENTS FOR 6 SERVINGS:

6 cups milk

¾ cup long-grain rice

1 cup heavy cream

¾ cup sugar

3 egg yolks, beaten

2 teaspoons vanilla

¼ teaspoon salt

1 teaspoon cinnamon

Old-Fashioned Rice Pudding

ALISON ELIZALDE

INSTRUCTIONS: In a large bowl, combine eggs, sugar, and salt. Mix well. Slowly stir in milk and vanilla. Add the remaining ingredients.

Pour into a buttered 1-quart casserole. Place casserole in a shallow pan filled with 1 inch of hot water. Bake at 325° for 1½ hours or until set. Serve warm or cool.

INGREDIENTS FOR 4 TO 6 SERVINGS:

2 eggs, beaten
½ cup sugar
¼ teaspoon salt
2 cups milk
1 teaspoon vanilla
1¼ cups cooked white rice, cooled
1 cup seedless raisins
dash of cinnamon
dash of nutmeg

Doughnut Pudding

DREESEN'S MARKET

INSTRUCTIONS: Combine all ingredients. Pour mixture into two 9x13-inch pans. Top with butter patties; sprinkle with cinnamon. Bake, covered, at 350° for 1 hour; bake, uncovered, for an additional hour.

INGREDIENTS FOR 30 SERVINGS:

20 stale doughnuts, coarsely chopped
1 quart milk
12 eggs
2 cups sugar
½ cup currants
2 tablespoons vanilla
butter patties
cinnamon

Indian Pudding

This recipe endeared me to my father-in-law because no one else would make it, and it was his favorite.

INSTRUCTIONS: Heat 2 cups of milk in the top of a double boiler; add molasses. Combine sugar, corn-meal, salt, and spices; add to the hot milk mixture, stirring constantly until thickened.

Add flour and 1 cup cold milk to beaten egg. Stir into hot mixture and cook for 15 minutes. Butter a 1½-quart casserole dish with some of the melted butter; add remaining butter to mixture.

Pour pudding into prepared casserole dish. Bake at 350° for 1½ to 2 hours, until firm and browned. Serve warm, topped with whipped cream.

INGREDIENTS FOR 4 SERVINGS:
2 cups milk
½ cup molasses
½ cup sugar
2 tablespoons cornmeal
½ teaspoon salt
½ teaspoon cinnamon
½ teaspoon ginger
1 tablespoon flour
1 cup cold milk
1 egg, beaten
2 tablespoons butter, melted
whipped cream

Queen of Puddings

MRS. FELIX DOMINY, 1916 L.V.I.S. COOKBOOK

One and a half cups white sugar, two cups fine dry bread crumbs, five eggs, one tablespoon-ful butter, vanilla, lemon or rose water flavoring, one quart sweet milk, half cup jelly or jam; rub butter into a cup of sugar, beat yolks very light and stir these together to a cream; bread crumbs soaked in milk come next, then the flavoring; bake this in a large but-tered pudding dish only two-thirds full, until the custard is set; then draw to mouth of oven; spread over with jam or jelly; cover this with a meringue made of the whipped whites and half cup sugar; close the oven down and bake till the meringue begins to color; eat cold with cream; fresh strawberries may be used, and it is then delicious.

Lemon Sponge Pudding

GINNY HEIGES

his is a family recipe given to me by a dear Delaware friend, Josephine Bayard, about 25 years ago. It was my late husband's favorite dessert, and he was a dessert freak! It is best to prepare this on the same day that it is to be served.

INSTRUCTIONS: In a large bowl, cream together sugar, flour, and butter. In a separate bowl, beat egg yolks and add milk. Add to creamed mixture. Stir in lemon juice and rind. Beat egg whites with salt until stiff; fold into mixture.

Pour into a buttered 1½-quart casserole. Set casserole in a pan of hot water. Bake, uncovered, at 350° for 45 minutes. The top should be lightly browned. There will be cake on the top, and pudding on the bottom. Let set for 3 hours before serving. Serve at room temperature.

INGREDIENTS FOR 6 TO 8 SERVINGS:
1 cup sugar
2 tablespoons butter
¼ cup flour
1 ½ cups milk
3 eggs, separated
5 tablespoons fresh lemon juice
grated rind of 1 lemon
⅛ teaspoon salt

STEAMED CHOCOLATE PUDDING

MARTHA MURRAY

his recipe is my grandmother's. The fun is cooking it in a coffee can. The taste is subtle.

INSTRUCTIONS: Cream together butter and sugar. Beat in egg. Add chocolate. Sift together flour, baking powder, and salt. Add to mixture. Blend in milk and vanilla.

Pour mixture into a coffee can. Place can upright in a pot of hot water or a steamer. Cover pot and steam for 1 hour. Remove steamed pudding from can, and slice like bread to serve. Top with sweetened whipped cream or softened vanilla ice cream.

INGREDIENTS:

1 tablespoon butter or shortening
½ cup sugar
1 egg
1 (1 ounce) square unsweetened chocolate, melted
1 cup flour
1 teaspoon baking powder
½ teaspoon salt
½ cup milk
1 teaspoon vanilla
sweetened whipped cream or softened vanilla ice cream

DANDELION WINE

MRS. LOUISA E. HASSELBERGER, 1939 L.V.I.S. COOKBOOK

Use only fresh blossoms and carefully remove all stems or the wine will be bitter. To every quart of blossoms, well packed, but not crushed, add 2 sliced lemons, 2 sliced oranges and 1 quart boiling water. Allow this to stand 24 hours, then drain off the juice. To every quart of juice add 1 cup sugar. Pour into jars and stand them in a granite pan. Let stand until fermenting is all done, fill up the jars every morning from 1 jar. After all the fermenting is done, empty the wine and wash the jars in hot water. Put on the rubbers and refill the jars to overflowing and seal them for storing.

Ginger Beer

1840 EAST HAMPTON COOK BOOK

Put 1 pint molasses and 2 teaspoon of ginger in a pail to be half filled with boiling water; leave room for 1 pint of yeast. Place it in a warm hearth for the night, and bottle it in the morning.

Hot Buttered Rum

RUTH MC CREA LIZARS

This recipe is from a dear old friend we called Erna the Burner and it is a testament to her warmth and fun. It makes a delightful hostess gift when accompanied by a package of cinnamon sticks and a bottle of rum.

INSTRUCTIONS: Mix all ingredients, except rum, together thoroughly. Place mixture in refrigerator overnight. This will keep well if refrigerated.

When ready to use, add about 1½ teaspoons of the mixture to a cup of hot water and an ounce of rum. Provide a cinnamon stick as a stirrer, if desired.

INGREDIENTS:
1 pound dark brown sugar
½ pound sweet butter, softened
8 ounces honey
1 teaspoon ground cinnamon
pinch of nutmeg
dark rum

OPTIONAL:
cinnamon sticks

Iced Tea for a Crowd

FAITH D. CHASE

erfectionists can use 1 cup of orange pe-
koe tea, but then you must strain the tea
after the hour's steeping.

INSTRUCTIONS: Bring water to a boil. Squeeze
oranges and lemons; strain juice and put aside.

Put rinds in the boiled water along with the tea and the
mint. Let steep for one hour. Remove rinds, squeezing
them out as you do it. Remove mint.

Add sugar and strained juices. Stir until sugar melts.
When cooled, bottle and refrigerate. Shake well before pouring tea over ice in glasses to serve.

INGREDIENTS FOR 1 GALLON:

20 cups water
10 oranges
7 lemons
20 tea bags
1 large bunch of fresh mint
3 cups sugar

North Carolina Eggnog

This is a traditional drink on New Year's Day when one goes from house to house to wish neighbors a Happy New Year. Use good bourbon and rum.

INSTRUCTIONS: Separate eggs. Put egg whites in tightly sealed jar in refrigerator. Beat egg yolks lightly. Very slowly, alternately add sugar and liquors to the egg yolks. An electric mixer can be used at low speed. Store this mixture in a covered quart jar in refrigerator for 24 hours. This is necessary to "cook" the egg yolks. When ready to serve, whip cream. Add egg yolk-whiskey-rum mixture. Beat egg whites until stiff and fold them in.

INGREDIENTS:
6 eggs, separated
1 pound confectioners' sugar
1 pint bourbon whiskey
½ cup dark rum
2 pints heavy cream

PLANTER'S PUNCH

ANNE TREGELLAS

INSTRUCTIONS: Mix sugar and lime juice. Add rums. Add remaining ingredients. Mix until thoroughly blended. To serve, pour into glasses over ice and garnish with fruit.

INGREDIENTS FOR 10 SERVINGS:
¼ cup sugar
¼ cup lime juice
2 cups dark rum
2 cups light rum
¼ cup Cointreau
¼ cup sweet vermouth
¼ cup crème de cacao
¼ cup Dubonnet
2¼ cups orange juice
2¼ cups pineapple juice
1¼ cups water
few drops Angostura bitters

GARNISH:
orange slices
maraschino cherries

Wild Cherry Bounce

MRS. DON FRANCISCO, 1965 L.V.I.S. COOKBOOK

Mrs. Francisco made this from an old family recipe this past autumn when the wild cherry crop was unusually plentiful. She says that in her New England childhood, her mother used to serve this at holiday time and even the small ones were allowed a tiny taste. Mrs. Francisco's ancestry goes back to East Hampton's first schoolmaster, Charles Barnes. He married Mary Hand of East Hampton in 1657 and they moved to Middletown, Connecticut about 1665.

INSTRUCTIONS: Put in wine bottle. Shake once or twice a day for a week or two. Store for a few months. Serve in small liqueur glasses with fruit cake at the Christmas and New Year holidays.

INGREDIENTS:
1 cup ripe but firm wild cherries
1 cup sugar
2 cups of Scotch whiskey or brandy

L.V.I.S. Members Judie Ackerman and Sandy Powell selling homemade canned goods at 1980 Summer Fair.

CONDIMENTS

Beach Plum

Beach Plum Jelly

MARILYN HUNTING

Now that Certo no longer prints instructions for making beach plum jelly, I guess it's up to us "old-timers" to see to it that this treat doesn't join the ranks of the dinosaur. It is for that reason I submit this recipe.

Beach plums may be bagged and frozen, unwashed, until the grey days of winter are upon us and making jelly seems more like fun.

INSTRUCTIONS: Wash beach plums in colander. Transfer to a very large pot. Thoroughly crush fruit. Do not pit or peel. Add 2½ cups water. Bring to a boil. Reduce heat and simmer, covered for 30 minutes.

Pour through jelly bag or several thicknesses of dampened cheesecloth and allow to drip. You may wish to hasten the process by squeezing the bag. However, this may cause the jelly to appear cloudy.

Measure 3½ cups juice into kettle. Add sugar and mix well. Place over high heat and bring to a boil, stirring constantly. Immediately stir in Certo; bring to a rolling boil and boil hard 1 minute, stirring constantly. Remove from heat. Skim off foam with metal spoon and pour into sterilized jars.

Place lid and cap on each jar as it is filled and invert jar. After all jars have been filled and capped, turn jars upright. Store in a cool, dry place.

INGREDIENTS FOR 6 CUPS:
3½ cups prepared juice (about 2 quarts fully ripe beach plums)
2½ cups water
6 cups sugar
1 packet Certo fruit pectin

Beach Plum Jam

BETTY TURI

Instructions: Wash and pit plums. This job will be easier if you have a pitter. Use 1 pound of pitted beach plums to 1 pound of sugar. Put both in a large pot, stir well and cook slowly until thick. Put into sterilized, hot jars and seal.

INGREDIENTS:

1 pound beach plums, pits removed

1 pound sugar

Plum Conserve

IDA D'ARCY

Wonderful when served with poultry or pork. I remember as a child eating it right out of the jar. Damson plums are available in August.

Instructions: Put Damson plums, pitted and cut into eighths, in a large pot. Add the oranges, cut into quarters and coarsely ground. Add raisins and sugar and let stand overnight.

Simmer for 2½ hours. Add walnuts. The mixture should be jelly-like in consistency when done.

Pour into clean, hot sterilized glasses and cover.

INGREDIENTS:

6 pounds Damson plums

4 navel oranges

2 pounds seeded black raisins

11 cups sugar

1 pound walnuts, coarsely chopped

Mother's Old-Fashioned Lemon Butter

MRS. SAMUEL DAVIS

This recipe has been a favorite in our family. My mother said she got it from one of her bridesmaids in 1915. Lemon butter was in the 1965 L.V.I.S. cookbook, which Craig Claiborne wrote a column about in The New York Times. He selected four recipes to write up, and this was one of them.

INSTRUCTIONS: Put sugar in top of double boiler. Add eggs, one at a time, mixing after each addition. Add grated rinds and lemon juice. Stir in butter, cut up. Cook and stir constantly over hot water until the mixture is thick enough to fall in two consecutive drops from a tablespoon. Do not let mixture boil.

Pour into sterile jars. Cover with paraffin and keep in refrigerator.

This is delicious with toast or as filling for sponge layers.

INGREDIENTS:

3 cups sugar

3 eggs, unbeaten

3 lemons, rinds finely grated and juice extracted

4 tablespoons butter or margarine, cut up

Fair Day Rum Mustard

LYS A. MARIGOLD

I started making this mustard about 15 years ago. It developed by trial and error. It's easy to make and everyone loves it. You can eliminate the rum and add more vinegar, or use another flavored liqueur.

INSTRUCTIONS: Blend together mustard, vinegar, and rum in the top of a double boiler. Whisk over hot water. Slowly add eggs, beating until completely blended. Do not let water boil.

Stir in sugar, butter, salt, and pepper. Heat for 5 minutes until thick. Refrigerate in a covered jar.

INGREDIENTS FOR 1 1/2 CUPS:
¼ cup dry mustard
6 tablespoons cider vinegar
2 tablespoons dark rum
3 eggs
6 tablespoons sugar
4 tablespoons sweet butter
½ teaspoon salt
½ teaspoon pepper

Mustard

ANN KIRK WILLARD

INSTRUCTIONS: Put mustard in mixing bowl. Pour vinegar over it. Do not stir. Cover. Let stand 3 hours or overnight. Put mixture in top of double boiler. Mix with wire whisk over hot water. Add eggs one at a time, whisking after each addition.

Add sugar, butter, and salt. Cook over hot water 5 minutes. Do not overcook. Put into jars and refrigerate. Will keep for months.

INGREDIENTS FOR 1 QUART:
1 (4 ounce) can Colman's mustard
1 cup tarragon vinegar
6 eggs
¾ cup sugar
½ pound butter
1 teaspoon salt

Lions' Club Barbecue Sauce

RAYMOND F. MEDLER, SAUCE DOCTOR

This recipe has been used in good stead for 30 years of Lions' Barbecues. It is enough sauce to grill 200 half-chickens. My wife, Rosita, makes up a fourth of the quantity. Refrigerated, it keeps well for a year of home use for grilled pork as well as chicken.

INSTRUCTIONS: Mix dry ingredients. Add vinegar and then oil. When blended, add eggs and mix thoroughly. Refrigerate.

INGREDIENTS:

2 cups poultry seasoning
4 cups salt
5 tablespoons black pepper
4 tablespoons paprika
2 gallons cider vinegar
1 gallon corn oil
20 eggs, well beaten

Big Jim's Onion Sauce

PAMELA VANDERBECK MC DONALD

Big Jim was a man big in stature and the Dad of a big family. The only cookin' feat that outdid his Sunday breakfast buffets was his secret onion sauce.

INSTRUCTIONS: Peel onions and cut into ¼-inch slices. Put them in a large frying pan with the oil. Simmer until translucent, not brown. Add remaining ingredients. Simmer 45 minutes to one hour, stirring frequently. This is best made a day ahead. Serve hot on hamburgers, hot dogs, or steak. Freeze unused sauce. To make it more zesty, you can add horseradish.

INGREDIENTS:

3 pounds Vidalia onions
3 tablespoons olive oil
2 tablespoons Worcestershire sauce
2 tablespoons white vinegar
2 tablespoons gravy seasoning sauce
4 (8 ounce) cans tomato sauce
2 medium cloves garlic, minced
1 bay leaf
½ teaspoon sage
½ teaspoon celery salt
½ teaspoon pepper

OPTIONAL:
1½ tablespoons prepared horseradish

Nelson's Bread and Butter Pickles

JOAN SHELT NELSON

This sweet recipe has been passed down [through] generations.

DIRECTIONS: Mix cucumbers, [peppers, and onions in a] large bowl. Add salt. Cover [with water and ice and re]frigerate for 3 hours. [Drain, rinse with cold w]ater and drain again. Place [garlic, sugar, turmeric, c]elery seed, mustard seed, and [vinegar in a large pot and] bring to a boil over high heat. [Reduce heat and cook 30] minutes, uncovered. [Add cucumber mixture. O]ver high heat, bring to a boil, [stirring occasionally. Ladle] hot mixture into sterilized hot

INGREDIENTS:
4 quarts medium pickling cucumbers, sliced
2 green peppers, diced
6 medium yellow onions, thinly sliced
½ cup salt
3 cloves garlic
5 cups sugar
1 ½ teaspoons turmeric
1 ½ teaspoons celery seed
2 tablespoons mustard seed
4 cups cider vinegar

Watermelon Rind Pickle

MRS. AMES H. MULFORD. 1939 L.V.I.S. COOKBOOK

Peel the rind and cut in 1 ½-inch squares. Cover with salt water (½ cup salt to 2 quarts water) and soak over night. In morning, drain, cover with cold water and boil until tender. Drain and boil in syrup until transparent. Syrup: 2 pounds sugar, 1 pint vinegar, 1 pint water, 1 lemon, thinly sliced, 1 tablespoon cinnamon sticks, 1 teaspoon white cloves, 1 teaspoon allspice (in cheesecloth bag). Boil until sugar is well dissolved.

COLUMBIA CHUTNEY

GRANDMA GLOVER. 1908 L.V.I.S. COOKBOOK

Two quarts tomatoes skinned and put on to boil, one cup raisins seeded and chopped, one quart vinegar, one pound brown sugar, two tablespoons salt, two teaspoonfuls each ground cinnamon and cloves, small teaspoonful pepper, fifteen large tart apples peeled, quartered, and chopped fine; boil all together till the apples are thoroughly cooked; bottle while warm; it is ready for use at once or will keep any length of time.

CRANBERRIES FOR A HOLIDAY DINNER

BEA LUCCI

INSTRUCTIONS: Wash berries in cold water discarding any berries which are soft. Drain. Transfer to an 8-inch glass pie plate. Sprinkle with sugar. Top with liqueur. Bake in 350° oven for 1 hour. The sugar should be melted and the berries a glistening red color. Remove from the oven. The condiment will thicken as it cools. Serve in a pretty glass bowl which shows the lovely color.

INGREDIENTS FOR 6 SERVINGS:
1 (12 ounce) package fresh cranberries
1½ cups sugar
½ cup orange liqueur

Corn Relish

MIKE BRAVERMAN

or the last 10 years or so, I have prepared this corn relish in large quantities for sale at the Food Booth of the L.V.I.S. Fair. I am told it quickly sells out. Don't hesitate to expand the recipe to the limits of your pots and endurance, which I find to be about 14 or 15 pounds at a time. In any case, always make some extra to give to friends.

INSTRUCTIONS: Combine all ingredients in a large saucepan, gradually stirring in vinegar. Bring to a boil. Reduce heat and simmer, stirring occasionally for 20 minutes or until liquid thickens somewhat.

Cool in a bowl and refrigerate. Yields about 2 quarts and keeps up to 10 days chilled. Flavors come through best when served at room temperature.

INGREDIENTS FOR 2 QUARTS:

6 cups corn kernels

1 green bell pepper, chopped

1 red bell pepper, chopped

3 carrots, chopped

2 medium onions, chopped

¼ cup celery leaves or parsley, chopped

¾ cup sugar

2 teaspoons dry mustard

1 teaspoon celery seeds

½ teaspoon turmeric

½ teaspoon cayenne

1 cup cider vinegar

East Hampton Point Cranberry Relish

GERARD HAYDEN, CHEF, EAST HAMPTON POINT RESTAURANT

 his relish goes well with game and poultry dishes. It also makes an excellent base for pastries and soufflés.

INSTRUCTIONS: Put wine and sugar in a heavy bottomed saucepan over high heat. Boil until sugar begins to caramelize to a light golden color.

Meanwhile, cut up oranges and lemons, including skin (but no pits) to a small ⅛-inch dice. Add oranges, lemons, and cranberries to caramelized sugar. Bring to a boil. Add spices.

Reduce heat. Simmer 30 minutes or until cranberries are soft and liquid is reduced by half.

INGREDIENTS:

2 cups Riesling wine (German or Californian)
1¾ cups sugar
5 oranges
2½ lemons
2 pounds fresh or flash frozen cranberries
1 cinnamon stick
1 fresh bay leaf
2 whole cloves

Fresh Watermelon Salsa

STEPHANIE TEKULSKY

INSTRUCTIONS: Combine all ingredients; mix well. Refrigerate for 2 hours. Add more balsamic vinegar to taste, if necessary.

Serve with chips, nachos, or raw vegetables. Celery is the best!

INGREDIENTS:

2 cups watermelon, seeded and coarsely chopped
2 tablespoons chopped onion
2 tablespoons water chestnuts
2 to 4 tablespoons chopped chilies
1 tablespoon balsamic vinegar
¼ teaspoon salt
½ teaspoon minced garlic

FULLING MILL RHUBARB OR CRANBERRY CHUTNEY

EUNICE JUCKETT MEEKER

his is excellent with roasts, Stroganoff, or cold meats. It also can be used in bite-size pastry tartlets.

INSTRUCTIONS: Mix all ingredients, except nuts, in a pot. Bring to a boil. Watch constantly and cook for 15 minutes. Remove from heat.

When it cools slightly add nuts if desired. Put in glass jars and store in refrigerator. It will keep several months, if your family and friends don't eat it before then.

INGREDIENTS FOR 2 QUARTS:

1 large onion, chopped

3 cups rhubarb, cut into small pieces, or cranberries

1 cup orange juice

2 cups sugar

2 chopped apples, skins on

⅔ cup black raisins

⅔ cup golden raisins

1 tablespoon dry mustard

1 tablespoon ground allspice

1 tablespoon cinnamon

½ tablespoon ground cloves

OPTIONAL:

1 cup chopped pecans or walnuts

Old South End Burying Ground, Gardiner Mill and Town Pond.

$\mathscr{S}$UPPORT

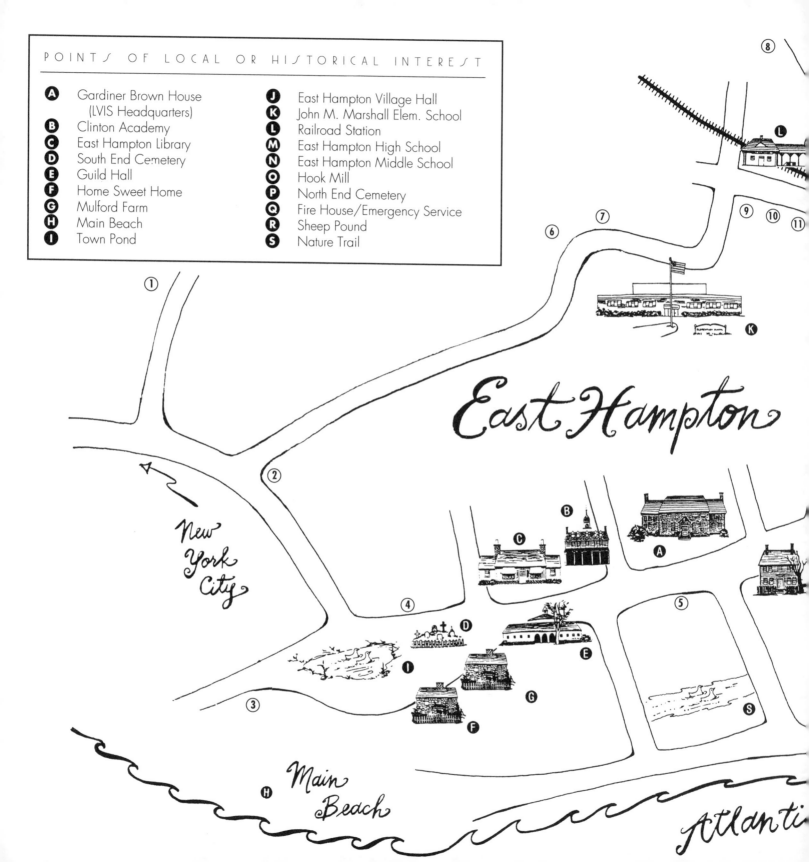

POINTS OF LOCAL OR HISTORICAL INTEREST

- **A** Gardiner Brown House (LVIS Headquarters)
- **B** Clinton Academy
- **C** East Hampton Library
- **D** South End Cemetery
- **E** Guild Hall
- **F** Home Sweet Home
- **G** Mulford Farm
- **H** Main Beach
- **I** Town Pond
- **J** East Hampton Village Hall
- **K** John M. Marshall Elem. School
- **L** Railroad Station
- **M** East Hampton High School
- **N** East Hampton Middle School
- **O** Hook Mill
- **P** North End Cemetery
- **Q** Fire House/Emergency Service
- **R** Sheep Pound
- **S** Nature Trail

East Hampton

New York City

Main Beach

Atlantic

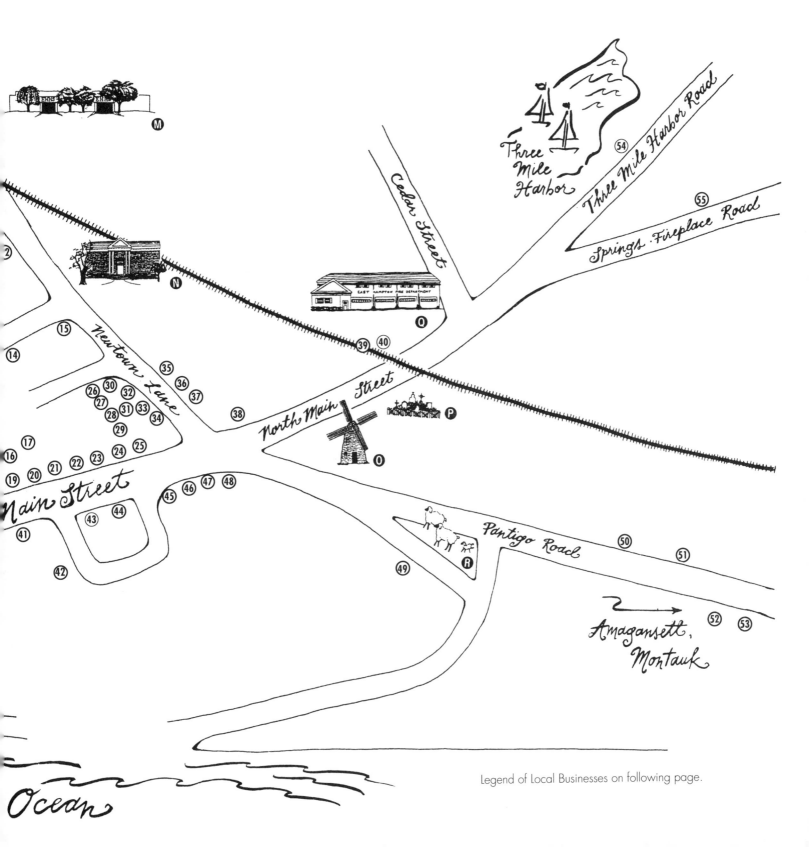

M

Three Mile Harbor

Three Mile Harbor Road

54

Springs Fireplace Road

55

Cedar Street

2

N

EAST HAMPTON FIRE DEPARTMENT

Q

15

14

Newtown Lane

35

36

37

39 40

26 30 32

27 31 33

28 34

29

17

16 25

24

19 20 21 22 23

41

43 44

42

45 46 47 48

Main Street

38

North Main Street

P

O

R

49

Pantigo Road

50

51

52 53

Amagansett, Montauk

Ocean

Legend of Local Businesses on following page.

ℒEGEND OF ℒOCAL ℬUSINESS 𝒮UPPORT

1. Wainscott Farms, Inc.
2. Jerry & David's Red Horse Market
3. MACCI Design Studio
4. The Maidstone Arms
5. The Palm at the Huntting Inn
6. Ben Krupinski General Contractor
7. The Golden Eagle
8. Whitmore's Tree Farm
9. Riverhead Building Supply Corp.
10. East Hampton Business Service
11. Villa Italian Specialties
12. Sotheby's International Realty
13. Mrs. Condie Lamb Agency, Inc.
14. East Hampton Industries, Inc.
15. Paine Webber/East Hampton
16. Bridgehampton National Bank
17. Markowitz Preische & Stevens, P.C.
18. Mark Fore & Strike
19. White's Pharmacy
20. Keesal & Mathews
21. Allan M. Schneider Associates, Inc.
22. Engel Pottery - Wendy Engel Gallery
23. Tennis East
24. The Osborne Agency, Inc.
25. Ralph Lauren Country Store
26. Suffolk County National Bank
27. Gubbins Running Ahead
28. Park Place Wine & Liquors
29. The Party Shoppe
30. Fenelon, Crowley & Tutino, C.P.A., P.C.
31. Dunemere Associates Inc. Real Estate
32. Entre Nous
33. Dreesen's Excelsior Market
34. Waves
35. Edwards & Duggan, P.C.
36. Village Hardware
37. Ann Crabtree
38. Devlin McNiff Real Estate
39. Thimbelina, Inc.
40. Della Femina Restaurant
41. E. T. Dayton Inc.
42. Jewels by Virtu
43. Village Realty
44. United Artists' East Hampton Cinemas
45. Coldwell Banker - Cook/Pony Farm Real Estate, Inc.
46. Cook Travel, Inc.
47. Book Hampton
48. Braverman Newbold Brennan Real Estate, Inc.
49. The Amaden - Gay Agencies
50. Suffolk County National Bank
51. Edward F. Cook Agency, Inc.
52. Hren Nurseries
53. Whitmore's Garden Shop
54. East Hampton Point
55. Bistrian Gravel Corporation

Congratulations to the

Ladies' Village Improvement Society

on your 100th Anniversary.

4 EAST 46 ST., NEW YORK, N.Y. 10017 687-0404-0111

Sony is proud

to support the

outstanding efforts of

The East Hampton Ladies'

Village Improvement Society

SONY

Congratulations from
America's number 1 name in nail care.

Sally Hansen

Donations

Mrs. John T. Allen
M.S. Amaden
Mrs. J. Paul Amaden
Madalyn Ammon
Mrs. Don L. Andrus
Bank of New York
Bebe Antell
Bryan Bantry
Mrs. Robert Benepe
K.E. Bennett
Babe Bistrian
Anne Bluedorn
May Ann Bozzi
Mike Braverman
Mary Brett
Marge Brinkley
Estrellita Brodosky
Olivia Brooks
Sue Bullock
Betty Cafiso
William Bernhard & Catherine Cahill
Kate Cameron
Mrs. Alexander P. Cannon
Pam Cataletto
Mrs. Girard Chester
Jean C. Clancy
Mrs. Bernard K. Clark
Mrs. Marshall Clark
Mrs. Lawrence Clarke
Piddy (Harriet) Clay
Karen Cohen
Sandra & James Conklin
Mrs. Edward F. Cook

Bella Coppia, Inc.
Leonard L. Cooper Sandblasting
Ann Creamer
E.T. Dayton, Inc.
Margaret D'Andrea
Jennifer & James D'Auria
Mrs. Samuel Davis
Del Laboratories
Judy Licht & Jerry Della Femina
Barbara Bolton Dello Joio
Mrs. Alfred Devendorf
Ruth Diefendorf
Marlene Dion
Lee Dunst & Lissie Diringer
DJM Films, Inc.
Clarisse Donaldson
Frances Ann Dougherty
Margot C. Dowling
Barbara Dubitsky
Mr. & Mrs. Wm. H. Duggan, Jr.
Diane & Larry Dunst
Mrs. Lee Eastman
East Hampton Independent News Co.
Charlotte Edison
Vivienne Evans
Marjorie C. Federbush
John L. Fenton
Patti & Ken Ferrin
Mrs. G.W. Fish
Mr. & Mrs. Lawrence Flinn, Jr.
Mrs. Robert R. Forrester, Jr.
Pierre L. Franey
Phyllis Frenkel

Abby Friedman
Eleanor Maloney Gaynor
Janet A. Geller
Kathleen R. Gerard
Mrs. S. George Gianis
Margot Gordon
Clorinda Gorman
Mrs. Gladys Gottlieb
Grand Cafe, Stephen & Ellen Gottlieb
Connie Gretz
Mrs. Walter S. Gurnee
Ann R. Halloran
Mrs. Donald M. Halsey
Nedenia H. Hartley
Virginia Heiges
Helen Hoie
Vivian Horan
Kim Hovey
Marilyn Hunting
Carl Icahn
Beverly Jablons
Lillian Jayne
Mrs. Edward H. Jewett, Jr.
Holly D. Johanson
Mrs. C. Lewis Johnson
Mrs. Benson E. Jones
Eleanore Kennedy
Olive Kennedy
Mrs. Donald Kirk
Lynn Kroll
Ben & Bonnie Krupinski
Mr. & Mrs. James R. Lamb
Lois Landauer

Donations

Mrs. Hal Lary
Mrs. Alexander M. Laughlin
Madeline Lawler
Suzanne & Brian Leaver
Phyllis & Bud Leventhal
Deborah Ann Light
Ruth & John Lizars
Loaves & Fishes, Anna Pump
Lobster Roll Restaurant
Mrs. Robert Loughead
Annette Lubin
Marilyn Lukashok
Dori K. Lyons
Leola Macdonald
Barbara Macklowe
Laura & Lance Maerov
Elizabeth J. Magill
Lysbeth A. Marigold
Charlotte Markowitz
John & Colleen Marshall
Ruth McCrea
Mrs. John I.B. McCulloch
Mrs. Pamela Anne McDonald
Mrs. Eunice Meeker
Mrs. Douglas Mercer
Albert S. Messina
Ruth Mueller
Jane Mulvihill
Audrey Nagel
Bruce & Nancy Nagel
Julia S. Neagle
Mrs. George Neff

Joan Nelson
Mrs. Eldo S. Netto
Nick & Toni's Restaurant
Mrs. Frederick H. Owen, Jr.
Gail Parker
Aubrey W. Peterson
Bonnie Pizzorno
Mrs. Robert Plitt
Mrs. John Putnam
Helen Rattray
Mr. & Mrs. Raphael Recanati
Michael Recanati
Phyllis A. Reid
Jean Rickenbach
Sheila Robbins
Dudley Roberts
Jill Rose
Mrs. N. Hilton Rosen
Ethel Rosner
Lee Radziwill Ross
Pat & Herb Rowland
Bill Ruder
Anne Sager
Ginnie (Mrs Virginia) Sauer
Mrs. Kennell I. Schenck
Robert G. Schwartz
Ellen & Phillip Schwartzman
Anne Schwenck
Mrs. Janet Schwitter
Robin N. Siegel
Patti Walton Silver
Helene Silverblank-Forst

Elise Simonds
Mrs. Harrison Skiba
James Alan Smith
SONY Corp. of America
Mrs. George Starke
James & Virginia Stier
Harry A. Striebel
Mrs. Jane Susskind-Narins
Mrs. Macrae Sykes
Jean Symer
Mrs. J.H. Taylor
Melissa & Mark Tender
Elsa Thayer
Thayer's Hardware
Dick Duane & Robert Thixton
Anne Tregellas
Mrs. Philip R. Tutino
Avis Usher
Lee Usher
Mrs. Oliver Vanderbilt
Stanley Wagman
Deborah Walter
Dan K. Wassong
Florence Fithian Stone Wessberg
Enez Whipple
Barbara D'Arcy White
Priscilla & Chris Whittle
Ann K. Willard
Mrs. David Williams
Mrs. Frederick S. Williams
Ann Wolfe
Mrs. John J. Yellott

$\mathcal{A}$CKNOWLEDGEMENTS

The Ladies' Village Improvement Society

ACKNOWLEDGEMENTS

WE THANK all those who contributed recipes for the L.V.I.S Centennial Cookbook. The recipes were chosen from over 600 submissions and from earlier L.V.I.S. Cookbooks. In some instances, recipes were edited after testing. We do not claim the selected recipes to be totally original.

A special thanks to our testers, The Gourmet Food Class, East Hampton High School: Johanna Anderson, Joel Anderson, Katherine Anderson, Jennifer Blume, Jennifer Boerem, Patrick Coyle, Maura Gledhill, Rhiannon Greene, Marcy Gross, Lynne Kulakowski, Kathleen Miller, Patricia Peters, Marlene Petykowski, Jesse Rothwell, Laura Uhll, Kevin Von Ohlen, Adam Willhite, and to Gerard Hayden and Chad Vanderslice of East Hampton Point Restaurant.

For the numerous photographs researched, collected, and ultimately selected and for sharing the wealth of knowledge, we wish to thank Dorothy King, the East Hampton Free Library, Long Island Room; Helen Rattray and Sheridan Sansegundo, The East Hampton Star; Steve Hadley, The East Hampton Historical Society; Mary Johnson and Virginia Schenck, L.V.I.S. Archives; Carlton Kelsey, Amagansett Library.

A special thanks to Eleanor Labrozzi, a gifted photographer, for all her beautiful East Hampton images; to Ric Cohn for his artful photography of the cover montage; to Beck Underwood for her fanciful map of East Hampton; to Priscilla Rattazzi for the use of her wonderful East Hampton beach photograph; and also to Jeffrey Frey for his fine photographic contributions.

COVER: Montage, Dolores Frey; Cover photo, Ric Cohn.
FRONT COVER: Clockwise starting at upper left: L.V.I.S. Charter Members in 1945 L.V.I.S. 50th Anniversary parade, photographer, Bert Morgan, C.F. Dayton Copy Collection, East Hampton Free Library; Hook Mill, photographer, Eleanor Labrozzi; Farmstand, photographer, Eleanor Labrozzi; photograph of Mrs. E. Hollingsworth Siter, L.V.I.S. Archives.

BACK COVER: Clockwise starting at upper left: Page from Mrs. J. Alexander Tyler's Receipt Book, East Hampton Free Library; Nature Trail Swans, photographer, Eleanor Labrozzi; Portrait of Julia Gardiner Tyler, L.V.I.S. Archives; Town Pond Painting by Arthur T. Hill; clams, photographer, Eleanor Labrozzi; Woman in leaf frame unknown, photographer, J.P. Condon, East Hampton Free Library; Private Home on East Hampton Beach, photographer, Priscilla Rattazzi.

PHOTOGRAPHY: Endpapers: Page from Mrs. John Alexander Tyler's Handwritten Receipt Book, Courtesy of East Hampton Free Library; Main Street, East Hampton, C.F. Dayton Copy Collection, East Hampton Free Library; L.V.I.S. Fair on the Village Green, C.F. Dayton Copy Collection, East Hampton Free Library; Heart of East Hampton Plaque, L.V.I.S. Archives; East Hampton Railroad Station, C.F. Dayton Copy Collection, East Hampton Free Library; Main Street, East Hampton, Unpaved, C.F. Dayton Copy Collection, East Hampton Free Library; L.V.I.S. Fundraiser Dinner Menu, 1910, L.V.I.S. Album, East Hampton Free Library; Picket Fence, courtesy of East Hampton Star; Early East Hampton Beach Scene, C.F. Dayton Copy Collection, East Hampton Free Library; Dancing on the Village Green, L.V.I.S. Fair, C.F. Dayton Copy Collection, East Hampton Free Library; L.V.I.S. Fair

Preparations, C.F. Dayton Copy Collection, East Hampton Free Library; Photo Concession, 1945 L.V.I.S. Fair, Photographer, Stanley Stady, L.V.I.S. Album, East Hampton Free Library; Artist Float, 1945 L.V.I.S. Anniversary Parade, Photographer, J.P. Condon, L.V.I.S. Archives; Jacqueline Kennedy Onassis, nee Bouvier, L.V.I.S. Fashion Show, L.V.I.S. Archives; Cookbook Booth, 1965 L.V.I.S. Fair, Photographer, C. Frank Dayton, L.V.I.S. Album, East Hampton Free Library; Watermelon Booth, L.V.I.S. Barbecue, Photographer, Rameshwar Das, Courtesy East Hampton Star; Main Street in front of L.V.I.S. Headquarters, Courtesy East Hampton Historical Society; Elm Tree Plaque, L.V.I.S. Archives; Flag, Photographer, Eleanor Labrozzi; Leaves, Photographer, Eleanor Labrozzi; L.V.I.S. Fair Committee, 1990, Photographer, David McHugh, L.V.I.S. Archives; Officer of L.V.I.S. in 1945 Anniversary Parade, Bert Morgan, Photographer, C.F. Dayton Copy Collection, East Hampton Free Library; Clam Bar at L.V.I.S. Fair, Courtesy East Hampton Star; Mrs. John Alexander Tyler's Receipt Book, Courtesy of East Hampton Free Library; Tomatoes, Photographer, Eleanor Labrozzi; F.H. Warner Bakery, Courtesy East Hampton Star; Chicken Coop, Photographer, James Jay Mackin, Courtesy East Hampton Star; Mrs. S. Kip Farrington & Party, L.V.I.S. Archives; Goose Shooters, L.V.I.S. Archives; C. Schenck's Market, Courtesy East Hampton Star; Corn, Photographer, Carol Kitman, Courtesy East Hampton Star; Child with Cookie, Courtesy East Hampton Star; Condiments Booth at Fair, Photographer, Cal Norris, Courtesy East Hampton Star; Town Pond, Photographer, Tet Borsig, Courtesy East Hampton Star; Thank You Card, Photographer, Ric Cohn; L.V.I.S. Headquarters, L.V.I.S. Archives.

L.V.I.S. Headquarters at Gardiner Brown House.

INDEX

Index

$\mathcal{L.V.I.S.}$ CENTENNIAL COOKBOOK

Post Office Box 1196, East Hampton, N.Y. 11937

Please send _____ copies	at $21.95 each	$ _____
Add postage and handling	at $4.00 each	$ _____
Add gift wrap (if desired)*	at $1.00 each	$ _____
	Sub-total	$ _____
New York State residents add 8½% sales tax on subtotal above		$ _____
	TOTAL	$ _____

☐ Enclosed find my check payable to L.V.I.S. CENTENNIAL COOKBOOK
☐ Please charge my American Express ☐ Mastercard ☐ Visa

Credit Card # _____ Exp. Date _____

Cardholder's Signature _____

Name (Print) _____

Address _____

City _____ State _____ Zip _____

Telephone _____

*Gift card to read _____

To order:
By TEL: 516-324-1220
By FAX: 516-324-1597

Ship to:
Name:
Address:
City _____ State _____ Zip _____

$\mathcal{L.V.I.S.}$ CENTENNIAL COOKBOOK

Post Office Box 1196, East Hampton, N.Y. 11937

Please send _____ copies	at $21.95 each	$ _____
Add postage and handling	at $4.00 each	$ _____
Add gift wrap (if desired)*	at $1.00 each	$ _____
	Sub-total	$ _____
New York State residents add 8½% sales tax on subtotal above		$ _____
	TOTAL	$ _____

☐ Enclosed find my check payable to L.V.I.S. CENTENNIAL COOKBOOK
☐ Please charge my American Express ☐ Mastercard ☐ Visa

Credit Card # _____ Exp. Date _____

Cardholder's Signature _____

Name (Print) _____

Address _____

City _____ State _____ Zip _____

Telephone _____

*Gift card to read _____

To order:
By TEL: 516-324-1220
By FAX: 516-324-1597

Ship to:
Name:
Address:
City _____ State _____ Zip _____

also a little wine

Soak the beans overnight; in the morning d[...]
off and put them into fresh water
Set them over the fire to boil slowly for fou[...]
Put in a separate kettle the meat, carrots an[...]
Strain the soup, when done, through a fine [...]
rubbing through all the beans that will go.
Pour into a Tureen adding in slices the [...]
and hard boiled eggs; — Sput in the win[...]
If it is too <u>thick</u> after straining, put it [...]
in the kettle and add hot water; if too
thin, let it boil until thick enough.

Take eight large mealy potatoes, pee[...]
and cut in small slices, slice one
large onion, boil in three pints of [...]
until tender, then pulp through [a]
cullender, add a small piece of butter[...]
little cayenne pepper and salt,
Just before serving add two table spoon[s]
full of cream. Do not let it boil
after the cream is added.
This is sufficient for three or four [...]